Reasons, Explanations and Decisions:
Guidelines for
Critical Thinking

Reasons, Explanations and Decisions: Guidelines for Critical Thinking

THOMAS MCKAY

Syracuse University

Wadsworth
Thomson Learning™

Australia • Canada • Mexico • Singapore • Spain
United Kingdom • United States

Philosophy Editor: *Peter Adams*
Assistant Editor: *Kerri Abdinoor*
Editorial Assistant: *Mindy Newfarmer*
Marketing Manager: *Dave Garrison*
Signing Representative: *Timothy Kenney*
Project Editor: *Marlene Vasilieff*
Print Buyer: *April Reynolds*
Permissions Editor: *Joohee Lee*
Production Service: *Pre-Press Company, Inc.*
Cover Designer: *Laurie Anderson*
Cover Image: *PhotoDisc*
Compositor: *Pre-Press Company, Inc.*
Printer/Binder: *Webcom*

For more information contact

Wadsworth/Thomson Learning
10 Davis Drive
Belmont, CA 94002-3098
USA
www.wadsworth.com

International Headquarters
Thomson Learning
International Division
290 Harbor Drive, 2nd Floor
Stamford, CT 06902-7477
USA

UK/Europe/Middle East/South Africa
Thomson Learning
Berkshire House
168-173 High Holborn
London WC1V 7AA
United Kingdom

Asia
Thomson Learning
60 Albert Street, #15-01
Albert Complex
Singapore 189969

Canada
Nelson Thomson Learning
1120 Birchmount Road
Toronto, Ontario M1K 5G4
Canada

Library of Congress Cataloging-in-Publication Data
McKay, Thomas J.
   Reasons, explanations, and decisions: guidelines for critical thinking / Thomas McKay.
     p.   cm.
   ISBN 0-534-57411-4 (alk. paper)
   1. Critical thinking.   I. Title
BC177M35   1999
160—dc21   99-35782

This book is printed on acid-free recycled paper.

TO MY FATHER

CONTENTS

REASONS, EXPLANATIONS, AND DECISIONS

CHAPTER 3
MATTERS OF MEANING   *54*

CHAPTER 4
INFORMAL FALLACIES   78

CHAPTER 5
ANALOGY   102

CHAPTER 6
UNDERSTANDING AND EXPLANATION   117

CHAPTER 7
EVALUATING EXPLANATIONS   128

CHAPTER 8
GENERALIZATION AND CAUSAL INFERENCE   *157*

CHAPTER 9
TESTING CAUSAL EXPLANATIONS   *176*

CHAPTER 10
DECISION MAKING   196

APPENDIX:
SOME SPECIAL CASES OF VALIDITY   241

Most of the goals of this book come together in the idea that it will help readers develop their abilities to evaluate and revise their beliefs in a mature and intelligent way. This means looking closely at the kinds of reasons that can be given for beliefs, thinking hard about how to evaluate reasoning, and developing the skill of effectively presenting that evaluation to others.

One of the great tools for developing your system of beliefs is discussion, and this book is unusual in its attention to familiarizing the reader with patterns for critical discussion that will help them make the best use of discussion as a tool for learning. This feature, and others mentioned below, encouraged me to think that I could write a book that would make a significant contribution, despite the existence of so many other books for the development of critical thinking.

Throughout the book, there are numerous examples and exercises. Readers who think hard about how the examples illustrate the discussion and who respond to the exercises will find that this activity strengthens their critical and expository abilities.

SPECIAL FEATURES

Over a thousand students in my courses have read drafts of this book. By seeing what is and what is not effective for my students, I have been able to find out much about how to present material in a way that produces learning, and I have been able to refine the exercises that go with each chapter. These well-tested exercises will enhance readers' understanding of the material and offer instructors an effective way to check on students' understanding.

Many of the arguments we wish to evaluate have conclusions that say that we *should* or *should not* do something. I provide (in Chapter 2) a pattern for constructing and evaluating such arguments. Keeping this pattern in mind will enable you to present better reasons for action, and it will enable you to know what questions to ask when others argue that something should be done. I have found this technique enormously useful in my teaching of this material, and it is not done in this way in any other text I know of.

The discussion of meaning (Chapter 3) takes context into account, and this enhances the discussion of vagueness and ambiguity. Readers learn to identify equivocations, and they also learn how to point out an equivocation in an effective way, a skill that enables them to carry discussion to a more productive level.

The treatment of fallacies of argument in Chapter 4 especially illustrates the idea of providing tools for discussion. Going beyond just identifying fallacies by name, we associate each name with an effective way of pointing out what is wrong with an argument. For example, a person who learns about the fallacy of *false dilemma,* should learn, as well, to articulate the alternatives actually being considered in the statement or argument being criticized (i.e., to identify the dilemma). She or he should also be prepared to point out alternatives that are being overlooked (to show why it is false).

The treatment of analogy (Chapter 5) is different from that in other texts. Here analogy is seen as a way of presenting general principles that can then be used in arguments. This treatment provides a much more effective and systematic means for evaluating and discussing analogies.

In Chapters 6–8, I emphasize explanations and their evaluation, and I encourage readers to see how the justification for causal claims is usually best evaluated as a type of inference to the best explanation. Chapters 7 and 8 include detailed applications of these ideas to the evaluation of reasoning.

Instructors who wish to discuss the evaluation of theories and theoretical change will find the material on the Copernican Revolution especially useful (Chapter 7).

Chapter 8 includes helpful tips on evaluating statistical information. This is no substitute for a statistics course, but it provides the orientation needed for picking out some of the most frequent problems in the use of statistical information in justifying causal claims.

Chapters 6–9 also use some ideas about causality to unify the discussion of the justification of causal claims, causal explanation, and testing causal hypotheses.

A full chapter (Chapter 9) is devoted to testing theories. Readers should come away with a strengthened ability to evaluate critically media reports of medical studies and other scientific studies. They will also develop an understanding of the basic elements of a good controlled experiment.

Chapter 10, on decision making, could be used on its own. The material in Chapter 10 also completes the discussion of *should* conclusions begun in Chapter 2. Here we develop the ability to deal with uncertainty in a systematic way, and we consider how to determine the relative value of various possible outcomes of action. The material on the prisoner's dilemma and related issues in Chapter 10 will provide a solid foundation for instructors who wish to discuss this topic.

I first taught a critical thinking course 25 years ago. I used Monroe Beardsley's *Thinking Straight,* an excellent text. Beardsley models the discussion of reasoning, and he provides interesting discussion of the epistemological background for the critical abilities being developed. I have found, though, that my students need an additional step. Modeling excellent discussion is one thing, but it is also enormously helpful to most students to point out the elements of good discussion of reasoning in a way that explicitly provides them with patterns to build on in discussions.

Instructors often note that the ability to point out fallacies effectively comes naturally to some people and not to others. I suspect that this is because some people are very good at *following* the model their teacher provides, whereas others need clearer, more explicit instruction about the elements of effective discussion of reasoning. (Some people can learn to play the piano by ear, but most of us need more explicit instruction.) I provide some of that instruction in this book.

As a result, this book is very effective for people studying on their own and for distance-learning situations. I have used drafts of this book with students who did most of the course by mail, and I have used it in an online version of the course. Because I do not rely on the students' ability to follow the model of the teacher, but instead give explicit instruction, people have been able to use this material very effectively in these kinds of situations. The presence of numerous exercises also enhances peoples' ability to engage in effective distance learning, and good feedback from an instructor, dealing with students' individual development, is of course an invaluable addition.

INSTRUCTOR'S MANUAL

For instructors, a manual is available through Wadsworth's Web Site. The manual includes answers to exercises and some useful tips on presenting some of the material for the course.

THANKS

In preparing this book, I owe my first debt of thanks to the many students and teaching assistants who have worked with me in developing the critical thinking course at Syracuse University. Examples from students sometimes appear in the book, usually with some editing, and I thank the many students who have made those contributions. Contributors include Emily Blitman, Tonette Chandler, Noah Goldman, Amanda Gordon, Carl Jetty, Russell Kincaid, Jason Powalisz, Jason Strangfeld, David Vacanti, and Jessica Vargas. I owe an even greater debt to the many students whose ideas, questions, suggestions, hesitations, and inability to understand have revealed where I needed to correct my own thinking or where my exposition needed improvement, and I thank them. In addition, my many conversations with teaching assistants about their experience with students in the course have contributed significantly to the ideas, the exposition, and the exercises that appear here. I am very grateful for their contribution to the book and for their fine work in general.

In the process of editorial review, many people provided helpful comments that have led to numerous changes, some of them quite significant. I thank them for their help.

I owe special thanks to my colleague in the Department of Physics, Peter Saulsen, who read the book and made many useful comments, encouraging me in the belief that this book can be helpful in developing critical thinking in many contexts.

Syracuse University has assisted considerably in the development of this text through their support of my teaching, and especially by providing the excellent office staff in the Department of Philosophy. Sue McDougal, Lisa Mowins, and Melissa Linde make it easy to keep producing new material for classes, and I thank them for their help.

Dianne Apter has made my life far better than it would have been without her, and I thank her most of all.

Reasons, Explanations and Decisions: Guidelines for Critical Thinking

CHAPTER 1

INTRODUCTION

WHEN SOMEONE IS LIKELY TO KILL OTHERS, WHATEVER IS THE LEAST EXPENSIVE, EFFECTIVE MEANS OF PREVENTING IT IS JUSTIFIED. THAT'S WHY I FAVOR CAPITAL PUNISHMENT FOR CONVICTED MURDERERS.

THE UNITED STATES IS NOT REALLY DEMOCRATIC, BECAUSE IF IT WERE, THEN EACH PERSON'S OPINION WOULD AFFECT GOVERNMENT SIGNIFICANTLY.

FOOTBALL SHOULD BE DISCOURAGED, BECAUSE IT MAKES PEOPLE AGGRESSIVE.

PEOPLE HAVE THE RIGHT TO DO WHAT THEY WANT WITH THEIR OWN BODIES, SO A PREGNANT WOMAN CAN HAVE THE FETUS ABORTED IF SHE WANTS.

ACTIONS BY CORPORATIONS AND GOVERNMENTAL AGENCIES THAT WOULD LEAD TO THE EXTINCTION OF A HARMLESS SPECIES OF PLANT OR ANIMAL CHANGE THE WORLD FOREVER, AND IF THEY CONTINUE WITHOUT CONTROL THEY WILL MAKE THE WORLD A PLACE IN WHICH NONE OF US WOULD WISH TO LIVE. THE ONLY EFFECTIVE WAY TO CONTROL THESE DAMAGING ACTIONS OF CORPORATIONS AND GOVERNMENTAL AGENCIES IS TO HAVE LAWS THAT PROHIBIT ACTIONS THAT WOULD LEAD TO THE EXTINCTION OF A HARMLESS SPECIES OF PLANT OR ANIMAL.

JUSTIFICATION

Whether you are watching television, reading a newspaper, attending a class, or studying a textbook, some person or institution is trying to influence your beliefs, attitudes, or actions. A person taking an *uncritical* attitude does not deliberately choose which of these will affect him or her. Instead, an uncritical person allows external factors to influence thought, attitude, and action in ways that might be unrelated to their value for that person's life.

Our general concern will be to understand the critical skills that we need for making more effective decisions about what to believe and what to do. Of course, we will not be deciding in detail what we should believe about every issue or listing appropriate ways to act in a variety of situations. Rather, we will be doing a more general study, illuminated by many examples, of the appropriate standards for determining what to believe and what to do. Studying the general standards for acquiring or changing belief means exploring the nature of *justification* and the giving of *reasons*. We can identify many subsidiary questions that are important to answer in making decisions about what to believe and how to act. What beliefs are justified? How do we tell whether a belief is justified? How do we develop and present reasons for a conclusion so that we can show others that a belief is justified? How do we evaluate the reasons that others present to justify beliefs? When should we adopt new beliefs? How do we justify a decision when our information is incomplete or imperfect? How do we tell whether an explanation is the best one available?

By encouraging reflective evaluation of the many sources that attempt to influence us, this study should encourage an attitude that gives individuals more control of their lives.

"Critical Thinking"

We will learn how to adopt a critical stance. Adopting a critical stance involves being open to all sorts of opinions and being ready to evaluate them to decide what beliefs best meet the standards we develop. It also involves the creative development of explanations that increase our understanding of our world and an active search for information that would cast doubt on explanations that are offered. It also involves the organization of information to make decisions more effective.

In reading and listening, being critical means taking an active role rather than being a passive absorber of information. We do not merely take in what people say, and we go beyond merely deciding whether we agree or disagree. We consider whether good reasons have been given (or at least can be given) for the claims that are made, and we try to base our own judgments on adequate reasons.

In writing and speaking, being critical requires that we make our justifications explicit, comprehensible, and persuasive. We can do more than just state our opinions. We try to use our knowledge of others in developing reasons that fulfill two conditions: that others will understand those reasons, and that those reasons will convince them that our claims are justified.

A critical stance helps us to move beyond sheepish acceptance of influences, beyond bare disagreement, and beyond dogmatic assertion, to the discovery of resources that can help in evaluating arguments and in advancing a discussion when there is a disagreement. A critical stance opens the possibility of substituting learning and discussion for unreflective belief, unconsidered action, or irresolvable disagreement.

Some of you may be seeing some negatives in this. Critical thinking can challenge our most dearly held beliefs, and it can sometimes make us aware that we are not able to justify any position at all on a subject that we would like to make a decision about. (People often criticize philosophers because philosophers seem to have plenty of questions but few answers.) Prepare to face some of these discomforts. Critical thinking puts you more in control of your beliefs, and that brings responsibilities and difficulties as well as benefits.

Reasons, Arguments, and Logic

When someone gives *reasons* to justify a belief, he or she is presenting an *argument*, and so we can also describe the study of the standards of reasoning as the study of the characteristics that distinguish acceptable arguments from those that are not acceptable. The study of reasoning will help us to evaluate sources of information (and misinformation), and it will also help us see how to justify our conclusions to ourselves and to others. In other words, we will be learning how to identify, develop, present, and evaluate arguments.

People often use the word *argument* to refer to a dispute. As we use the word *argument,* however, not every dispute involves arguments. A dispute can be a futile clash of dogmatically maintained positions, for example. If neither side gives reasons for the positions held, then there is no argument (in our sense of the term *argument*). Dogmatic clashes of opinion tend to produce conversations that make no progress—if they manage to allow conversation at all. When we present and consider arguments, we can understand each other's opinions better and see how beliefs connect. This enables us to see more clearly where our important disagreements are, and it provides a basis for detailed, productive conversation. When people are willing to give reasons and discuss them, they are usually open to considering the possibility that the reasons for their conclusions might not be good reasons, and so someone might even change an opinion on the basis of considered argument.

It is also important that an argument need not involve any dispute. For example, an argument could consist of reasons for an old, uncontroversial belief.

1. Jennifer advised me to invest in this company, I followed her advice, and now I am rich because of it. As I have always done, I should trust her financial advice.

Or an argument could consist of reasons leading to a completely new belief that no one disagrees with because no one had any opinion about it before.

2. The blue feathers and the particular kind of nest found here clearly show that blue jays lived here last summer.

The study of argument involves learning how to identify and appraise reasoning and how to reason effectively.

An argument has two components. The reasons presented as justifications are the *premises* of the argument, and the claim they are intended to justify is the *conclusion.*

3. Because almost everyone is disappointed with Democratic policies (premise), the Republicans will score significant gains in the next election (conclusion).

4. The cost of transporting needed raw materials to our manufacturing plant has become high (premise). There are other regions nearer to the source of supply, where transportation costs are low (premise). In addition, construction costs are low there (premise), and labor costs will be lower than at our present location (premise). Thus we should consider moving (conclusion).

5. The new drug RXQ should not be sold to the public (conclusion), because it contains three known carcinogens and has not been sufficiently tested (premise).

6. Someone is knocking at the back door (premise). The meter man must be here (conclusion).

Note that the conclusion does not need to be at the end of the presentation of an argument. (See example 5.)

Formal logic is the discipline that systematically describes the relationship between premises and conclusions, telling us when the premises and conclusion connect in a way that makes for valid reasoning. In studying reasoning in a more informal way in this book, we will learn how to appraise arguments even when we cannot apply formal techniques. A thorough knowledge of formal logic and its limits is an extraordinarily valuable tool, but it needs to be supplemented by other skills of argument evaluation, and we can usefully develop many of those skills apart from the detailed study of the methods of formal logic.

Of course, people are not always presenting arguments when they speak or write. We tell stories, present facts without argument, ask questions, make exclamations, express admiration, and much more. However, whenever someone presents reasons for accepting some claim, we have an argument, and giving and evaluating reasons is a key element of intelligent belief formation. When we are using arguments to convince others of a conclusion, the premises and conclusion will be assertions we make to convince others. When we are confirming our own beliefs or developing new beliefs on our own, we might never state the premises and conclusion aloud. (Consider examples 1 and 6 above. Most often, we could come to such conclusions without saying or writing anything.)

In developing and appraising arguments, we will sometimes focus on how we use language in formulating arguments. Even though many arguments are not stated aloud (or in print), it is very valuable to see how to use the resources of language in drawing conclusions and presenting arguments.

Recognizing Arguments in Ordinary Language

Most often, someone is interested in a particular argument because he or she is thinking of presenting that argument, or because someone else has presented it as a reason for accepting the conclusion. In presenting an argument, the speaker or writer needs to state the premises and conclusion in a way that enables the audience to tell what the argument is. To consider a paragraph or series of paragraphs presenting an argument and to evaluate whether the argument presented is a good argument, we must be able to identify the premises and conclusion of the argument. Several indicator words aid us in doing this. If we see one of these, we can suspect that a conclusion is about to follow.

So

Hence

Thus

Therefore

It must be that

"The President is very unpopular, *so* the opposition party will make significant electoral gains." The word *so* helps to make it clear what is premise and what is conclusion. We also have words indicating that a premise is about to follow.

> For
>
> Since
>
> Because
>
> Due to the fact that

"*Since* the President is very unpopular, the opposition will make significant electoral gains." These indicator words aid in identifying premises and conclusion.

We must use all of these aids with care, though. Many of these words, especially *since, because* and *so,* have other uses to indicate temporal, causal, or other types of connections.

> *Since* Tuesday he has not studied.
>
> It broke *because* it dropped.
>
> He shouted 'Help!' *so* that everyone would look at him.

These statements of temporal relationship and causal sequence are not arguments. Nothing is presented as a reason (a premise) for thinking that some other thing (a conclusion) is true.

It is also important to note that we can present an argument without any of these indicator words.

> The President is very unpopular, and his party has not used its legislative majority effectively. The opposition will make significant gains in the next election.

As long as we find some sentence or sentences asserted as reasons for believing some further claim, we know that we have an argument. Here, what is said in the first sentence seems to be offered as a reason for accepting the second. Still, the absence of indicator words can make it harder to know whether an argument is being given, and it is generally better to use indicator words to let your audience see clearly when you are offering premises in support of a conclusion.

Even when it is clear that an argument is being presented and the conclusion has been clearly stated, the other elements of the argument are not always perfectly explicit. Sometimes we can leave critical premises unstated because they are general knowledge or because they are assumptions indicated in an obvious way by the rest of what we say.

> Whales must have lungs, because all mammals have lungs.

Clearly the conclusion is that whales have lungs. The word *must* in a sentence frequently indicates that the sentence is a conclusion, and the word *because* is being used here to indicate the premise of an argument (a reason for accepting the conclusion). However, we can connect the conclusion with the explicitly stated premise, "all mammals have lungs," only if we assume that whales are mammals. The speaker does not need to make that premise explicit, because it is generally known to be true, and because the rest of what is said clearly indicates that the speaker is making this assumption. (In Chapter 2 we will look more closely at the process of identifying missing elements of arguments.)

EXERCISE 1A

For each passage below, determine whether it presents an argument. If it does, then indicate what the conclusion is.

1. Flutes must use reeds, because all woodwind instruments use reeds, and flutes are woodwind instruments.

2. No brass instruments use reeds, and flutes don't use reeds, so flutes must be brass instruments.

3. After a hard day of rehearsals, John loves to sit in a quiet meadow where he can hear only the birds.

4. Since last summer, when he hitched around Europe playing music on the street, he takes his flute everywhere.

5. Since a clarinet requires reeds, it must not be a brass instrument.

6. Betty will be angry unless someone else brings the music stands. But if Ann doesn't bring them, no one will. So either Ann will bring the music stands or Betty will be angry.

7. Carl was angry because he had no music stand.

8. When I hear you play like that, it makes me so angry that I want to smash your flute and break your jaw.

9. Hector hates jazz, so he shouldn't play jazz.

10. If Hector hates jazz, then he shouldn't play it.

11. Hector hates jazz. Because of this, he didn't play with our group.

EXERCISE 1B

List three claims that you agree with but that most people disagree with. (Later we will ask you to construct an argument for one or more of these opinions. Right now, though, we just want your instructor to have a chance to make suggestions about which of these claims will be most promising for further development and about how you can formulate your claim in the most useful way.)

More on Identifying Arguments

When reading a passage, you can tell if there is an argument by determining whether some statements in the passage are given as reasons for accepting a conclusion. A passage may have a definite *point* and yet not offer any reasons for accepting that point. Compare these paragraphs:

> Charles Brown is running for Congress this year in the 27th Congressional District. He is the Democratic candidate, running against Ike Mason, the Republican. Both are lifelong residents of the district. I urge you to vote for Charles Brown.

You should vote for Charles Brown in the upcoming election. He has devoted his entire adult life to public service, and he will represent your interests with the same energy and influence that have always characterized his work. Unlike his opponent, he is a real friend of working people, and he owes nothing to big business.

The second passage provides reasons why you should vote for Charles Brown, so it contains one or more arguments. The first makes some factual claims, but the passage provides nothing as a reason for voting for Charles Brown, so there is no argument in the first example.

A passage may contain an argument along with other material; examples, clarification, or comments on related matters may occur. Once you have identified a conclusion, you cannot assume that everything else in the passage is a reason for accepting that conclusion. In the following paragraph, we label each statement so that we can discuss them more easily and show their relationship in a diagram.

[S1] An issue has arisen in connection with our plans to build a new school. [S2] The site selected includes marsh habitat that will be destroyed if the school is built. [S3] Some people believe that this marsh habitat is critical for the survival of several bird species in our area. However, [S4] I think that we should go ahead and build the school there anyway. [S5] That is the only convenient location available at a reasonable price, and [S6] there is plenty of marsh habitat in neighboring counties. [S7] The species in question will thrive in the habitats still available, and [S8] the taxpayers will not approve funds for a school at a more expensive site.

The first three sentences are background information. They are not part of the argument that is presented in the rest of the paragraph. Once we identify [S4] as the conclusion, we can see that [S1], [S2], and [S3] are not reasons for thinking that the conclusion is true. If we indicate premise–conclusion relationships by drawing an arrow from a premise to a conclusion that it supports, we can simply leave [S1], [S2], and [S3] out of the argument diagram.

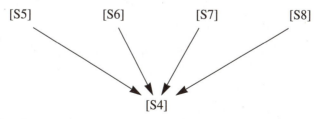

A passage may contain more than one argument, and the conclusion of one argument in a passage may be the premise of yet another argument.

[S1] You should vote for Alicia Williams and Carla Sanchez. [S2] Both are lifelong Democrats who will fight for your interests. [S3] Alicia Williams will use her government experience in the State Attorney General's Office in the Senate. [S4] Carla Sanchez has a thorough knowledge of the people of this community and their needs; [S5] no one could be a better representative for us.

We can break [S1] into two conclusions:

[S1a]   You should vote for Alicia Williams.

[S1b]   You should vote for Carla Sanchez.

The entire passage then has this argumentative structure:

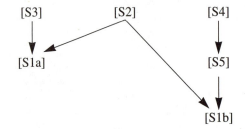

[S2] is a premise for two arguments. (We could also have broken [S2] into two separate parts, as we did with [S1].) Note too that [S5] is both a conclusion and a premise. [S4] is a premise for the conclusion [S5], and [S5] is then a premise for the conclusion [S1b].

The conclusion of an argument might not be explicitly stated if the passage makes it clear what the conclusion is. In the following case, there are two clear unstated conclusions.

Professor Gould has said that Julius Caesar ordered that giraffes be presented at the Colosseum. But Caesar died early in the first century A.D., and the Colosseum was not built until the third century A.D.

Two conclusions are clear here:

[C1]   Caesar could not have ordered that giraffes be presented at the Colosseum.

[C2]   Professor Gould is wrong about this.

Our diagram would include both of these.

[S2] Caesar died early in the first century A.D.   [S3] The Colosseum was not built until the third century A.D.

[C1] Caesar could not have ordered that giraffes be presented at the Colosseum. (unstated)

[S1] Professor Gould has said that Julius Caesar ordered that giraffes be presented at the Colosseum.

[C2] Professor Gould is wrong about this. (unstated)

EXERCISE 1C

Read each of the following passages. Is there an argument? For each argument, answer these questions:

What is the main conclusion?

What are the premises?

(Remember that the premises are the statements that are intended to support the conclusion. A paragraph may include some statements that are background information or even just irrelevant comments. Remember also that the conclusion may be unstated and that a paragraph may contain more than one argument.)

Draw a diagram to indicate the premise–conclusion relationships in the passage. (In your diagram, use the labels provided for the sentences.)

1. [S1] All people should have equal political rights, because [S2] there is nothing that differentiates people at a birth in a way that is relevant to their political rights.

2. [S1] The taxpayers must not be forced to bear new taxes, and [S2] the city has made all of the cuts that it can. [S3] Unless there are additional cuts in school district or city programs, there will have to be new taxes. Thus [S4] the school district must cut its programs.

3. [S1] If we don't consolidate city and county school systems, the city school system will continue to deteriorate, producing a large number of young adults who are not equipped to find work that will keep them out of poverty. [S2] We must not allow this disastrous social situation to occur, so [S3] we must consolidate city and county schools.

4. [S1] We—the governors in a democracy—must make intelligent decisions when we vote. [S2] Without a free flow of information, we cannot make intelligent decisions. Thus [S3] there must be freedom of speech in a democracy.

5. [S1] The other day, my wife and I tried to take a boat ride that would ordinarily last just 20 minutes. [S2] As we left our marina, we were stopped by the county sheriff's boat for a sobriety test and a thorough safety inspection. [S3] As we re-entered the marina, we were stopped by the state police boat for another sobriety test. [S4] We support the enforcement of safety laws, but [S5] when boaters who have not been drinking and who show no signs of intoxication are stopped twice, increasing a 20-minute outing to an hour-long ordeal, that is harassment.

6. [S1] Many herbs are known to have medicinal properties. So [S2] it is not a waste of taxpayer dollars to finance trials of herbal treatments that appear implausible. [S3] Open-mindedness is a friend of scientific investigation, and since [S4] herbal treatments are widely used, [S5] it is important to determine whether they work and whether they have any harmful effects.

7. [S1] Abortion is the destruction of an unborn baby. [S2] A new human life begins as soon as the egg has been fertilized. [S3] Science reveals without question that once the egg is fertilized, every identifying characteristic of a

brand new human being is present, even the color of the eyes and hair, the sex and everything else. [S4] Pregnancy is the period for this new human life to mature, not to "become human"—[S5] it already is. (From "Abortion: Questions and Answers," Cardinal John J. O'Connor.)

8. [S1] A steady movement of people from the city to suburban and rural areas has decreased the city's population, increased the percentage of its population that are poor, and increased the percentage of its population that are African-American and Hispanic. [S2] If the tax base continues to shrink, then the resulting poor support for education and services, combined with racial and ethnic polarization, will lead to increasing tension between city and suburban populations. [S3] We must stop this trend. [S4] The only way to stop it is by consolidating city and county governments, so that there is a single tax base in support of a unified, high-quality system of education and a uniform level of municipal services.

Maintaining Coherent Belief

The evaluation of our beliefs can give us reason to revise or withdraw beliefs when we see that they stand in conflict. Thus I might believe these two things:

> Al is trustworthy.
>
> No one trustworthy would take the books from my room without asking.

Later I may find evidence leading me to believe the following:

> Al took the books from my room without asking.

I now have a problem (in addition to the missing books). At least one of these three beliefs is false; the three sentences are logically connected in a way that makes it impossible for all of them to be true. Perhaps Al is not worthy of continued trust; perhaps there is some special reason that could lead someone trustworthy to take the books without asking (maybe the room was flooding); or perhaps the evidence is misleading and Al didn't really take them. I may resolve to look for further information to help me to decide which of the three claims is false, but even without further information, logic is sufficient to establish that they cannot all be true.

The principles at work in arguments are also at work here. Some *sets* of beliefs are logically acceptable, but others are not. The analytical techniques that help us distinguish acceptable arguments from unacceptable arguments also help us distinguish logically unacceptable sets of beliefs from logically acceptable sets. A set of sentences or beliefs like those in our example is an *inconsistent* set, because there is no possible way for all of them to be true; at least one is false.

This is an inconsistent set of sentences:

> {Al is trustworthy.
>
> No one trustworthy would take the books from my room without asking.
>
> Al took the books from my room without asking.}

Once you uncover the inconsistency, it is not acceptable to continue to believe all three. You are sure to be wrong about at least one of them if you do. Although our main focus will be the study of arguments, we will sometimes apply our analytical skills to discovering or showing the inconsistency of sets of sentences.

VALIDITY AND SOUNDNESS

We need additional precise terminology to help us to focus on justification. Consider the following two arguments. (Here we will adopt the useful practice of writing premises separately and marking the conclusion with a special symbol, $\therefore$. Ordinarily, when we present arguments in English, we use words like *therefore, thus,* and *so* to indicate the conclusion. The special symbol $\therefore$ makes the conclusion stand out more visibly.)

A. If Socrates was human, then he was warm-blooded.
Socrates was human.
$\therefore$ Socrates was warm-blooded.

B. If Socrates was a plumber, then he used a plunger.
Socrates was a plumber.
$\therefore$ Socrates used a plunger.

We can all readily recognize A to be a good argument. Is B a good argument too? That question should not be quite so easy to answer, because the question itself is too crude. There are two importantly distinct factors that go into making an argument good.

Argument B has both bad features and good features. On the bad side, it has a false premise, so it cannot be a convincing argument among those of us who recognize the premise's falsity. On the good side, the premises are appropriately connected with the conclusion. *If the premises were true, the conclusion would have to be true as well*. If we were studying formal logic alone, we would study this *connection* between premises and conclusion—that is, what it would be for premises to support or justify a conclusion if they were true. This central concept of logic is the concept of a *valid* argument—an argument in which the premises *support* the conclusion—and this concept can be explained in either of two ways:

> In a valid argument, any possible situation in which the premises are true is also a situation in which the conclusion is true.

> In a valid argument, it is not possible for the conclusion to be false when all the premises are true.

Understanding these characterizations enable us to *understand* what makes some arguments valid and provides the foundation for *showing* that arguments are valid or showing that they are invalid. Validity and truth are the two important but separable components of good argument. In our studies, we will be concerned with both of these aspects of good argument.

Examples A and B are both valid arguments. The premises and conclusion are connected in the right sort of way; it is not possible for the conclusion to be false when the premises are true. (In other words, in any possible situation in which the premises are true, the conclusion is also true. The premises imply the conclusion.)

Still, A can be seen to be a much better argument than B when we consider the other evaluative factor, the facts about Socrates (i.e., whether the premises are true). Every premise of A is true, but at least one premise of argument B is false. There are two features of good argument, validity and truth, and when an argument has both features, we call it a sound argument.

A *sound* argument has both of the following features:

1. It is valid.
2. All of its premises are true.

In seeking to establish new truths based on things already known, we are seeking sound arguments. Because sound arguments are valid and have true premises, they must also have true conclusions. Valid argument preserves truth, so that if we start with all true premises in a valid argument, we are certain to have a true conclusion.

An *unsound* argument, on the other hand, is one that fails to meet one or both of the conditions for soundness; either it is invalid or it has one or more false premises. Although both arguments A and B above are valid, only A is sound.

When it is possible for an argument to have true premises with a false conclusion, the argument is *invalid*. In an invalid argument, no special relationship guarantees that if the premises are true, then the conclusion must also be true.

C. Some ancient Greeks were philosophers.
   Socrates was a philosopher.
   ∴ Socrates was an ancient Greek.

D. All Babylonians were philosophers.
   Socrates was a philosopher.
   ∴ Socrates was a Babylonian.

Neither of these two arguments is valid. In other words, there is no guarantee that truth will be preserved when the step is taken from the premises to the conclusion in these arguments. Even if the premises are true (as in C), they do not provide an adequate justification for the conclusion. In our studies, we will be developing a keener sense of when an argument is invalid, and it is mainly through this that we will enhance our abilities to develop and appraise arguments. (C and D, of course, are unsound arguments, because they are invalid.)

In studying critical thinking, we will try to develop an ability to make judgments about soundness (i.e., about both validity and truth) in as wide a range of cases as possible. This practical ability will not have the systematic organization of formal logic, and we must often settle for less certainty in our judgments. However, we will be able to apply our skills directly in a wide range of cases that we actually encounter in deciding what to believe.

We must learn to look at the two features of arguments separately; in other words, we must learn to make judgments about validity that are independent of our judgments about truth. We can evaluate an argument for validity independently of trying to determine whether the conclusion is actually true or false and independently of trying to determine the actual truth-values of the premises. That skill can often help us in criticizing arguments and in developing arguments. It helps in the criticism of arguments, because it enables us to pinpoint the exact source of our disagreement. When we can show that a speaker has argued invalidly, we avoid *mere* disagreement and make it possible for the discussion to advance; the speaker can identify the gap that needs to be filled or the revision that is required to make the argument more convincing. When we are developing arguments, the ability to test them for validity enables us to make sure that there are no inferential holes, and so it enables us to present our conclusions more effectively. We can focus on arguments that are at least valid and so have a chance of being sound.

Since we can make judgments about the validity of an argument without knowing whether the premises are true, we can often show that an argument is unacceptable without ever having to enter into any factual dispute about the truth of its premises. This is a valuable ability, because our knowledge of the subject matter may be imperfect, or the beliefs that serve as premises for an argument may be controversial. Neither of those things will matter (to the adequacy of the argument) if the argument is not valid. If it is not valid, then it cannot be a sound argument, and we do not need to decide whether the premises are true.

> If we were at the beginning of a long-term global warming trend, then El Niño would be causing a northern shift in the jet stream. We have seen just such a northern shift. Therefore, we must be at the beginning of a long-term global warming trend.

The first sentence of this is a claim about weather systems that requires considerable knowledge of meteorology to evaluate. Nevertheless, a person who doubts the existence of such a global warming trend does not need to know whether the first sentence is true in order to begin criticism of this argument. The argument is not valid, so even if the premises are true, they do not provide a compelling reason to accept the conclusion. The northern shift could be caused by something else (even if a similar shift would also be caused by a long-term global warming trend). Thus the recognition that this is not a valid argument provides a basis for questioning the conclusion, and resolution of the factual, meteorological questions is not yet relevant.

(Even though this argument is not valid, it might seem to you that it provides *some* support for its conclusion. That question will be taken up later, when we discuss the evaluation of explanations and their importance in justifying beliefs. For now, we can say that the above argument would at least need to have the added premise that global warming is among the best explanations for the change in El Niño and the jet stream.)

Considering the Possibilities

Validity is an independent component of soundness, and it involves the full range of truth-value possibilities. The *actual* truth-values represent *just one* truth-value possibility. In a valid argument, the premises and conclusion constitute a unit such that *in every possible situation*, if the premises were true, then the conclusion would be true. In showing that an argument is valid, one must somehow consider the full range of possibilities, checking to see whether connections exist that rule out the possibility of true premises with a false conclusion.

Some examples may make it clearer how we are concerned with truth-value possibilities, not with actual truth-values.

   a. If John were to fail chemistry, he would not graduate. John will not fail chemistry. Therefore, he will graduate.

   b. All primates have some broad teeth. All mammals that eat vegetables have some broad teeth. So all primates are mammals that eat vegetables.

   c. Some senators won't dance unless they get their bills passed. Anyone who won't dance will be painted blue. So some senators will be painted blue unless they get their bills passed.

Only example c is valid, even though the individual sentences in example b are true, the sentences in c are false, and we don't know the actual truth-value of the sentences in a. In examples a and b, we can think of possible situations in which the premises would be true and the conclusion false. In example a, John might pass chemistry but fail some other course he needed for graduation. In example b, it might have been that many creatures that did not eat vegetables, including some primates that did not eat vegetables, had broad teeth. Nothing in the premises rules out this possibility, so the premises do not guarantee that the conclusion is true. For example c, though, there is no possible situation in which the premises are true with the conclusion false. That is why c is valid. (Of course, none of these examples are sound arguments. Examples a and b are invalid, and example c has one or more false premises.)

    For examples a and b, we were able to describe possible situations in which the premises would be true with the conclusion false. Our doing this makes the case that the argument is invalid, and the possible situation described is called a "counterexample" to the claim of validity. It is also called a "model" that shows invalidity for that type of argument.

    The definition of validity in terms of possible situations tells us immediately how we could show someone that an argument is *invalid*: An example of just *one possible situation* in which the premises are true with the conclusion false will guarantee invalidity.

    Suppose that someone were to argue in the following way:

    Since some lawyers are senators (premise), and since some senators are old (premise), it must be that some lawyers are old (conclusion).

One way to see that this is *invalid* is to envision a possible situation in which the premises would be true with the conclusion false. For example, if things became so bad with the law profession that we decided to kill off all the lawyers and start over again, allowing no one over thirty to become a lawyer, then after a short while we might have a situation in which the premises were true with the conclusion false. If a few of the new, young lawyers were elected to the Senate (joining some of the old non-lawyers already there), then there could be a situation in which these were true:

    Some lawyers are senators.

    Some senators are old.

The following, though, would be false:

    Some lawyers are old.

Thus the argument cannot be valid, because it is possible for the premises to be true with the conclusion false. The premises alone do not *guarantee* the truth of the conclusion.

Note how we need just *one possible situation* to show *invalidity*. This situation can be very far-fetched as long as it is clearly a possible situation.

If we try to describe a situation in which some simple *valid* argument has true premises with a false conclusion, we will not succeed. For example, imagine a situation in which these sentences are true:

> If Socrates was human, then he was warm-blooded.
>
> Socrates was human.

Now try to add to the situation that the following sentence is *false* (while the others are still true):

> Socrates was warm-blooded.

There is no such possible situation. To make the conclusion false, one must also falsify at least one of the premises, so attempts to show invalidity fail.

With more complex arguments, it is not so obvious when the attempt to describe a possible situation succeeds and when it fails. We will develop techniques of argument evaluation that can be applied to both simple and complex arguments, but often we use public discussion as the testing ground for validity, relying on those who challenge an argument's conclusion to show that the argument is unsound. They can do so by describing a (possible) situation in which the premises are true with the conclusion false (showing invalidity), or they can try to show that at least one premise is actually false.

Inductive Strength

Working with the concept of validity is an important way to develop your understanding of good argument and your ability to analyze arguments. Nevertheless, we need to note here that not every strong argument is a valid argument. If I have seen the same professor come into my classroom every Tuesday when my class is done (to set up for her own class, I have presumed), then I have good reason to think that she will be there at the end of my class this Tuesday. But this argument is not valid.

> P1   She has been there at that time every Tuesday so far this semester.
>
> ∴   She will be there this Tuesday.

It is certainly possible for the premise to be true with the conclusion false.

If an argument is not valid, but nevertheless the premises support the conclusion to some degree, the argument is *inductively strong*. Arguments that are intended to be inductively strong (but not valid in our very stringent sense) can be called *inductive* arguments. We will look closely at the concept of inductive strength of arguments in Chapters 6–9.

EXERCISE 1D

In this chapter, we introduced some special terminology:

> true statement
>
> valid argument

sound argument

consistent set of statements

The special terms introduced here have uses in other contexts: a lover can be true (or untrue) to his or her beloved, a passport can be valid (or invalid), a ship's hull can be structurally sound (or unsound), and a car can be consistent (or inconsistent) in its performance. Such uses are relatively easy to distinguish from our uses of these terms, because they apply to entirely different sorts of things. We have to be more careful, however, about other familiar uses of terms, because sometimes people say that a conclusion is sound or that a statement is valid, and this conflicts with our usage in a way that is potentially more confusing. In our discussions of justification, it is important to stick to the usage conventions we have established, and part of that is to notice that we will apply the words *valid* and *sound* only to arguments. We will never say that a person has made a valid point or that an argument has a valid conclusion, for example, because those uses differ from our use; points and conclusions are not arguments. Similarly, the word *consistent* will be applied to some sets of statements, but never to arguments. The phrase *consistent argument* would be an incorrect use of our terminology.

We have talked about three different kinds of things: statements (or beliefs), sets of statements (or sets of beliefs), and arguments. Different terminology applies to each, and the terminology for one should not be applied to the others.

A **statement** or **belief** may be

> **true** or **false**
>
> **justified** or **unjustified**

A **set of statements** or **set of beliefs** may be

> **consistent** or **inconsistent**

An **argument** may be

> **valid** or **invalid**
>
> **sound** or **unsound**

For each of the following statements, indicate whether it is a correct or an incorrect use of our terminology. (In this exercise, we are not concerned with which of these statements are actually true. We are concerned only with whether they use our terminology correctly.)

1. Alice presented a true argument.

2. Bernardo's statement is valid.

3. Clara's premises were unsound.

4. Denzel's conclusion is false.

5. Eduardo's conclusion is invalid.

6. The premises of Felicia's argument are consistent, though not all of them are true.

7. Giorgio gave a valid argument.

8. Herman's assumptions are invalid.

9. Irma's argument is consistent.

10. Jared's beliefs are sound.

EXERCISE 1E

For each argument, indicate whether it is valid or invalid. If the argument is invalid, give a counter-example to show invalidity. That is, if the argument is invalid, describe a possible situation in which the premises are all true and the conclusion is false.

A. Every dog is a mammal.
No pets are mammals.
So no dogs are pets.

B. All Olympic skiers train hard.
Some people who train hard ride bicycles when training.
So some Olympic skiers ride bicycles when training.

C. All doctors are musicians.
Some doctors play chess.
So some musicians must play chess.

D. Some dogs howl.
Some dogs swim.
So some dogs that howl swim.

E. All faculty members support the main goals of the striking workers.
Every department chair is a faculty member.
So every department chair supports the main goals of the striking workers.

F. All faculty members support the main goals of the striking workers.
Some department chairs are faculty members.
So some department chairs support the main goals of the striking workers.

EXERCISE 1F

Examine each passage below, and for each, answer the following questions:
(a) Is there an argument? If so, what is the conclusion?
(b) If there is an argument, is it valid?
(c) If there is an argument, is it sound? (Answer with a "?" if you do not know whether the argument is sound.)

1. All doctors have degrees, and all lawyers have degrees. So at least some doctors must be lawyers.

2. Not all doctors have degrees, but all lawyers have degrees. Also, since 1900, no doctors have been lawyers.

3. Since all doctors have degrees, and anyone who has a degree has attended school, every doctor must have attended school.

4. Every doctor is a lawyer. Every lawyer has a degree. So every doctor must have a degree.

5. Some surgeons are lawyers, but no lawyers have studied medicine. So some surgeons haven't studied medicine.

6. Every surgeon in New York is licensed to do surgery. Some doctors are surgeons in New York. Thus some doctors are licensed to do surgery.

7. Doctors and lawyers have clients, and they are also similar in other ways.

8. At least some doctors perform surgery, so, since no lawyers perform surgery, not all doctors are lawyers.

9. Not all doctors do surgery. Some lawyers do medical counseling. But every doctor who does surgery does medical counseling.

10. Whenever a person eats broccoli often, he or she is able to play the saxophone. George Bush was not able to play the saxophone. So George Bush must not have eaten broccoli often.

EXERCISE 1G

Indicate each choice that completes the sentence correctly.

1. Whenever an argument is valid:
   a. it has a true conclusion.
   b. it has true premises and a true conclusion.
   c. it has true premises if it has a true conclusion.
   d. it has a true conclusion if all its premises are true.
   e. it is sound.
   f. it is sound if all its premises are true.
   g. it has a true conclusion if it is sound.
   h. it has a false conclusion if it has a false premise.
   i. it either has a true conclusion or has at least one false premise.
   j. it does not have all true premises and a false conclusion.

2. Every invalid argument:
   a. has a false conclusion if all its premises are true.
   b. has true premises and a false conclusion.
   c. has inconsistent premises.
   d. has a false conclusion.
   e. is unsound.

CHAPTER 2

CONSTRUCTING AND ANALYZING ARGUMENTS

C LINTON SHOULD HAVE BEEN REMOVED FROM OFFICE, BECAUSE HE LIED TO A GRAND JURY, AND THAT ACTION VIOLATES HIS OATH TO UPHOLD AND DEFEND THE CONSTITUTION OF THE UNITED STATES.

CONGRESS'S VOTE TO IMPEACH CLINTON SET A VERY BAD PRECEDENT. NOW, WHENEVER THE CONGRESS IS OF A DIFFERENT PARTY FROM THE PRESIDENT, THEY WILL FEEL FREE TO IMPEACH THE PRESIDENT FOR ANY KIND OF MISCONDUCT, EVEN IF IT HAS NO RELATIONSHIP TO THE PRESIDENT'S OFFICIAL ACTIONS.

I SHOULD STUDY TONIGHT, BECAUSE I HAVE AN IMPORTANT EXAM TOMORROW.

UNMARRIED YOUNG PEOPLE SHOULD NOT HAVE UNPROTECTED SEX, BECAUSE THAT CAN LEAD TO PREGNANCY OR DISEASE THAT CAN GRAVELY DISRUPT THEIR LIVES.

You may have found yourself in the position of presenting or evaluating arguments like these. We use very similar skills when we construct an argument to establish a conclusion and when we analyze someone else's argument. Either way, we must try to construct the best argument we can from the materials immediately available.

When we are constructing arguments, the materials are our own first thoughts; and these usually require some supplementation and some finer crafting before they can fit together to make a sound argument. Sometimes we even find that there is no supplementation or finer crafting that can turn those first thoughts into a sound argument, because there is no way to shape those materials to fulfill the joint goals of validity and truth. Then we must give up the argument.

When we interpret others' words, we usually find a similar incompleteness in our basic material, the actual sentences that we are trying to interpret. In such cases, we must try to supplement those sentences with additional sentences that can link them together into a valid argument. In supplementing what is there, we should try to preserve the truth or reasonable plausibility of the premises as much as possible, to see whether we can construct a sound argument based on the materials that the author of the argument has provided.

IDENTIFY THE CONCLUSION AND THE PREMISES

The construction or analysis of an argument must begin with *identification of the argument's explicit components*. We must ask, "What is the conclusion?" and "What is offered in support of that conclusion?" (that is, "What are the premises?"). The indicator words mentioned in Chapter 1 help us to identify the broad outline of the argument by helping us to identify the conclusion and the premises when we are analyzing others' arguments.

> Since all doctors have studied anatomy, my friend Alice will know whether the femur is a leg bone.

Here, for example, the use of the indicator word *since* makes it clear that "all doctors have studied anatomy" is a premise and that "my friend Alice will know whether the femur is a leg bone" is a conclusion. Even when there are no indicator words, we can still identify the components by asking what is being supported (the conclusion) and what is offered as support (the premises).

> The economy is improving again, with lower unemployment and a strong dollar. We will soon see some inflation, if nothing is done to prevent it.

It is clear that the second sentence is intended to be the conclusion of an argument that has the first sentence as a premise, even though there is no indicator word. The observed state of the economy (described in the first sentence) is mentioned as a reason for thinking that there will be inflation if nothing is done to prevent it. In reading, we can generally get a good start on finding the conclusion if we ask the question "What is this person (the speaker or writer) trying to convince me of?" (In Chapters 3 and 4, we will also look at some methods of persuasion other than argument.)

FILL IN CONNECTING PREMISES

Once the conclusion and explicit premises are identified, we must ask whether any unstated supplementary material must be included as a part of the argument. Is the speaker making some assumptions that are needed in the argument? In identifying what supports the conclusion that "my friend Alice will know whether the femur is a leg bone" in the example above, we must find more than the stated premise "all doctors have studied anatomy." If this argument is to have a chance of being valid, it must also involve some *unstated premises* connecting the stated premise with the conclusion. In this case, it seems that the speaker is probably assuming two things: that Alice is a doctor, and that any doctor who has studied anatomy will know whether the femur is a leg bone. In this example, what has been said is a pretty clear indicator of what supplementation is needed to construct a valid argument. What the speaker says makes little sense unless he or she is making these assumptions or something very much like them. The whole argument is this, then:

[P1]   All doctors have studied anatomy.

[P2]   Any doctor who has studied anatomy <u>will know whether the femur is a leg bone</u>. (unstated premise)

[P3]   <u>My friend Alice</u> is a doctor. (unstated premise)

∴ [C]   My friend Alice will know whether the femur is a leg bone.

Note how the added premises [P2] and [P3] connect [P1] with the conclusion. The argument's premises include every part of the conclusion (underlined in [P2] and [P3]), and the remaining elements of the premises connect the parts of the conclusion together in a way that is appropriate to support the conclusion validly.

The question "What additional premises are needed to establish validity?" is of course not the only important question about an argument. We also want to know, for example, what reason we have to believe that the premises are true. That, however, is a very different question; it is a question about the soundness of the argument. To answer it, we would need to identify the reasons for believing that all doctors have studied anatomy. Most often, though, it is better to take up the question of the validity of the stated argument first. Identifying any unstated premises that are required to make the argument valid makes it clearer to us what the fundamental elements of the argument are. We can take up the question of soundness later, looking into the reasons to accept the premises we have identified.

Of course, there are times when we cannot simply fill in the supplementary premises that would make for a complete valid argument and make clear how the whole argument goes. This may happen because we just don't know enough about the speaker or the subject matter to guess what was intended or know what premises would be reasonable. At other times, we are unable to use the materials given to construct a valid argument simply because the materials cannot be suitably connected. There are invalid arguments.

If John passed chemistry, then he will graduate. But he did not pass chemistry, so he will not graduate.

This argument is invalid, and there is no evident way to revise it to make a valid argument. The best we can do is to point out its invalidity and ask the person who offered it how he would like to revise it. (We determined how to show invalidity in Chapter 1.)

In constructing your own arguments, you may sometimes begin with just a conclusion that you wish to support.

[C]   Capital punishment is sometimes justified.

If you wish to support such a conclusion, you should try to think of a statement that you might use to support that conclusion and then continue to fill out the argument much as you would if you were analyzing someone else's argument. For example, if you think that [C] is true, it might be because you feel that the cost of maintaining the very worst criminals in prison for life is excessive. Then you would have this premise as a part of your reason for accepting [C]:

[P1]   The cost of maintaining the very worst criminals in prison for life is excessive.

You would then need to find other premises that would connect that premise validly to your conclusion, and of course these other premises would also have to be claims that you felt you could defend.

[P2]   Some criminals, the very worst, must receive capital punishment or be maintained in prison for life.

[P3]   Any punishment is justified if it is the only alternative to a punishment that has excessive costs.

The argument with premises [P1] through [P3], and conclusion [C] now seems valid. This can provide a beginning for a dialogue on the substantive issue. We can start to evaluate whether these premises are really true.

In discussion, those who wish to criticize an argument can do several different things.

Critics can try to show that the argument is not really valid even though it appears to be at first glance. (That will not work in this particular example, because the argument is valid. Unless you can show validity, however, you should consider such criticisms.)

Critics can try to show that one of the premises is false and that therefore the argument is not sound. [P3] is likely to be the most controversial premise in our example. Faced with this challenge, you would have to try to give reasons for accepting [P3] or at least try to show that the critics' reasons for doubting [P3] are not well founded.

More weakly, a critic can suggest that one of the premises is unjustified; we do not have adequate reason to think that it is true (even if it is true). In this case, your response will again be to give an argument in support of that premise, to convince the critic that acceptance of that premise is justified.

Critics may also suggest that some element of the argument is vague—that the argument is not persuasive simply because it is not at all clear what is being said. For example, the claim that the cost of a punishment is excessive is somewhat unclear. (In Chapter 3, on meaning, we will discuss in some detail this kind of criticism and the responses to it.)

In constructing an argument, you may also wish to consider other approaches to your conclusion. For example, the following argument patterns are validating patterns. Any argument that fits one of these patterns will be valid, so they can be used as a basis for constructing arguments that capital punishment is sometimes justified. The argument based on one of these general patterns will be convincing only if the general pattern can be filled out in a way that makes the premises acceptable. You should not expect your audience to accept an argument until it meets both conditions: It must be accepted as valid, and the premises must be accepted as true.

A. [P1]   Anything fulfilling condition X <u>is justified</u>.
  [P2]   <u>Capital punishment sometimes</u> fulfills condition X.
  ∴ [C]   Capital punishment is sometimes justified.

B. [P1]   Any punishment fulfilling condition X <u>is justified</u>.
  [P2]   <u>Capital punishment sometimes</u> fulfills condition X.
  ∴ [C]   Capital punishment is sometimes justified.

C. [P1]   In certain conditions Y (when certain kinds of crimes have been committed), any punishment fulfilling condition X <u>is justified</u>.
  [P2]   <u>In cases of type Z</u>, conditions Y exist and <u>capital punishment</u> fulfills condition X.
  [P3]   There are cases of type Z.
  ∴ [C]   Capital punishment is sometimes justified (i.e., in cases of type Z).

D. [P1]   <u>Capital punishment is justified</u> if it is the only way to achieve certain goals W.
  [P2]   <u>In certain conditions Y</u>, capital punishment is the only way to fulfill goals W.
  [P3]   Situations fulfilling the conditions Y occur.
  ∴ [C]   Capital punishment is sometimes (under conditions Y) justified.

Each of these patterns for the premises would validly yield the conclusion in question. Note that the elements of the conclusion occur in the premises in a way that links the premises together and links the premises to the conclusion. The trick, then, is to find ways to fill in one of these patterns (or some other validating argument pattern) in such a way that the premises are *true*, so that you have a sound argument for your conclusion. Some patterns are more promising than others. For example, Pattern A has a very general first premise, and it will be hard to fill in "conditions X" in Pattern A in a way that is clear and specific enough to be convincing. Pattern B is only slightly different, but it seems more likely that we can find a true statement with the general form of its first premise, because we now need only a general statement about punishments, not a general statement about all things. (Note that the premise [P3] in the argument recently discussed is an example of a premise with the same general form as [P2] of argument schema B. Making it explicitly of that form requires only slight restatement: "Any punishment that is the only alternative to a punishment that has excessive costs is justified.")

  These patterns do not exhaust the possibilities. The idea here is to come up with some *valid* argument patterns that might underlie a sound argument for the conclusion. You can revise as you work, as long as you are still working with a *valid* pattern after your revision.

EXERCISE 2A

Use each of the general patterns B, C, and D above, and construct a *valid* argument for the conclusion that capital punishment is sometimes justified. In other words, replace X, Y, Z, and W with suitable material so that you have a specific valid argument.

Note: This does not have to be a sound argument. For the purposes of this exercise, we are concerned only with validity. (However, if you think that capital punishment is sometimes justified, then you should be able to come up with some argument that you believe is sound. Perhaps your argument will fit one of these patterns, or perhaps it will be based on a different valid argument pattern.)

Here is one set of answers for this question. (Note that B has a very implausible first premise, but the others improve on this. D is an argument that might be worth genuine discussion in a debate about capital punishment.)

Pattern B

[P1]   Any punishment that serves as an effective deterrent to criminal behavior is justified.

[P2]   Capital punishment sometimes serves as an effective deterrent to criminal behavior.

Therefore, capital punishment is sometimes justified.

Pattern C

[P1]   When crimes of an abnormally inhuman nature are committed, any punishment that will put an end to the criminal behavior is justified.

[P2]   In cases of excessively brutal slayings, a crime of an abnormally inhuman nature has been committed, and capital punishment will put an end to the criminal behavior.

[P3]   There are cases of excessively brutal slayings.

Therefore, capital punishment is justified (in cases of excessively brutal slayings).

Pattern D

[P1]   Capital punishment is justified if it is the only reasonable way to prevent a violent felon from striking again.

[P2]   When a violent felon has been convicted and punished several times and this has not affected that person's behavior, capital punishment is the only reasonable way to prevent that violent felon from striking again.

[P3]   Sometimes violent felons who have been convicted and punished several times do not change their behavior at all.

Therefore, capital punishment is justified (when a violent felon has been convicted and punished several times and has not changed his or her behavior).

More on Validity

In deciding whether an argument is valid, we can rely on many different resources to help us. Some argument forms are validating argument forms, and it can be helpful to recognize some of the most common of these.

Disjunctive syllogism

X or **Y**   Either we will maintain serial killer Smith for life or we will execute him.

| not-**X** | We will not maintain Smith for life. |
| So **Y** | So we will execute him. |

(A *disjunction* is a compound sentence in which the word *or* is the connective word. A *syllogism* is a valid argument (according to Aristotle). This, then, is a fundamental valid argument form involving disjunction.)

Modus ponens

If **X**, then **Y**	If Bill has bought a new hat today, then we do not have enough money to go to the movies.
X	Bill has bought a new hat today.
So **Y**	So we do not have enough money to go to the movies.

Modus tollens

If **X**, then **Y**	If Bill had bought a new hat today, then you would have seen him wearing it.
not-**Y**	You didn't see Bill wearing his new hat today.
So not-**X**	So Bill didn't buy a new hat today.

Hypothetical syllogism

If **X**, then **Y**	If Bill has bought a new hat today, then we do not have enough money to go to the movies.
If **Y**, then **Z**	If we do not have enough money to got to the movies, then Arnie will be angry.
So if **X**, then **Z**	So if Bill has bought a new hat today, then Arnie will be angry.

(Like *modus ponens* and *modus tollens*, this is a fundamental argument pattern for hypothetical—that is conditional—sentences.)

Universal syllogism

All **A** are **B**.	All doctors golf.
All **B** are **C**.	All golfers are wealthy.
So all **A** are **C**.	So all doctors are wealthy.

Universal-particular syllogisms (two types)

All **A** are **B**.	All doctors golf.
Individual **i** is **A**.	Carla is a doctor.
So individual **i** is **B**.	So Carla golfs.

All **A** are **B**.	All doctors golf.
Individual **i** is non-**B**.	Danielle does not golf.
So individual **i** is non-**A**.	So Danielle is not a doctor.

Continuing to list valid argument forms is a futile exercise, however, because there are an infinite number of valid argument forms. The principal value of formal logic is that it systematically organizes large classes of valid argument forms and develops techniques for showing validity.

For much of our ordinary discussion of argument, though, we rely on a little help from our friends in deciding what is valid. If an argument seems valid, a person can propose it and see whether anyone can think of a way to show invalidity. ("Raise it up the flag pole and see if anyone revolts.") There are two ways to show invalidity.

> We can show invalidity by describing a possible situation in which the premises are true with the conclusion false.

> We can also show invalidity by showing that the argument has no validating features. We do this by trying to isolate all of the logical features of the argument, and then showing that those are not validating features. (Of course, this leaves open the possibility that someone will show us that we have not uncovered all of the logically relevant features, and the discussion will then continue. . . .)

For example, suppose someone argues in the following way:

> If the ambassador were unhappy with her position in Portugal, she would be willing to take the position in Ireland. And she was willing to take the position in Ireland, so she must have been unhappy with her position in Portugal.

We can show the invalidity of this in two ways. The situation could be this: The ambassador was very happy in her position in Portugal, but she was willing to take the position in Ireland because the President said that he needed her special skills there. In such a situation, the premises would be true and the conclusion would be false. So the argument is invalid.

Alternatively, we can note that this argument exhibits the following pattern:

> If **X**, then **Y**
>
> **Y**
>
> So **X**

This is not a validating pattern of argument (and there does not appear to be anything else that would make this argument valid). [We can show that this is not a validating pattern of argument by giving a clear counter-example: an example of an argument that fits that pattern and is obviously invalid. For example,

> If Julia Roberts is a lawyer, then she has gone to school.
>
> Julia Roberts has gone to school.
>
> So Julia Roberts is a lawyer.

Such an example makes it clear that this is not a validating argument pattern, because it makes it clear that not every argument fitting this pattern is valid.]

The first of these methods was discussed in Chapter 1. The second is more readily available to those who have studied formal logic, because they can have more confidence that they have uncovered all of the logically relevant features of an argument. Nevertheless, we may sometimes want to use this method, especially in simple cases like the one just discussed.

Some Patterns That Will Not Validate an Argument

In pointing out that a pattern of argument is not a validating pattern, it is useful to have some of the common examples named. Once we have seen that the pattern is not a validating pattern, we can identify it by name; thereafter, we need not show the same thing every time we see the pattern. At the end of the last section, we showed that the following pattern is *not* a validating pattern:

Affirming the consequent

> If **X**, then **Y**
>
> **Y**
>
> So **X**

An *if-then* sentence is called a *conditional*, and the conditional has two parts: the *antecedent,* which is the clause after the word *if*, and the *consequent*, the clause after the word *then*. The invalid pattern just mentioned is called *affirming the consequent* because its premises are a conditional sentence and the affirmation of its consequent. This is never a validating pattern.

It is worthwhile to note another pattern that does not validate arguments. Like affirming the consequent, this pattern recurs in ordinary discussion even though it is not a validating pattern.

Denying the antecedent

> If **X**, then **Y**
>
> not-**X**
>
> So not-**Y**

This is not a validating pattern. (You should be able to think of an example that will show that it is not a validating pattern. Find two sentences, **X** and **Y**, that will fit into this pattern and will make the premises true and the conclusion false.) Its name comes from the fact that its premises consist of a conditional and the denial of the antecedent of that conditional.

Compare these two patterns, denying the antecedent and affirming the consequent, to the *validating* argument patterns *modus ponens* and *modus tollens*. (The two validating patterns could be called *affirming the antecedent* and *denying the consequent*, although those names are not generally used.) Make sure you know which patterns are validating and which are not.

In making judgments about what pattern applies to an argument, it is important to identify correctly the elements of the conditional. The antecedent is the clause after *if*, even when the order of presentation is reversed in the sentence.

> If Senator Alvarez voted against the treaty, the President will be angry.
>
> The President will be angry if Senator Alvarez voted against the treaty.

These sentences make the same conditional statement, and in each case the antecedent of the conditional is "Senator Alvarez voted against the treaty." In English we can freely change the order of the clauses, but that does not affect their logical roles. The clause with *if* is the antecedent. Thus the following would count as a case of *denying the antecedent:*

> The President will be angry if Senator Alvarez voted against the treaty.
>
> Senator Alvarez did not vote against the treaty.
>
> So the President will not be angry.

And of course this argument is not valid.

EXERCISE 2B

Each of the following passages contains an argument that has a conditional premise. Classify each argument as an example of *modus ponens* (MP), *modus tollens* (MT), affirming the consequent (AC), denying the antecedent (DA) or "other." Indicate whether the argument is valid or invalid.

1. If Alice is planning to go to the party with John, then John is a happy man. John is a happy man. So Alice must be planning to go to the party with him.

2. If Barney went to the party with Carla, then David is angry now. Barney went to the party with Carla. So David must be angry now.

3. If Alice and Betty are both at the party, then Ernie is embarrassed now. But I see that Ernie is not embarrassed now, so it must not be true that Alice and Betty are both at the party.

4. If John passed chemistry, then he will graduate on time. John passed chemistry. So John will graduate on time.

5. Federico will throw a tantrum if the cinematographer is late. But the cinematographer is not late, so Federico will not throw a tantrum.

6. If John has taken good care of his car, then it runs well now. So he must have taken good care of it, since it does run well now.

7. If all of the President's advisors publicly defend him against recent charges, then we know that he thinks that those charges are serious. Since his advisors are not publicly defending him, he must not think that those charges are serious.

8. The power outage would have lasted a long time if the storm had been severe. It did not last a long time, though, so the storm must not have been severe.

9. If the storm had not been severe, then the power outage would not have lasted a long time. It did last a long time, though, so the storm must have been severe.

EXERCISE 2C

Give an example, different from any in the book, that shows that affirming the consequent is not a validating pattern of argument.

Give an example, different from any in the book, that shows that denying the antecedent is not a validating pattern of argument.

CLARIFY

At almost any stage in the analysis or construction of an argument, we may need to *clarify* what is said so that the connections within the argument become clear. We may need to paraphrase or qualify the speaker's words, and we may need to make the terminology more uniform. For example, it is not immediately apparent why the following argument is valid:

> The economy will be in big trouble, because it cannot tolerate a continuation of low interest rates, but such rates will continue.

Identifying premises and conclusion in the stated material gives us this:

> [P1]   The economy cannot tolerate a continuation of low interest rates.
>
> [P2]   Low interest rates will continue.
>
> ∴ [C]   The economy will be in big trouble.

Rather than trying to fill in supplementary premises to connect the words in [P1] with the words in the conclusion, I would suggest paraphrasing [P1] so that it connects with the conclusion in a more obvious way.

> [P1*]   If low interest rates continue, then the economy will be in big trouble.

Premise [P1] is stylistically nicer than [P1*] in the ordinary presentation of this argument, but [P1*] connects [P2] and the conclusion in a clear and evidently valid way. Also, [P1*] seems to say the same thing as [P1]—it is a paraphrase of [P1]. As long as we are sure that [P1] and [P1*] say the same thing, we can see why the argument is valid. The argument with [P1*] as its premise is an instance of a very basic, validating argument pattern, *modus ponens*:

> If **X**, then **Y**
>
> **X**
>
> ∴ **Y**

No matter what sentences we put in place of **X** and **Y**, we will get a valid argument from this pattern. And the argument with [P1] as its premise really says the same thing as the one with [P1*] as its premise, so it is valid too.

We will see many examples of paraphrase and other kinds of clarification as we do our argument analyses. Putting a sentence into other words helps us to focus more clearly on the meaning of the sentence and can help us to see its logical connections with other sentences.

EVALUATE THE PREMISES

Once you have identified a valid argument, you must evaluate the premises. Are the premises true? This takes you more directly into the particular subject matter of the argument. In this text we often stop here, because of course it is not our goal to tell you the truth about all subject matters. You will use the specific knowledge you have to evaluate the premises of arguments, and sometimes you will construct a further argument for one or more of those premises (i.e., an argument in which that premise is the conclusion).

CONSTRUCTION AND ANALYSIS: EXAMPLES

When we construct arguments, we need to try to approach our arguments with the same critical attitude that others will apply (and that we apply to the arguments of others). It is important for us to recognize the two distinct components of sound argument:

> The premises are true.
>
> The premises are appropriately connected to the conclusion (so that the argument is valid).

In developing arguments for presentation to others, these two components require work of very different kinds.

> We must ask whether the audience will accept the premises.
>
> We must try to determine whether it would be possible for the conclusion to be false in some possible situation in which the premises were true. (That is, we must try to determine whether there is a way to show that the argument is invalid.)

If the premises are not wholly acceptable, we must support or revise the premises. If the argument is not valid, we usually need to identify additional premises, revise our premises so that they "fit together" properly, or formulate an entirely new argument for our intended conclusion. We use these guidelines in constructing arguments and in the evaluation of arguments that others present.

> Suppose we start with this statement of an argument:
>
> Abortion is always wrong, because it is always wrong to kill an innocent human.

The conclusion is that abortion is wrong, and the premise is that it is wrong to kill an innocent human. Some of the supplementation that is needed here is apparent. One easy way to supplement this would be to add the premise:

> An abortion is the killing of an innocent human.

This makes the argument valid, but it combines several ideas that we might want to consider separately.

> Every abortion is the killing of a fetus.
>
> A fetus is a human.
>
> A fetus is innocent.

We can make it easier to discuss this argument if we write those as separate premises. Thus the argument could be reconstructed in the following way:

[P1]   It is always wrong to kill an innocent human.

[P2]   Every abortion is the killing of a fetus.

[P3]   Every human fetus is a human.

[P4]   Every human fetus is innocent.

∴ [C]   Every abortion is wrong.

This might serve as a beginning of discussion, but many opponents of abortion would want to qualify [P1] and the conclusion, because most believe that some abortions are justified—for example, when the pregnancy threatens the life of the mother, in cases of rape, etc. Therefore, you might want instead to consider some argument that fits this pattern:

[P1*]   Except in situations of type X, it is wrong to kill an innocent human.

[P2]   An abortion is the killing of a fetus.

[P3]   Every human fetus is a human.

[P4]   Every human fetus is innocent.

∴ [C*]   Abortion is wrong, except in situations of type X.

A valid argument of this type, with suitable qualifications in place of X, can launch discussion of the substantive question. Once such an argument is presented, someone who favors the view that abortion is not wrong must explain which premise is false. Such a person is likely to give reasons for thinking that [P1] or [P3] is false. (Note that [P3] is not so trivial as it may first appear. For example, it is not true that every human liver is a human. You must establish something special about fetuses in order to justify [P3].) The abortion opponent must then defend the challenged premise. As we all know, this is a very difficult topic to discuss. The process of constructing arguments and evaluating them carefully can help to uncover the fundamental points of disagreement that underlie differences of opinion on this topic. It provides a way to move beyond mere disagreement to reasoned discussion.

As we have been developing this argument, we have also begun to see the development of more complex argument structure. The principal argument that we presented against abortion could be represented in this way:

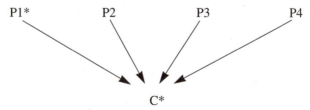

P1*   P2   P3   P4

C*

Each premise contributes to the justification of the conclusion. We also mentioned, and set aside, another premise:

[P5]   An abortion is the killing of an innocent human.

This combines the material of [P2] through [P4], so we set it aside. In fact, [P2] through [P4] validly support [P5], so another way to think of the argument is to see [P5] as the premise linking [P1*] to the conclusion.

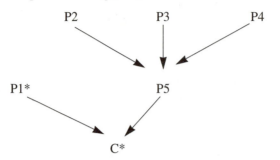

This breaks our argument into two separate sub-arguments, an argument for [P5] and an argument for [C*], and that suggests how we could break the presentation of the argument into separate paragraphs. If we were to add an argument for P1*, then we might have a third paragraph. The structure of the argumentation might then be this (where [P7] and [P8] are reasons for [P1*]) :

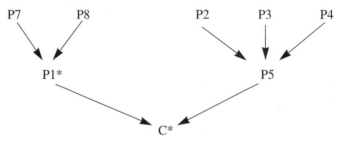

In an essay, we must make all of this linear. Sentences come one after another, of course, not in a diagram, so we must decide which argument to present first. A diagram like this, though, can help us to get the general structure of the argumentation clear in our minds, so that we will know what decisions need to be made about the presentation of the argument. Premises for the separate parts can then be presented in an orderly way, rather than in a tangled web that is difficult to follow.

It is important to note that if all three of the arguments (with conclusions P1*, P5, and C) above were valid, then so would be the argument that has premises P7, P8, P2, P3, and P4 and conclusion C*. We can preserve validity even if we omit the intermediate steps. But the reasoning is often easier to follow when those intermediate steps are included. They provide a way to break the discussion into smaller parts that can be presented in separate paragraphs.

Some Examples of Argument Analysis

Example 1

Sometimes it is not clear what mistake is being made in an argument. In such cases, we need to consider multiple possibilities in criticizing the argument.

I thought that I needed to go to the bank, because I thought that I needed some money. One premise of my reasoning is clear: that I need some money. My conclusion is that I must go to the bank. My reasoning was not sound, however, because I was overlooking the fact that I could get money from a nearby ATM.

When I consider my own reasoning, it is not obvious which of two mistakes I was making. I might have been making the mistake of reasoning from a false premise: that I must go to the bank to get money. On the other hand, fully stated, my argument might have been invalid: perhaps my principal inexplicit premise was that if I go to the bank, then I can get money. In that case, my argument was invalid because that premise is not sufficient to support the conclusion that I *must* go to the bank for money. (For that conclusion, I would need a premise saying that I can get money only by going to the bank). Either way that I try to make my reasoning clear, I find that it does not work.

Usually, the best way to approach the analysis of an argument is to follow these steps, as we did in discussing most of the examples in this chapter:

1. Identify the conclusion.
2. Identify the premises that are stated in support of the conclusion.
3. If the argument with that conclusion and those premises is not yet valid, then try to identify reasonable unstated premises that will connect the stated premises to the conclusion. (Sometimes the argument is just invalid, so that this cannot be done in any reasonable way. In such cases, we will often find that the argument fits one of the invalid patterns denying the antecedent or affirming the consequent, or that it commits one of the irrelevant appeals discussed in Chapter 4.)
4. Once you have a valid argument, you can ask whether the identified premises (whether explicitly stated or unstated) are really true. If not, consider whether any modifications would make the premises more acceptable *while preserving validity.*

Example 2

Suppose someone argues in the following way:

> Couples should live together before getting married. That way many of them will find out about some of the things that might lead to divorce.

As it stands, this is not close to being valid, simply because it leaves much unsaid. We can rewrite it to indicate the explicit structure more clearly.

> [P] If couples live together before getting married, then many of them will find out about some of the things that might lead to divorce.
>
> Therefore, [C] couples should live together before getting married.

If someone asked, "Why should they find out about some of the things that might lead to divorce?" or "How does that premise support the conclusion?", then the person giving the argument would have to say more about how the premise and the conclusion are connected. The argument might be filled out in the following way:

> [P] If couples live together before getting married, then many couples will find out about some of the things that might lead to divorce.

[P2]   If many couples find out about some of the things that might lead to divorce, then in many cases, couples will avoid marriages that would end in divorce.

[P3]   All couples should do all those things that might enable many of them to avoid marriages that would end in divorce.

Therefore, [C]   couples should live together before getting married.

This is now a valid argument. We have identified some additional premises that connect our original premise with the conclusion.

Now that we have identified these additional premises, we can begin to raise questions about their truth. This will open up a real discussion of the topic.

Premise [P] is stated in a very cautious way (". . . they will find out about *some* of the things that *might* lead to divorce"). Because of this caution, it is probably true. But [P2] and [P3] are not so acceptable.

[P2] has two problems. It does not seem true that finding out about things that *might* lead to divorce would (or even should) lead many couples to avoid marriage; and it is not clear that it is the couples whose marriages would end in divorce who would do the avoiding. Someone would have to do empirical research (or argue in ways that are not evident to me) in order to make a very convincing case that the marriages that would end in divorce would often be avoided.

But even if that case could be made, [P3] has some problems too. First, one might question whether all marriages that would end in divorce should be avoided. It may be that in many cases the marriage, even though it ends in divorce, has value that would not have been adequately replaced if the marriage had never occurred. In addition, we should note that [P3] is much too broad. Eliminating marriage entirely would cut down drastically on the number of divorces. We may not want to do *all* things that would cut down on the number of divorces.

If we wish to develop a better argument along these lines, we need to go back and formulate more acceptable premises. For example, a reformulation of [P3] might make it more acceptable:

[P3*]   Couples should do all those things that would enable them to avoid exactly those marriages that would end in divorce and in which avoidance of the marriage is better than having the marriage with its ending in divorce.

This premise avoids the problems raised above, and it seems true. Unfortunately, the premises no longer fit together in a way that yields a valid argument, and it will be difficult to revise [P1] and [P2] so that we have a valid argument again. There is nothing that couples can do that will have the miraculous result that [P3*] requires. Certainly, there is no reason to think that living together before marriage will have this remarkable consequence.

People sometimes find this process of constructing arguments frustrating, because we often end up seeing that the line we are following cannot be made convincing. Even when we run up against this problem, though, the process of trying to develop an adequate argument should make the issue much clearer and should open our minds and our discussions to important considerations that we had not previously taken into account. This has value of its own.

Example 3

Here is an example of a difficult argument analysis involving several related conclusions, some argued for, some not. We must clarify the conclusion and identify missing links in the argument.

> But the peculiar evil of silencing the expression of an opinion is, that it is robbing the human race; posterity as well as the existing generation; those who dissent from the opinion, still more than those who hold it. If the opinion is right, they are deprived of the opportunity of exchanging error for truth: if wrong, they lose, what is almost as great a benefit, the clearer perception and livelier impression of truth, produced by its collision with error. (John Stuart Mill, *On Liberty*)

In trying to analyze this passage, you should first try to identify the conclusion or conclusions. That seems pretty clear here, because the entire first sentence seems to be offered as a conclusion, with the entire second sentence in support of it. The first sentence, however, really breaks up into several parts.

  A. Silencing the expression of an opinion robs the human race.
  B. Silencing the expression of an opinion robs posterity.
  C. Silencing the expression of an opinion robs the existing generation.
  D. Silencing the expression of an opinion robs those who dissent from the opinion.
  E. Silencing the expression of an opinion robs those who dissent from the opinion more than it robs those who hold it.

It would be difficult for Mill to argue for all of these things in so short a passage, and he doesn't really do it here. If he had established B and C, that would give us A; but he really argues for D, not C, and so he does not really establish B or A in full generality.

> [P1]   If an opinion is right, then silencing it deprives people [who do not already believe it] of the opportunity of exchanging error for truth.
>
> [P2]   Depriving people of the opportunity of exchanging error for truth robs existing generations [of the truth].
>
> [P3]   Depriving people of the opportunity of exchanging error for truth robs their posterity of the benefits that come from their ancestors' having believed the truth.
>
> ∴ [C1]   If an opinion is right, silencing it deprives those who do not believe it and their posterity.
>
> [P4]   If an opinion is wrong, then if it is silenced, people [those in the current generation who do not believe it] lose the clearer perception and livelier impression of truth, produced by the collision of truth with error. [That is, people lose the best opportunity to understand why this erroneous opinion is wrong.]

[P5]   If the current generation loses the best opportunity to understand why an opinion is wrong, then their posterity is also robbed of the benefits that come from their ancestors' having understood this.

∴ [C2]   If an opinion is wrong, silencing it deprives those who do not believe it and their posterity.

[P6]   Every silenced opinion is right or wrong. (unstated)

[P7]   Every silenced opinion has some people who do not believe it. (unstated)

∴ [C3]   Silencing any opinion harms some people [those who do not believe it] in current generations and their posterity.

The structure of the argumentation, then, is:

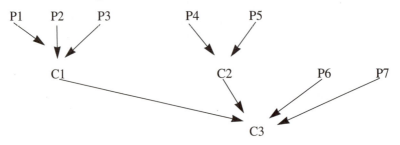

Nothing in this argument actually supports Mill's claim that suppressing an opinion harms those who believe it. Once we identify the premises, it becomes clear that he didn't even try to support this. (It is a much more generally accepted view, so perhaps he felt no need to defend it.) Presumably he would give different reasons for that conclusion if he wanted to support it. Also, nothing in this passage justifies the actual quantitative judgment that he makes: that silencing an opinion robs "those who dissent from the opinion, still more than those who hold it." Nothing here could serve as a basis for such a quantitative comparison.

EXERCISE 2D

Construct an argument for one of the controversial opinions that you listed for Exercise 1B. Think about why you believe the conclusion, and then try to connect your reasons for believing the conclusion with that conclusion by finding plausible premises that will serve as the basis for a valid argument.

EXERCISE 2E

For each of the following passages, (a) identify the conclusion (or conclusions), (b) identify all of the explicitly stated premises, and (c) fill in unstated premises, trying to fulfill these conditions:

The resulting argument is valid.

The unstated premises that have been filled in are as plausible as possible or are indicated in an especially clear way by the other things that are said.

1. All pornography should be banned. Thus *The National Geographic* should be banned, since it contains pictures of naked people.

2. We should engage in war only as a last resort, because every war has many innocent victims.

3. If I believe that I exist, then I exist. Thus I must exist.

4. Every medical doctor deserves to make a lot of money, because every medical doctor has survived a long period of rigorous training, and every medical doctor has a great deal of responsibility.

5. We can be sure that no one has been here. Nothing was disturbed.

6. Every holiday brings her a strange feeling of loneliness, even when many people are around her. Since it is Thanksgiving, she must be feeling that way again.

7. Remodeling the town square would be as expensive as maintaining our fire department for a year. Remodeling the town square is unnecessary. So we shouldn't remodel the town square.

8. Rights are either God-given or evolve out of the democratic process. Most rights are based on the ability of people to agree on a social contract—the ability to make and keep agreements. Animals cannot possibly reach such an agreement with other creatures. They cannot respect anyone else's rights. Therefore they cannot be said to have rights. (From Rush Limbaugh, *The Way Things Ought To Be*, Pocket Books, 1993, p.103.)

ARGUING FOR A *SHOULD* CONCLUSION

Some words, such as *and, or, every, some,* and *if,* play critical roles in valid arguments, and much about those roles is understood well. Thus some patterns of argument, like *modus ponens*, can be identified as validating argument patterns. Whenever an argument fits the pattern, it is valid.

Many of our arguments, however, involve the introduction of words like *can* and *should* that are not understood as well. We need especially to look at *should*, because many of the conclusions we wish to argue for are about what people should or should not do, and we need some guidelines concerning the kinds of considerations that are important in such arguments.

Sometimes, of course, a conclusion with *should* follows for reasons that have nothing to do with the special features of that word.

If Carlos brought dip, then Boris should bring out the potato chips.

Carlos brought dip.

∴ Boris should bring out the potato chips.

This is simply a valid instance of *modus ponens*, and no special features of *should* play a role in the argument.

Often, however, we argue for *should* conclusions in other ways. Sometimes, for example, we argue for a *should* conclusion even when there is no *should* in the premises. At other times, we have a premise that we *should* achieve a certain goal and a conclusion about what we *should* do. In what follows, we will explore some of the ways in which such arguments can be effective. We will also see how to uncover the common defects in such arguments.

Although the arguments below are not valid, they represent some typical sorts of arguments with *should* conclusions. Let's consider how to evaluate these arguments and how to strengthen them.

A. Dennis should take his mother to work.
Dennis can take her to work if he borrows Ernie's car.
∴ Dennis should borrow Ernie's car.

B. Barney wants a pair of skates.
He will get a pair of skates if he whines a lot.
∴ Barney should whine a lot.

C. Carla wants to play in Carnegie Hall.
The only way to get to Carnegie Hall is to practice.
∴ Carla should practice.

These arguments connect (1) a premise about what we want or what we should achieve, and (2) a premise about how the goal can be attained, with a conclusion about what we should do. Consideration of these arguments will make it clear that something more needs to be said about when this connection is acceptable. The ends do not always justify the means, and we need to try to say more about when they do and when they don't.

Consideration of argument A should immediately suggest one thing about what is needed to justify a conclusion about what should be done. We need to know at least that borrowing Ernie's car is the best way for Dennis to get his mother to work. If it isn't (if Dennis has no license, or if the bus is easier and faster, etc.), then Dennis should select the better means. Thus we at least need a premise that says that the means suggested is best, not merely that it will achieve the goal.

Looking at argument B, we see what some of the other connecting premises should be. Before we conclude that Barney should start whining, we would want to know whether that is the best way for him achieve the goal, just as we wanted to know this in the case of argument A. He should not just choose a means; he should choose the best means. And even if whining *is* the best way (for example, it might be the best way because it is the only way), we would want to know whether Barney should have the skates. The fact that Barney *wants* the skates is not sufficient to justify the claim that he should have them. Perhaps skates are uncontroversial, but if Barney wanted drugs or deadly weapons instead, and if the best way to get them was to whine, then we still shouldn't advise Barney to start whining. We should instead try to get him to stop wanting the drugs or the deadly weapons. Schematically, we might begin to develop a pattern of argument that indicates what to look for.

[P1] Barney wants to achieve **X**.

[P2] Doing **Y** will achieve **X**.

[P3] Doing **Y** is the best way to achieve **X**.

[P4] Barney's desire to achieve **X** should be satisfied.

∴ [C] Barney should do **Y**.

This pattern seems promising, but a look at Carla's situation (in argument C above) suggests that this still needs some more premises, or at least some clarification of the ones we have.

If we follow the pattern just outlined, and if we take X to be *playing in Carnegie Hall* and we take Y to be practicing, and we substitute *Carla* for *Barney*, then we get this argument:

[P1]   Carla wants to get to Carnegie Hall.

[P2]   Practicing will get her to Carnegie Hall.

[P3]   Practicing is the best way to get to Carnegie Hall.

[P4]   Carla's desire to achieve the goal of getting to Carnegie Hall should be satisfied.

∴ [C]   Carla should practice.

[P1] and [P3] are true. Carla wants to get to Carnegie Hall, and practicing is the best way (in fact, it is the only way) to get there. Still, we have no guarantee that [P2] is true. In saying that practicing is the only way to get to Carnegie Hall, we point out the necessity of it, but we are not saying that it is a guarantee.

Should Carla practice even if we cannot say for sure whether she will get there? This is a hard question that we will take up again later in Chapter 10, when we say more about balancing our estimate of the value of an outcome with our judgment of the probability that it will actually occur. It might be worth a try for her, or it might not. For now, we will assume that we have knowledge of the outcomes of actions and will postpone consideration of the complications that uncertainty imposes.

Still, even if we imagine that we know for sure that [P2] is true—if Carla practices (a lot) she definitely will get to play at Carnegie Hall—the ordeal might not be worth it to Carla. Even though she wants to get there, and even though practicing is the best way (in fact the only way), and even though it would work, maybe she shouldn't practice because there are much better things that she could do with her time and effort. Perhaps this is a failure of [P4] again. All things considered, this isn't what she should do. The problem here, however, is really with the difficulty (cost) of **Y** (the means), and a different version of [P4] will make this clearer.

[P4$^+$]   All things considered, doing **Y** (and achieving **X**) is better than not achieving **X**.

In this case,

[P4$^+$]   All things considered, practicing a lot and getting to Carnegie Hall is better than not getting to Carnegie Hall.

This is a much more formidable premise, but it captures the conditions we need to fulfill much more adequately. We want to know whether the goal is sufficiently valuable so that the means to obtain it are justified. Hence we can call this the condition that the ends justify the means (**EJM**).

In fact, [P4$^+$] even takes over the ground covered by [P1]. Whether Barney wants to achieve the goal Y or not, achieving it is better than not achieving it if [P4$^+$]

is true. (The fulfillment of Barney's desires is one factor that goes into deciding which action is better, but it is not usually the only one.) Thus we begin to develop a general pattern for arguments for conclusions about what we *should* do.

Should **Pattern**

> [P2]   Doing **Y** will achieve **X**.
>
> [P3]   Doing **Y** is the best way to achieve **X**.
>
> [P4$^+$]   All things considered, doing **Y** (and achieving **X**) is better than not achieving **X**.
>
> ∴ [C]   **Y** should be done.

When someone argues for a conclusion that someone *should* do something by indicating a goal that is to be achieved, there are three questions that we should ask:

> Will the suggested action achieve the goal?
>
> Is it the best way to achieve the goal?
>
> Is the goal valuable enough to justify the action required to attain it?

An argument that fits our *should* pattern will provide a "yes" answer to each of those questions, and this will ordinarily be a very powerful argument for that action. We can call our three premises the *success condition* (**SC**), the *optimal means condition* (**OMC**), and the *ends justify the means condition* (**EJM**). This pattern will be very useful in arguing for *should* conclusions and in evaluating others' arguments. When someone says that we should do something in order to achieve a particular goal, we should ask whether all three of these important conditions are fulfilled. The conclusion about what should be done will not be justified if these three conditions are not fulfilled.

In general terms, our *should* pattern is

> **SC**   Doing **Y** will achieve **X**.
>
> **OMC**   Doing **Y** is the best way to achieve **X**.
>
> **EJM**   All things considered, doing **Y** (and achieving **X**) is better than not achieving **X**.
>
> ∴   **Y** should be done.

In most cases, however, we will use a version that mentions a particular person or group of people as the agents of the action. We can refer to them in place of **A** in the following version of the *should* pattern.

> **SC**   **A**'s doing **Y** will achieve **X**.
>
> **OMC**   **A**'s doing **Y** is the best way to achieve **X**.
>
> **EJM**   All things considered, **A**'s doing **Y** (and achieving **X**) is better than not achieving **X**.
>
> ∴ [C]   **A** should do **Y**.

In the next section, we will discuss some variations and complications of this pattern that might be useful for some circumstances. Nevertheless, the pattern just discussed is the principal one to keep in mind when you are constructing or evaluating an argument that someone should do something in order to achieve a particular goal.

This is not the only way to justify a *should* conclusion. Any validating argument pattern might have a *should* statement as its conclusion. Arguments that cite one or more of the premises of the *should* pattern above, though, are among the most common types of argument for a *should* conclusion. If the premises in such an argument are not all explicitly stated, then we know that there are questions to be asked about the adequacy of the argument. For example, if only the **SC** is stated, then we will want to know whether the means suggested to achieve the goal are the best means (Is **OMC** true?) and whether the goal is worth it (Is **EJM** true?). This pattern provides us with a very automatic way to see what questions to raise in appraising others' arguments that something should be done to achieve a certain goal. Just as important, it reminds us what conditions need to be fulfilled when we are arguing for doing an action in order to achieve a goal. As soon as we have formulated goal **X** as a reason for doing action **Y**, we can ask whether the three premises of this argument are true.

Some Related Patterns

The *should* pattern that we have identified is not the only way to argue for a *should* conclusion. As we have already mentioned, sometimes a *should* conclusion follows from premises from a very ordinary inference pattern, such as *modus ponens*. We can also identify some other patterns that are closely related to the *should* pattern we have examined. For example, sometimes we wish to know only that doing **Y** is *part of* the best way to achieve a goal. Thus we will want a somewhat qualified version of the *should* pattern.

Should **Pattern** (with *completion condition*)

SC'	Doing **Y** is *part of a course of action* **Q** that will achieve **X**.
OMC	Doing **Q** is the best way to achieve **X**.
EJM	All things considered, doing **Q** (and achieving **X**) is better than not achieving **X**.
CC	The other elements of **Q** are, or will be, in place for achieving **X**.
∴ [C]	**Y** should be done.

The *completion condition*, **CC**, is added because there is no point in starting your car if the wheels have been removed, even if starting your car (when the wheels are on) is part of the best way to get somewhere. The fact that an action would be valuable if the world were different is not enough to justify it, so we need **CC** to justify doing **Y** to achieve **X** if there are other significant conditions involved in bringing **X** about.

Should*

A slightly different variation on our basic *should* pattern can also be useful in some cases. Sometimes (though not often), we can justify a premise that is much stronger than **EJM**.

> All things considered, doing **Y** (and achieving **X**) is better than any course of action that would be precluded by doing **Y**.

Saying that **Y** is better than any course of action it precludes means that doing **Y** won't prevent you from doing anything that would be as good or better. There is no downside to doing **Y**. Such a premise will take over the job of **OMC** and **EJM**. (If doing **Y** and achieving **X** is better than doing **Z** and achieving **X**, no matter what **Z** is, then **Y** is the best way to achieve **X**.) We will call it the *global optimality* (**GO**) condition. Here is the *should** pattern:

SC	Doing **Y** will achieve **X**.
GO	All things considered, doing **Y** (and achieving **X**) is better than any course of action that would be precluded by doing **Y**.
∴ [C]	**Y** should be done.

Because that new **GO** even takes over the work that is done by **OMC**, we can rely on just **SC** and **GO**.

The *should* patterns that include **CC** or **GO** can be useful, but far more often it is better to argue for a *should* conclusion based on a particular goal by using the basic *should* pattern of the preceding section.

Arguing for a *Should* Conclusion: Points to Cover

We can summarize our results with the following guidelines for arguing for a conclusion that something should be done to achieve a goal.

If you wish to use some goal **X** as a basis for arguing that **B** should do **Y**, then you should make sure that the following points are covered in the premises:

> **Success Condition**: Doing **Y** will achieve **X**.
>
> [In some cases: **SC'**: Doing **Y** is a part of a course of action that will achieve **X**.]
>
> **Optimal Means Condition**: **Y** is [part of] the best way to achieve **X**.
>
> **Ends Justify Means**: Doing **Y** (and achieving **X**) is better than not achieving **X**.
>
> [When **SC'** replaces **SC**, add the **Completion Condition**: Other factors required to achieve **X** are satisfied.]

The **OMC** and the **EJM** can be replaced by a broader condition that entails them both:

> **Global Optimality**: Doing **Y** (and achieving **X**) is better than any course of action that it precludes.

Ties: A Slight Complication

This needs to be made more complicated if there are two or more "equally optimal" ways o f achieving **X**. Suppose that **Z** = {**Y1, Y2, Y3**, . . .}, where **Y1, Y2, Y3**, . . . are different ways of trying to achieve **X**. Then the following conditions must hold for some set **Z** of possible actions:

Success Condition: Each member of **Z** will achieve **X**.

Optimal Means Condition: All members of **Z** are equally good, and nothing outside **Z** is a better way to achieve **X** (they are all optimal).

Ends Justify Means: Doing any member of **Z** (and achieving **X**) is better than not achieving **X**.

The **OMC** and the **EJM** can again be replaced by a broader condition that entails them both.

Global Optimality: Doing any action in **Z** (and achieving **X**) is at least as good as any course of action precluded by doing that action.

Our conclusion, in the case of ties, is that **B** should do (at least) *one* of the actions in **Z**.

The Relationship of This to Formal Validity

Working with our basic *should* pattern, we can now identify a formally valid schema for justifying *should* conclusions.

Should

SC

EJM

OMC

Whenever a set of actions **Z** satisfies **SC**, **EJM**, and **OMC**, one of the actions of **Z** should be done.

∴ [C]   One of the actions of **Z** should be done.

Ordinarily, we will omit the last premise of this schema, and we will generally use the simpler version of the schema that applies when there is just one optimal action **Y**, rather than a set **Z**, to consider. Usually, then, we can use the basic pattern as our guide:

Basic *should* pattern

SC	Doing **Y** will achieve **X**.
EJM	Doing **Y** (and achieving **X**) is better than not achieving **X**.
OMC	**Y** is the best way to achieve **X**.
∴ [C]	Action **Y** should be done.

Examples

When you wish to argue that something should be done in order to meet a certain goal, you will probably find it useful to formulate an argument along these lines, most often using the **basic *should* pattern,** with or without the completion condition **CC**. For example, if you believe that the President should convene a Middle-East conference in order to help remove tension in that part of the world, then you will have a very convincing argument if you can establish all of these things:

SC   Calling a Middle-East conference will contribute to removing tension in that part of the world.

OMC   Calling a Middle-East conference is a part of the best course of action for contributing to the removal of tension in that part of the world.

EJM   Calling a Middle-East conference and contributing to the removal of tension in that part of the world is better than not contributing to the removal of tension in that part of the world.

CC   The other factors required for having the Middle-East conference contribute to removing tension are in place.

The *should* elements of an argument may interact with other elements. For example, in the following argument, the conclusion is that whenever certain conditions are fulfilled, medical assistance in bringing about the death of a mortally ill person should be provided. In the following argument, let's use the words *mortally ill person* to describe any person fulfilling these conditions:

A. The person has an incurable disease and will die soon.

B. The person has unbearable pain, and the remainder of life will consist only of suffering.

The argument is as follows:

1. Providing medical assistance in bringing about death will reduce the mortally ill person's pain and suffering.

2. Providing medical assistance in bringing about death is the best way to reduce the mortally ill person's pain and suffering, as long as all of the following conditions are fulfilled:
    (a) A patient requests medical assistance in bringing about death.
    (b) This is the patient's free will, expressed in his or her right mind with witnesses appointed by a court.
    (c) The medical assistance is administered by at least two doctors, with independent observers.

3. Providing medical assistance in bringing about death and relieving the person's pain and suffering is better than not relieving the mortally ill person's pain and suffering, as long as conditions a, b, and c are fulfilled.

∴ If conditions a, b, and c are fulfilled, then medical assistance in bringing about death should be provided for the mortally ill person.

The general pattern here is

> **SC**
>
> If a, b, and c are fulfilled, then **OMC**.
>
> If a, b, and c are fulfilled, then **EJM**.
>
> So, if a, b, and c are fulfilled, then the action should be done.

As usual, this is just the beginning of discussion. The advantage of structuring the argument in this way is that it presents one view clearly, so that precise points of disagreement can be identified for further discussion.

Uncertainty (a Big Complication)

We have formulated conditions to be fulfilled by arguments justifying *should* conclusions, but so far our formulation is based on the assumption that we are not in doubt about the outcomes of the actions in question. Later (in Chapter 10), we will learn some approaches to the accommodation of uncertainty. For now, it may be useful to identify the problem more clearly.

If I have just a few dollars on hand, I may have to choose between using that money to buy a lottery ticket and using it to go to a job interview (in order to pay my rent and buy food in the future). Both of these actions may fail the success condition (**SC**) of our argument schemas. Neither the interview nor the lottery purchase guarantees success. Still, if there is a reasonable chance of getting the job, it will in most cases be clear that it is better to go to the job interview than to put the money into lottery tickets. We have not allowed for uncertainty, and we have not provided any basis for balancing the much greater uncertainty involved in playing the lottery against the more ordinary uncertainty that goes with job interviews.

Really, there is a more general question here about balancing the estimated probability of success with the value of success and the costs of employing the particular means under consideration. We do not want to rely on just considering what *will* work (for sure), but we should not be willing to consider everything that *might* work (no matter how remote the chances of success and no matter how great the cost of the means).

Later (Chapter 10) we will examine more thoroughly the balancing of probabilities and values in making decisions, and we will leave the full consideration of dealing with uncertainty until then.

Evaluative Terms

In considering arguments for *should* conclusions, we have freely used evaluative expressions such as *good*, *better*, and *should*. These terms work together and shift around together. Fundamentally, our guidelines are based on the idea that you *should* do whatever is *best* (or at least, if there are ties, something that satisfies the condition that nothing is better). When you are considering ways of achieving a goal, this means picking the best way to achieve the goal (optimality) and making sure that there is nothing better that you could be doing instead. Do not lose sight of the fact that this all amounts to saying that you should do what is best. Breaking that advice into its separate components is a way of making sure that you cover all of the elements that go into making something the best choice of action. We have not given you value-neutral criteria for deciding what you should do, of course. We have merely identified elements that can go into an argument once you have determined what you value.

I also want to emphasize again that the patterns we discussed are not the only ways to argue for *should* conclusions. These patterns can be called into play when you are arguing that you should do something on the basis of some goal to be achieved. This is one very common way to argue for such a conclusion, but it is not the only way.

CHAPTER SUMMARY

In Chapter 2, we learn some key ideas and techniques for the analysis, construction, and evaluation of arguments.

> In analyzing and evaluating an argument, we must identify the stated premises and conclusion and then try to fill in any unstated premises that would be required to make the argument valid. If we can identify a valid argument to consider, then we can evaluate the premises to determine whether they are true. This may lead us into the consideration of other arguments (arguments in support of the premises).

> Although we cannot list all of the validating argument patterns, it is helpful to list some of the more common types of valid arguments. It is especially important to be sensitive to the simplest argument patterns involving a conditional, knowing which are validating patterns (*modus ponens* and *modus tollens*) and which are not validating patterns (denying the antecedent and affirming the consequent).

> One way to argue that an action should be done in order to achieve a particular goal is to argue that the action will achieve the goal, that it is the best way to achieve the goal, and that achieving the goal in this way is worth it. This pattern of argument provides a good guideline for constructing such arguments and for evaluating others' claims that an action should be done in order to achieve a particular goal. It is important to remember, though, that this is not the only way to argue that an action should be done.

EXERCISE 2F

The following sentences present brief arguments. Use the basic *should* pattern, which includes the **SC, OMC,** and **EJM** conditions, to write out a full *should* argument based on these passages. (For example, sentence 1 presents the success condition for a *should* argument. Once you have that, you can write out the whole argument. The argument will have three premises—**SC, OMC,** and **EJM**—and a conclusion.) Evaluate the resulting arguments. Are the premises plausible?

1. We should execute murderers, because doing so will prevent them from killing again.
2. You should buy a lottery ticket, because you won't win unless you play.
3. We should release almost all prisoners, because doing so is the only way to cut down on prison costs.

EXERCISE 2G

Develop an argument fitting one of our patterns for *should* arguments. You may wish to use one of these topics, for example:

> High school biology classes that include the study of evolutionary theory should include the study of creationist alternatives.

> The minimum drinking age should be changed . . . [Specify the way it should be changed, and argue specifically for that.]

> There should be no laws against abortion in the early stages of pregnancy.

> Prostitution should be legal.

> Slavery should be illegal.

> No one should be drafted into military service.

EXERCISE 2H

Fill in any missing premises in these arguments. Make the argument valid, and make the missing premises as plausible as possible. (If the argument is valid as it stands, then just note that it is valid.)

A. [P1]   Sales taxes are not collected on the basis of how much a person is able to contribute.

∴ [C]   Sales taxes are unfair.

B. [P1]   Raising state taxes will make the state less able to attract and retain businesses.

[P2]   If the state is less able to attract and retain businesses, then jobs will be lost and the economy will suffer.

[P3]   If jobs are lost and the economy suffers, the poor will be harmed along with everyone else.

∴ [C]   Raising state taxes will harm the poor.

C. [P1]   When a woman becomes pregnant because of rape, she did not choose to be pregnant.

∴ [C]   In the case of pregnancy due to rape, abortion is a woman's right.

D. [P1]   Requiring four philosophy courses would significantly increase almost every student's ability to read and analyze difficult material.

∴ [C]   We should require four philosophy courses.

E. [P1]   Almost every doctor opposes additional federal control over the system of health care.

[P2]   Any doctor who opposes additional federal control over the system of health care has good reasons to want success for insurance companies' managed care plans.

∴ [C]   So we can expect to find most doctors cooperating in the administration of insurance companies' managed care plans.

F. [P1]   Raising social security taxes is the only way to save the social security system.

∴ [C]   We should raise social security taxes.

G. [P1]   Cutting the police force in half would reduce the city budget significantly and produce considerable tax relief.

∴ [C]   We should cut the police force in half.

H. [P1]   Here is another secret to a woman's success. The best way to keep your man feeling that he is in control is to greet him at the door wearing your sexiest nightie, when he comes home from work, at least a couple of times each month.

∴ [C]   You should greet your man at the door wearing your sexiest nightie, when he comes home from work, at least a couple of times each month.

I. [P1]   Every war has many innocent victims.

∴ [C]   We should engage in war only as a last resort.

J. [P1]   The spread of new ideas about sex roles diminishes the value placed on the traditional family.

[P2]   Encouraging traditional ideas about sex roles will stop the spread of new ideas about sex roles.

∴ [C]   Traditional ideas about sex roles should be encouraged.

EXERCISE 2I

The following arguments are invalid. In each case, identify the conclusion, and then show that the argument is invalid.

1. If Alice failed biology, then she didn't graduate.

   She didn't graduate.

   So she must have failed biology.

2. Some doctors are Republicans.

   Some Republicans are wealthy.

   So some doctors are wealthy.

3. If the President signs the bill, it will become law. So it won't become law, since the President won't sign it.

4. If the federal government supports the states in encouraging new industry, then we will survive the national crisis of lagging economic development. But it is a time of budget cutting in Washington, and the federal government will not support states in encouraging new industry. So we will not survive the crisis, and recession is ahead for us.

EXERCISE 2J

Find an example of an argument in the newspaper, a magazine, or a textbook. Identify the conclusion and the stated premises. Can you fill in unstated premises that will make this a valid argument? How plausible are the premises? What is your over-all evaluation of the argument?

APPENDIX TO CHAPTER 2:
AN EXTENDED EXAMPLE

On January 16, 1991, President George Bush argued for attacking Iraq in order to end Iraq's control over Kuwait, a control that Iraq had achieved by invasion. In the next chapter, we will discuss "loaded" language, a prominent feature of this speech. For now, though, you should take care to observe the way in which Bush's argument can be seen to fit our pattern for *should* conclusions. Bush states the success condition (**SC**), and he gives reasons for accepting the **OMC** and **EJM** conditions.

Here is one way that we might outline his argument.

Bush Argument: January 16, 1991

[P1]   All reasonable diplomatic options have been exhausted.

[P2]   Waiting longer to decide will lead to several grave problems with little hope of benefit.

[P3]   If all reasonable diplomatic options have been exhausted and waiting longer to decide will lead to several grave problems with little hope of bene-fit, then the use of force now is the best way to free Kuwait.

∴ [C1]   The use of force now is the best way to free Kuwait.

[P4]   Using force now and liberating Kuwait has several benefits: stopping ag-gression, interfering with the build-up of arms in Iraq, and saving the Kuwaitis from further atrocities and from the forced imposition of a foreign government. These benefits outweigh the (admittedly grave) costs of waging this war.

[P5]   Whenever the benefits of an action outweigh its costs, it is better to perform that action than not to perform it.

∴ [C2]   The use of force now, liberating Kuwait, is better than not liberat-ing Kuwait.

[C1] = **OMC**   The use of force now is the best way to free Kuwait.

[C2] = **EJM**   The use of force now and the liberation of Kuwait is better than not liberating Kuwait.

[P6] = **SC**   The use of force now will free Kuwait.

∴ [C3]   We should use force now.

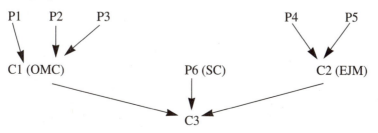

Many people disagreed with Bush's decision in this case. Each of the six premises was called into question by some group. Our analysis makes it clear that there are many different bases for disagreement here, and thus it helps focus discussion of the argument and the actions taken.

Address to the Nation Announcing Allied Military Action in the Persian Gulf

January 16, 1991

President George Bush

Just 2 hours ago, allied air forces began an attack on military targets in Iraq and Kuwait. These attacks continue as I speak. Ground forces are not engaged.

This conflict started August 2nd when the dictator of Iraq invaded a small and helpless neighbor. Kuwait—a member of the Arab League and a member of the United Nations—was crushed; its people, brutalized. Five months ago, Saddam Hussein started this cruel war against Kuwait. Tonight, the battle has been joined.

This military action, taken in accord with United Nations resolutions and with the consent of the United States Congress, follows months of constant and virtually endless diplomatic activity on the part of the United Nations, the United States, and many, many other countries. Arab leaders sought what became known as an Arab solution, only to conclude that Saddam Hussein was unwilling to leave Kuwait. Others traveled to Baghdad in a variety of efforts to restore peace and justice. Our Secretary of State, James Baker, held an historic meeting in Geneva, only to be totally rebuffed. This past weekend, in a last-ditch effort, the Secretary-General of the United Nations went to the Middle East with peace in his heart—his second such mission. And he came back from Baghdad with no progress at all in getting Saddam Hussein to withdraw from Kuwait.

Now the 28 countries with forces in the Gulf area have exhausted all reasonable efforts to reach a peaceful resolution—have no choice but to drive Saddam from Kuwait by force. We will not fail.

As I report to you, air attacks are underway against military targets in Iraq. We are determined to knock out Saddam Hussein's nuclear bomb potential. We will also destroy his chemical weapons facilities. Much of Saddam's artillery and tanks will be destroyed. Our operations are designed to best protect the lives of all the coalition forces by targeting Saddam's vast military arsenal. Initial reports from General Schwarzkopf are that our operations are proceeding according to plan.

Our objectives are clear: Saddam Hussein's forces will leave Kuwait. The legitimate government of Kuwait will be restored to its rightful place, and Kuwait will once again be free. Iraq will eventually comply with all relevant United Nations resolutions, and then, when peace is restored, it is our hope that Iraq will live as a peaceful and cooperative member of the family of nations, thus enhancing the security and stability of the Gulf.

Some may ask: Why act now? Why not wait? The answer is clear: The world could wait no longer. Sanctions, though having some effect, showed no signs of accomplishing their objective. Sanctions were tried for well over 5 months, and we and our allies concluded that sanctions alone would not force Saddam from Kuwait.

While the world waited, Saddam Hussein systematically raped, pillaged, and plundered a tiny nation, no threat to his own. He subjected the people of Kuwait to unspeakable atrocities—and among those maimed and murdered, innocent children.

While the world waited, Saddam sought to add to the chemical weapons arsenal he now possesses, an infinitely more dangerous weapon of mass destruction—a nuclear weapon. And while the world waited, while the world talked peace and withdrawal, Saddam Hussein dug in and moved massive forces into Kuwait.

While the world waited, while Saddam stalled, more damage was being done to the fragile economies of the Third World, emerging democracies of Eastern Europe, to the entire world, including to our own economy.

The United States, together with the United Nations, exhausted every means at our disposal to bring this crisis to a peaceful end. However, Saddam clearly felt that by stalling and threatening and defying the United Nations, he could weaken the forces arrayed against him.

While the world waited, Saddam Hussein met every overture of peace with open contempt. While the world prayed for peace, Saddam prepared for war.

I had hoped that when the United States Congress, in historic debate, took its resolute action, Saddam would realize he could not prevail and would move out of Kuwait in accord with the United Nation resolutions. He did not do that. Instead, he remained intransigent, certain that time was on his side.

Saddam was warned over and over again to comply with the will of the United Nations: Leave Kuwait, or be driven out. Saddam has arrogantly rejected all warnings. Instead, he tried to make this a dispute between Iraq and the United States of America.

Well, he failed. Tonight, 28 nations—countries from 5 continents, Europe and Asia, Africa, and the Arab League—have forces in the Gulf area standing shoulder to shoulder against Saddam Hussein. These countries had hoped the use of force could be avoided. Regrettably, we now believe that only force will make him leave.

Prior to ordering our forces into battle, I instructed our military commanders to take every necessary step to prevail as quickly as possible, and with the greatest degree of protection possible for American and allied service men and women. I've told the American people before that this will not be another Vietnam, and I repeat this here tonight. Our troops will have the best possible support in the entire world, and they will not be asked to fight with one hand tied behind their back. I'm hopeful that this fighting will not go on for long and that casualties will be held to an absolute minimum.

This is an historic moment. We have in this past year made great progress in ending the long era of conflict and cold war. We have before us the opportunity to forge for ourselves and for future generations a new world order—a world where the rule of law, not the law of the jungle, governs the conduct of nations. When we are success-ful—and we will be—we have a real chance at this new world order, an order in which a credible United Nations can use its peacekeeping role to fulfill the promise and vision of the U.N.'s founders.

We have no argument with the people of Iraq. Indeed, for the innocents caught in this conflict, I pray for their safety. Our goal is not the conquest of Iraq. It is the lib-eration of Kuwait. It is my hope that somehow the Iraqi people can, even now, con-vince their dictator that he must lay down his arms, leave Kuwait, and let Iraq itself rejoin the family of peace-loving nations.

Thomas Paine wrote many years ago: "These are the times that try men's souls." Those well-known words are so very true today. But even as planes of the multina-tional forces attack Iraq, I prefer to think of peace, not war. I am convinced not only that we will prevail but that out of the horror of combat will come the recognition that no nation can stand against a world united, no nation will be permitted to bru-tally assault its neighbor.

No President can easily commit our sons and daughters to war. They are the Na-tion's finest. Ours is an all-volunteer force, magnificently trained, highly motivated. The troops know why they're there. And listen to what they say, for they've said it better than any President or Prime Minister ever could.

Listen to Hollywood Huddleston, Marine lance corporal. He says, "Let's free these people, so we can go home and be free again." And he's right. The terrible crimes and tortures committed by Saddam's henchmen against the innocent people of Kuwait are an affront to mankind and a challenge to the freedom of all.

Listen to one of our great officers out there, Marine Lieutenant General Walter Boomer. He said: "There are things worth fighting for. A world in which brutality and lawlessness are allowed to go unchecked isn't the kind of world we're going to want to live in."

Listen to Master Sergeant J.P. Kendall of the 82d Airborne: "We're here for more than just the price of a gallon of gas. What we're doing is going to chart the future of the world for the next 100 years. It's better to deal with this guy now than 5 years from now."

And finally, we should all sit up and listen to Jackie Jones, an Army lieutenant, when she says, "If we let him get away with this, who knows what's going to be next?"

I have called upon Hollywood and Walter and J.P. and Jackie and all their coura-geous comrades-in-arms to do what must be done. Tonight, America and the world are deeply grateful to them and to their families. And let me say to everyone listen-ing or watching tonight: When the troops we've sent in finish their work, I am deter-mined to bring them home as soon as possible.

Tonight, as our forces fight, they and their families are in our prayers. May God bless each and every one of them, and the coalition forces at our side in the Gulf, and may He continue to bless our nation, the United States of America.

Note: President Bush spoke at 9:01 P.M. from the Oval Office at the White House. In his address, he referred to President Saddam Hussein of Iraq; Secretary of State James A. Baker III; United Nations Secretary-General Javier Perez de Cuellar de la Guerra; and Gen. H. Norman Schwarzkopf, commander of the U.S. forces in the Persian Gulf. The address was broadcast live, nationwide, on radio and television.

CHAPTER 3

MATTERS OF MEANING

THAT DEPENDS ON WHAT THE MEANING OF "IS" IS.
— PRESIDENT BILL CLINTON, AUGUST 17, 1998

The ability to use words comes to us naturally and plays a central role in nearly all our activities. The critical evaluation of reasons and beliefs requires an understanding of some of the ways in which this resource affects our cognitive life.

The value of language is most apparent in its use in communicating with others; but even when we think to ourselves, language plays a crucial role in the development of many of our ideas. An examination of some of the problems and resources associated with the words we use will enhance our ability to use language in a clear and effective way in formulating, presenting, and evaluating reasoning. We need to develop our sensitivity to ambiguity and vagueness and the effect these have on argument; we need to practice clarifying our own arguments and learn to be aware of multiple possibilities in the interpretation of others' words; and we need to learn the power of suggestion inherent in the connotations of our words, so that we can identify some poor substitutes for justification and so that we can control the effect of our own words.

WORDS, CONTEXT, MEANING, AND REFERENCE

We use words in particular conversational contexts to convey meanings, make contrasts, or refer to particular things or sets of things. Most words have a considerable range of uses in these activities.

Take a simple word like *she*, as used, for example, in the sentence "She will win a prize." The word *she* refers to some female the speaker is calling attention to in the situation in which the word is used. That is the principal general role, the principal *meaning*, of the word. A particular utterance (or inscription) of it will refer to just one female, though different utterances have referred to many different individuals. (English speakers have probably used this word in referring to almost every female person they have ever spoken about.) The situation, or *context*, in which the word is used plays a key role in determining the reference of each particular use of this word. (There is no general answer to the question "Who is the referent of the word *she*?" We can only identify the referent of a particular use of that word.)

Consideration of the word *now* reveals a different way in which context plays a role in determining what is being said. The word *now* always refers to some time period that includes the time at which it is uttered. That, however, is not very specific. Any particular spoken use occurs at a particular moment, and that establishes one feature of the reference: The word *now* refers to a time period that includes that moment. Full communication must also give some clue about the extent of the time period under discussion. Consider the contrasting periods that these uses refer to:

> I just pushed up my glasses, but *now* they are down my nose again.

> I am working at the pharmacy *now,* but this evening I will party.

> I worked in a pharmacy last year, but *now* I am studying law.

> Some of our ancestors lived in an ice age, but *now* our lifestyles are evolving in a more hospitable interglacial climate.

The meaning of *now* does not change here. Rather, its meaning is not the only factor involved in determining what it applies to. When we hear a use of a word like *now*, we must apply our knowledge of the speaker and the context to determine (at least roughly) the extent of the period referred to.

As we have seen, the context determines one feature of *now* in a very systematic way: the moment of utterance must be included in the time period referred to. Another feature, the extent of the time period (this moment, this hour, this day, this week, this year, or this meteorological period), is not determined in such a systematic way from the conversational context, but it must still be appropriate to the content of the conversation.

Note how a lack of adequate context can make this unclear. If we overhear Carlos saying, "Now I am studying law," we do not know whether he is in the act of studying right at the moment he says it. He could instead be using the word *now* to make a contrast between his principal activity last year and his principal activity this year (even if he is not studying at the moment he says it, or even on that day or in that week).

Words like *now* and *she* are especially useful in illustrating the way that meaning and context are used in determining what is being referred to. They have a meaning—we would not use *now* to refer to a person or *she* to refer to a time, for example—but that meaning must interact with the relevant context to determine the content of a particular use of the word.

General terms, such as *green*, *square*, *doctor*, *friend*, and *city*, apply to the particular things they do because of the meanings they have and the contrasts they are used to make. The word *green* may apply to an apple for a time and then stop applying when the apple ripens. In this case, the meaning of the word determines its range of applicability.

Context plays a role in our determination of what contrasts are relevant, and so of what a word applies to. Without context, it is difficult to answer even such simple questions as "How many fingers do you have?" The answer could be ten or eight, depending on whether or not I am to count my thumbs as fingers. Sometimes we count them in this way, and sometimes we don't.

Even with color words, the needs of the particular conversation can play a role in determining whether it is appropriate to apply a term. If there are two wines, a Chablis and a Bordeaux, and I ask for the red one, it is clear that I want the Bordeaux. However, if the wines are a Bordeaux and a Beaujolais, and if I ask for the red one rather than the purple one, then I want the Beaujolais rather than the Bordeaux. The word *red* is used to make contrasts among the things being discussed, and it is conversationally appropriate if the contrast is clearly made. For a use of a term to be conversationally appropriate in a context, what it applies to in that context should be clear.

VAGUENESS

The uses of the words *now* and *red* also illustrate that the use of a word can be meaningful even when no precise, general application exists. A particular use of a word has an application that should be contextually appropriate; it should make a contrast or apply to some individual or set that is salient in the particular context of conversation. Once we have the idea of the relevant contrast being made (this afternoon, not tonight; this year, not last; this meteorological period, not the ice age), we do not need to know the precise boundaries of the time period. This holds true for much of what we say. If I say that my sister wore red lipstick, I mark a contrast (with white, black, orange, and so on), even if I am somewhat uncertain about whether I would apply the term *red* to certain shades of magenta. Clear discussion does not require precise limits for the set of things I would apply *red* to, as long as my use of the word makes an adequate contrast in the situation at hand.

Words and conversational context together should enable an audience to figure out, well enough for the conversational purposes, what the speaker is talking about. This process can misfire, however; vagueness can be inappropriate. If Uncle Bill says to his young nephew, "You have certainly grown bigger," that is precise enough. If Uncle Bill is a laboratory technician, then he will probably find it inappropriate to report, "We heated the piece of titanium quite a bit, and it certainly grew bigger." In understanding people's statements and arguments, we must use our good judgment about the purposes at hand in determining what the appropriate standards of precision are.

AMBIGUITY

There are at least three ways for a sentence to be ambiguous.

Lexical Ambiguity

A sentence can be ambiguous because a word in it has multiple meanings.

The banks were important to the town.

This could be true because of the town's financial situation or because it is near a high river. The word *bank* has multiple meanings, and in this sentence (without additional context), it is not clear which meaning is intended. Ambiguous words create the possibility that the sentences that contain them will also be ambiguous. Of course, the context of discussion will often make it clear which meaning is intended, so that the audience often has no difficulty in understanding the speaker. (We usually know whether the news story we are hearing is about finance or floods.)

Syntactic Ambiguity

Some sentences have more than one structural interpretation and consequently have multiple possible meanings. There does not need to be any ambiguous word. The word *syntax* refers to the way words (or symbols) are put together, so we call the existence of multiple structural interpretations *syntactic ambiguity*.

> Judy and Alice or Jane will clean your engine.

That sentence is ambiguous because we do not know what its structure is. Although no word is ambiguous, there are two possible structures, which we can indicate with brackets:

> [Judy and Alice] or Jane will clean your engine.
>
> (Either Judy and Alice will do it (together) or Jane will do it.)
>
> Judy and [Alice or Jane] will clean your engine.
>
> (Judy will do it, and either Alice or Jane will do it with her.)

From the original sentence alone, we cannot tell what the speaker meant.

Modifying phrases can often be a source of syntactic ambiguity, because often we can find more than one way to apply the modifier.

> John attacked the woman with a knife.

It is not clear who has the knife. Careful presentation of ideas requires a sensitivity to such ambiguities, so that we can rewrite (paraphrase) the sentence in question in a way that makes the meaning clear.

> Seeing that the woman had a knife, John attacked her.
>
> Using his knife, John attacked the woman.
>
> Sometimes underlying structure is not so easily shown.
>
> Every Englishman loves one woman above all others:
> > the Queen.
> > his mother.

These are two ways to complete the sentence, corresponding to distinct interpretations. In the first case, we interpret the sentence as saying of one particular woman (the Queen) that every Englishman loves her above all others.

> One particular woman x satisfies this condition: Every Englishman loves x above all other women. (That woman is the Queen.)

In this first case we cannot go on to say, "Each loves his own mother best." Then it would not be about one particular woman anymore. In the second case, though, we interpret the sentence as being about Englishmen and not about any particular woman.

> Every Englishman x satisfies this condition: x loves one woman above all others. (Each loves his own mother best.)

In this case, there can be different women for different Englishmen, so each could love his own "Mum" best, and the second completion becomes possible. No single word within the sentence is ambiguous, but the structure of the original sentence (before the colon) allows these two different interpretations. (This ambiguity is very easy to represent using the tools of formal logic, but that is beyond our scope here.)

Contextual Ambiguity

When conversational context needs to play a role, contextual unclarity can infect a sentence, creating an ambiguity.

> Alice wanted Mary's father to go with her.

Here the word *her* needs to refer to some contextually apparent female. It could refer to Alice, to Mary, or even to some other female the speaker points at when speaking the sentence. Context could provide multiple candidates, so the application of the word *her* could be unclear.

It might be argued that context plays a role in the application of most words. Two classes of words, adjectives and comparatives, are worth special mention in that regard. Bertha saw a rat in her basement. It was a

> small mammal
>
> large rodent
>
> large household pest
>
> small adult rat

Just calling it *small* would be misleading. Whether we apply *small* depends on our comparison class. When the comparison class is unclear, the applicability of the adjective can be in doubt, and the meaning of a statement can be left uncertain. If someone says,

> John is a high school basketball player. He is tall.

we really do not get a very good idea of John's height. Is he

> tall for a basketball player
>
> tall for a high school basketball player
>
> tall compared to most adult males
>
> tall for a high school male
>
> tall for a high school student

or what?

Explicitly comparative words, such as *more* and *less* and words with *-er* endings (*prettier*, *slower*, etc.), need a comparison class. For years, advertisements said "Colgate kids get fewer cavities." Fewer than whom? Fewer than kids who don't brush their teeth? That would not be very surprising, but it is also not relevant if you are deciding which brand of toothpaste to buy. (It is relevant if you are deciding whether to buy toothpaste.) Without a clear comparison class, we do not know how to evaluate the importance of the claim because we do not really know what is being said.

The unstated item of comparison can mislead. Consider this statement from a memorial service:

> Alex worked all of his life to make the world a better place. When he died, however, it certainly wasn't better than it was when he was born. I guess that there is little that a person can do.

When you see the word *better*, you should ask, "Better than what?" In evaluating Alex's good works, we would ordinarily want to know whether the world was *better than it would have been* if Alex had not lived and done what he did. That is the sensible comparison to be making in the first sentence. In the second sentence, though, the speaker is evaluating the world in comparison to *how it was when Alex was born*. That is an entirely different comparison.

When we closely examine arguments, we often need to eliminate another common type of unclarity. Often we omit quantifiers like *all*, *some*, *many*, and *nearly all* when we make assertions. We say, "Lions are warm-blooded" rather than "All lions are warm-blooded." Our audience would know that this property is uniform in lions, so the word *all* is unnecessary. Omission of a quantifier word should not always be taken as an omission of *all*, however. We also say, "People have seen my dog catch a Frisbee in midair." In some cases, therefore, an omission can leave an ambiguity.

> Lions like to have their tummies scratched.

> People will be glad when we get a new mayor.

Here it is genuinely unclear what the quantifier word should be. Probably the speakers in these cases do not mean *all*. Perhaps they mean *some*, *many*, or *most*. In cases of this kind, questioning often reveals that even the speakers are not too sure what they meant. Such unclarities can seriously mislead hearers (or readers) and can perniciously infect an argument.

AMBIGUITY IN ARGUMENT

When ambiguity infects an argument, we have an *equivocation*. We have already seen that validity requires a close interconnection of premises and conclusion. An equivocation occurs when the *words* that appear in the premises and conclusion *appear* to link in the right way but when this appearance of validity is superficial because there is an ambiguity. When there is equivocation, words that appear to be the same really have a different meaning, so there is no real linkage of meaning. This is a *fallacy* of argument—a way of arguing that may at first appear adequate but really is not. In ordinary cases of validity, the *meanings* of the premises and conclusion must be appropriately connected; similar words without an appropriate connection of meaning are ineffectual in producing validity.

This is easiest to see in the case of simple examples.

> Cassandra: The stability of the banks is threatened. Everyone should take precautions.
>
> Simon: So I should get my money out now.

If Cassandra was warning about a danger of flooding, then Simon has drawn the wrong conclusion from the premises she offered. Cassandra's predictions would be much more useful if she were careful to avoid such misleading ambiguity.

Equivocations occur with distressing frequency. Identifying them and making them clear to others are important skills of inquiry and discussion.

John Stuart Mill once argued in the following way:

> The utilitarian doctrine is, that happiness is desirable. . . . What ought to be required of this doctrine . . . to make good its claim to be believed?

> The only proof capable of being given that an object is visible, is that people actually see it. . . . In like manner, I apprehend, the sole evidence it is possible to produce that anything is desirable, is that people do actually desire it. . . . This being a fact, we have not only all the proof which the case admits of, but all which it is possible to require, that happiness is a good.

Mill links two arguments here.

> [P1]   People desire happiness.
>
> [P2]   Whatever is desired is desirable (capable of being desired).
>
> ∴ [C1]   Happiness is desirable.

> [P3]   Whatever is desirable is a good. (unstated)
>
> [C1]   Happiness is desirable.
>
> ∴ [C2]   Happiness is a good.

Each of these seems like a valid argument. [P1] and [P2] are used together to establish [C1]. [P3] and [C1] are then the premises of an argument to establish the ultimate conclusion, [C2].

The problem is that the word *desirable* must have different meanings in [P2] and [P3] if these are both to be acceptable premises. Note that in [P2], *desirable* is given a special meaning—"capable of being desired." This is not a common meaning for it, and Mill presents some analogies to get us to focus on that meaning and accept it. (*Visible* does mean "capable of being seen.") Thus [C1] is established with this special meaning for *desirable*. But [C1] is used again in the second argument, where it must connect with [P3]. But [P3] is plausible only with a more ordinary meaning for *desirable*—"worthy of being desired." Note that substituting the special meaning gives us something that is evidently false.

> [P3*]   Whatever is capable of being desired is a good.

People are certainly capable of desiring things that are not good. Similarly, substituting the ordinary meaning in [P2] would also yield something evidently false.

[P2*]   Whatever is desired is worthy of being desired.

People have desired many unworthy things. But [C1] appears in each of these arguments, and if Mill's argumentation is to be successful, the meaning of *desirable* in [C1] must connect appropriately with each of these other premises. That is not possible, because if [P2] and [P3] are both to be true, *desirable* must be used in different ways in the two arguments. The argument that establishes [C1] establishes it with a different meaning from what is required for the second argument, and there is no uniform meaning that connects all of these together.

How to Point Out an Equivocation

I have given a full analysis of Mill's argument to show how equivocation interferes with validity and soundness of argument. But in convincing someone that this argument is unsuccessful, we would ordinarily like to be able to make the problem clear in a simpler, more compact way, without using concepts and techniques of analysis that might be unfamiliar to our audience or unnecessary for making our case. Often we can do that. In the case of Mill's argument, it would usually suffice to say that a key word shifted meaning and to identify the word and cite the two meanings.

> Mill's argument fails because the word *desirable* is used with two different meanings. First it seems to mean "capable of being desired," but to get the conclusion to follow plausibly, it must later mean "worthy of being desired."

This will usually be enough to make the situation clear. If it is not enough, then you can go on to show that neither of these meanings would work throughout the discussion.

> If *desirable* means "capable of being desired," then Mill is wrong: It is not true that whatever is desirable (capable of being desired) is a good. If *desirable* means "worthy of being desired," then Mill is wrong again: It is not true that everything that is desired is desirable (worthy of being desired). No uniform meaning can be carried through Mill's discussion.

The following general pattern is a very successful way to point out equivocations.

> *Phase 1:*   Identify the word or phrase that has multiple meanings, and identify the distinct meanings.

If that does not make the situation sufficiently clear, then move on to phase 2.

> *Phase 2:*   Eliminate the word in question and substitute a clear phrase that expresses one of the meanings. Then note how the argument fails (is not sound) if we stick to that uniform meaning. Note also how it fails (is not sound) if we substitute a phrase that expresses the other meaning and carry that meaning through the arguments.

We tried the Mill argument with each of the meanings for *desirable* substituted in, and it didn't work either way. That is generally a very effective way to show that no interpretation of the passage can turn it into a successful argument.

We have mentioned several distinct types of ambiguity (lexical, syntactic, and contextual). Any of these can be a source of equivocation in argument. (The word *amphiboly* is sometimes used for equivocations that are due to syntactic ambiguity.) Mill's argument involves a lexical ambiguity, but a syntactic or contextual ambiguity could also cause a similar problem. In the example that follows, a syntactic ambiguity leads to a misunderstanding. One speaker uses a sentence with one particular meaning, and then a second speaker draws a conclusion from that sentence, but understanding it to have a different meaning.

> John: All of the witnesses say that they saw someone commit the crime.
>
> Alice: With such uniformity of judgment, it should be easy to convict the perpetrator.

But if each of the witnesses says that it was someone different, and John meant only that each has an opinion about who was seen (though the opinions may differ), then Alice's conclusion is not at all justified. She apparently believed John to be claiming that some particular person is such that all of the witnesses say that they saw that person. But John might not have meant to say that at all.

Often an equivocation occurs when a term in the conclusion is given a "special meaning." The conclusion might follow with that special meaning, but it does not follow with the ordinary meaning of the term, and yet the speaker wants the audience to accept the conclusion with the ordinary meaning. For example:

> There are a large number of political prisoners in the United States. Thousands are in jail because they are too poor to pay bail bond. Thousands are in jail because of delayed trials. Thousands are in jail because they don't have the political clout to be released on personal recognizance. That is political.

The conclusion that follows from these premises is that many people are in jail for reasons that are related to politics. The phrase *political prisoner*, however, does not ordinarily mean "a person who is in jail for a reason related to politics." Ordinarily it means something much more specific: "a person who is in jail because of his or her political views." We strongly condemn countries that imprison people for their political views. In this passage, the speaker has tried to carry the strong condemnation for that over to condemnation for people who are jailed for other "political" reasons. That, though, is an equivocation.

SUMMARY OF IMPORTANT CONCEPTS

Kinds of Unclarity

Vagueness   There is no clear boundary between the things the expression applies to and the things it does not apply to. (Vagueness is normal. Contextually inappropriate vagueness is a problem.)

Ambiguity   multiple meanings. In a sentence, we can distinguish three kinds of ambiguity:

Lexical ambiguity: due to a word with multiple meanings

Syntactic ambiguity: due to multiple possibilities for the structure of the sentence

Contextual ambiguity: due to multiple ways of applying a word in a particular situation

Equivocation

A word or phrase is used in an argument with more than one meaning or application. The argument may appear superficially valid, because the premises and conclusion have properly connected words or phrases, but it is not really valid, because the words or phrases are not used in a uniform way. (Proper connection of the meanings of the expressions is ultimately the important thing for validity of argument. Multiple meanings and shifts of meaning can cause a failure of connection for the meanings even when the expressions appear to be appropriately linked.)

EXERCISE 3A

Identify the conclusion of each argument and evaluate the argument. Point out the most significant weakness. Note any equivocations. (Examples 10 and 11 are difficult. Some answers are provided at the end of the chapter, but try to think them through yourself before you look at the answers.)

1. The law says that insane people should not be punished but should be treated instead. Anyone who murders is insane. So murderers should be treated for their problems, not punished with prison sentences.

2. We have seen miracles—like people walking on the moon. So we know that we can believe in the miracles that the Bible describes.

3. Equal rights for women should not be constitutionally guaranteed. Men and women are different, physiologically and emotionally. If this is so, then men and women are not equal; and if men and women are not equal, then the law should not treat them as equals.

4. Although the President traveled around the nation promising that his administration would enhance our security, we don't see it in our neighborhood. Our cars and homes are subject to regular vandalism, making us feel nervous and angry every day. Security needs to begin at home, and we should not re-elect a President who can't keep his promises.

5. I don't think that Peter is being paid enough. In his new job, he gets additional responsibilities every day, and people with greater responsibility should get higher pay.

6. Last week my father said that he could afford only an inexpensive graduation present for me. Yesterday he said that some of the new cars being imported from central Europe will be very inexpensive. So I guess that he will buy me something that costs about the same as one of those. That will be just fine.

7. Our curriculum requires the study of basics, such as English composition, mathematical skills, and use of a foreign language. Philosophy, which is the most basic study of all, should be included in this category.

8. Professors and other teachers should not try to cultivate independent thinking in their students. Independent thinkers would have to start from scratch, and there would be no point in that. Students should forget about trying for independence and should learn from their masters.

9. Many Americans are proud that their country is based on individualism, the idea that society is made up of individual people and that the government should be designed to serve the needs of the people. But we should reject individualism, because the doctrine that each person can stand alone is inimical to the sense of community that a smoothly functioning society requires. As President Kennedy said, "Ask not what your country can do for you, but rather ask what you can do for your country."

10. Trees have a very meaningful language. When they turn up their leaves, that means that it will rain. When they lose their leaves, that means that winter is coming. A language like that tells us something important in a very clear way.

11. When the President makes his next appointment to the Supreme Court, he should appoint a strict constructionist. Faithful adherence to the text of the Constitution and the intentions of the original framers is really the only defensible principle of Constitutional interpretation. And strictness is what our country needs now. Criminals' rights, minority demands, and individual freedoms have been enhanced at the expense of victims' rights, the will of the majority, and the need to preserve order in the state. That is why the President should appoint someone who will take a strict and narrow view when an individual claims that the state or federal government has infringed on his rights.

12. By asking good questions, a student can make his or her professor more able to provide help. Since the professors who are more able to help are the ones who should get tenure, students ultimately determine who should get tenure.

EXERCISE 3B

John Smith approached an undercover agent and traded his rifle, an automatic, for two ounces of cocaine. Smith then sold some of the cocaine (to another undercover officer) at a profit. Smith was charged with "using a firearm during and in relation to a drug trafficking crime."

> For his drug trafficking alone, Smith would ordinarily receive a sentence of at most 2 years.
>
> Using a firearm in such a crime carries a mandatory penalty of 5 years.
>
> Using an automatic firearm in such a crime carries a mandatory penalty of 30 years.

What penalty should the judge give Smith? Why? (This account is based on a case that actually went to the United States Supreme Court. Why would there be controversy about this?)

CONNOTATION AND SUGGESTION

In using words, we classify individuals, apply general concepts, and relate general concepts to one another. But these cognitive activities are only one aspect of the power of words. Words can also call forth attitudes and emotional responses that may be related or unrelated to their cognitive content. This power can reinforce or undermine an argument, and often it is used in place of real argument.

Bertrand Russell pointed out some "irregular verbs" in calling attention to the fact that two words may apply to the same (or almost the same) things, and express the same property of those things, yet differ greatly in the attitude they express. When two words differ in the attitudes and emotional responses they express or evoke, they are said to have different *connotations*, and words with the same content (or denotation) may have very different connotations indeed.

I am firm; you are obstinate; he is a pig-headed fool.

I have reconsidered; you have changed your mind; he has gone back on his word.

When we choose one word or phrase instead of another, we can convey a great deal about our attitudes toward our subject, and we can cause very different reactions in the people we are speaking to. Consider some of these contrasting words for similar things:

clever	sly	cunning
associate	fellow traveler	crony
public servant		government bureaucrat
career	job	grind
key figure	important person	big cheese
aroma	smell	stench
trusting		gullible
stand up to pressure		persist in a desperate mission

Whether I choose the "assertive aroma of his pipe," the "strong smell of his pipe," or the "foul stench of his pipe" can convey my attitude toward the smell, and my listener is likely to react initially with a similar attitude. When a factual evaluation is important, a critical listener must get past that initial reaction and sort out the factual content from the expression of attitude. In each of these cases, the listener would know that the pipe had a noticeable smell, but the listener cannot say much more about the quality of this smell (unless he or she is well acquainted with my olfactory preferences). Because people have very different attitudes toward similar smells, we cannot tell much about the objective features of the smell from these descriptions.

There are several reasons for us to become sensitive to the attitudes that the connotations of words convey. In evaluating arguments, we need to be able to identify the extent to which the factual content is influencing us and the extent to which we may be reacting in an unjustified way to attitudes associated with the words used. Sometimes we will find that there is little or no substantive content in what is said, or that no reason has been given for a conclusion, but rather that words are being used to convey an attitude without any factual basis. In addition, in our own writing we want the connotations of the words we use to work in support of the claims and arguments we present.

Euphemism

Often a familiar word for something carries a definite impact and a set of associations that a speaker wishes to avoid. Politicians know well that the terms used for things can make a big difference in the impact of a statement or an argument.

> Tax increases have been called *revenue enhancement*, *receipts strengthening*, and *tax surcharges*.

> To avoid the word *recession*, those in office have used other words, like *slump*, *flat economy*, *correction*, *downturn*, *slowdown*, *spasm*, or (creatively) *sidewise waffling*.

> A blockade is an internationally recognized act of war. So in the period before the 1991 war with Iraq (oops! the "military action" in Iraq), the United States carried on "interdiction" of shipments to Iraq. In responding to a question in which the word *blockade* was used, Secretary of State James Baker said frankly, "Let's not use the word *blockade*."

In any debate, both sides want to be identified as being in favor of something good. That is usually even better than being opposed to something bad. Thus, for example, opposing parties in the abortion debate identify themselves as "pro-choice" and "pro-life." The term *pro-abortion* is much less favorable than *pro-choice* because *abortion* is much less positive than *choice*. It is also misleading because it suggests a position in favor of women's having abortions, when only the existence of the option to have abortions is supported. Of course the term *anti-life* would be even more negative and even more inaccurate. The *pro-life* side avoids *anti-abortion* and *anti-choice* in order to have the advantage of a positive ("pro") portrayal of their position.

The language of military briefings is an interesting case to consider. During a military action, grim events must often be reported, and those who make the reports often have many reasons to minimize attention to the loss of life involved. In addition, these events generally have a strategic significance that must be reported. Excessive attention to the strategic role of military action can distract us from the human toll, and the use of strategic terms to describe events contributes to this tendency. Terms like *interdiction*, *incursion*, and *protective reaction* indicate something about the strategy involved, but we must keep in mind that they usually refer to events that involve considerable destruction and loss of life. These words do not call our attention to this destruction in the way that words like *bombing* and *attack* do. And in a jargon-filled briefing, terms like *capability attrition*, *degradation of our personnel aggregate*, *KIA* and *collateral damage* (civilian casualties) can pass right by us without evoking the deep feelings that other descriptions of the incidents would call up. Emotionally loaded language would convey the impact on our lives better than the strategy-oriented description does.

Connotation in Place of Content

"Coke has life." What does that mean? Not much. It conveys a very positive attitude toward Coke (Coca-Cola), but we would find it difficult to specify the actual information conveyed by this claim.

CALVIN AND HOBBES © Watterson. Reprinted with permission of UNIVERSAL PRESS SYNDICATE. All rights reserved.

You might think that the goal of advertising is to convince you that you should buy a product. But that is not quite right. The goal is to *get you* to buy the product. Convincing you that you should buy it is just one way to do that, and it is often not the most effective way. If you will buy the product in an unthinking way because of favorable associations with it (an "image"), then your action is not under your immediate cognitive control, so reasons alone will not lead you to change your practice so readily. Reasoned actions change under the influence of information; unreasoned actions are less flexible.

Favorable language can lead to favorable associations, even when no good reason is given and even when the factual content of the claim about the product is unimportant, negative, or nonexistent. "Come to Marlboro country." "You've come a long way, baby." Nabisco crackers: "Crisper, Tastier, Premiumer." It may be easier to make a sale by manipulating customers than by convincing them of anything. A typical ad for clothing in the *New York Times* (July 28, 1996) showed sketches of three outfits, with the following text:

casual pursuits

slim khakis, crisp cottons—
perfect to play out all your day's plans

Lord & Taylor
The SIGNATURE of American Style

In such an ad, developing image is much more important than giving arguments.

Overblown Jargon

Academic prose is sometimes awful. Ponderous abstract terms are used when simpler descriptions are available, and in the worst cases, obscure terminology masks the fact that very little is being said. This overburdened prose is apparently impressive to some people, and it can insulate writing from substantive criticism by making the substance extraordinarily difficult to identify.

CALVIN AND HOBBES © Watterson. Reprinted with permission of UNIVERSAL PRESS SYNDICATE. All rights reserved.

Consider these sentences that begin a section in *Critical Existentialism*, by Nicola Abbagnano (translated by Nino Langiulli, Anchor Books, 1969, p. 89).

> Freedom, then, can only be the result of freedom. It demands an effective comprehension of its own fundamental nature, as well as of the concrete historical modes in which it is actually manifest.

Here we see some common problems. When an author uses an abstract concept as the subject of a sentence, it is easy for the reader to lose contact with the concrete meaning of the sentence. Instead, words flow past in an incomprehensible stream. A serious reader must look elsewhere to find more specific claims that give content to the sentence in question. In this particular case, the first sentence follows a discussion in which the author claims that *people must be free in order to be able to understand freedom.* By using *then* (in the first of the sentences quoted here), the author suggests that this is a summary of that point. But in the next sentence he seems to be making an entirely different (and perhaps even conflicting) point: that *a person must understand freedom in order to be free,* and this understanding must include both the general concept and the way that particular cases illustrate that concept. In this and adjacent passages, the author has not given reasons to believe either of these claims but has merely asserted them without justification. Thus the slogan "Freedom can only be the result of freedom" is obscure in its meaning, and the use of this sloganeering and pretentious language obscures the fact that no reasons are being given for accepting the claim (or claims) in question. Because it is unclear, it serves as a pivot point for shifting from one unjustified assertion to another, while giving the impression of having legitimately connected the claims in one section with those of the next.

An author can also achieve this nebulous lack of concreteness by talking of the *characteristics* of a group, a nation, or a period of time, when it is the *actions* of people in those groups, nations, or periods of time that are really under discussion. By speaking of something larger than the individuals, the author leaves obscure the question of which or how many individuals are being discussed (some? most? all? the influential ones? etc.). In the following passage, an ill-defined "epoch of the logos" is the subject of some claims about writing and meaning, but neither the passage nor the surrounding text makes clear the extent of the epoch or the claims being made about it.

> The epoch of the logos thus debases writing considered as mediation of mediation and as a fall into the exteriority of meaning. To this epoch belongs the difference between signified and signifier, or at least the strange separation of their "parallelism," and the exteriority, however extenuated, of the one to the other. This appurtenance is organized and hierarchized in a history. (*Of Grammatology*, Jacques Derrida, translated by Gayatri Chakravorty Spivak. Baltimore, MD: Johns Hopkins University Press, 1976, p. 13.)

All of this is supposed to have something to do with people writing and using language, but this passage gives us very few clues to the intended meaning. To some people, the pretentious fog of abstract language may make the author seem impressive and may make unsubstantiated claims seem wise and important.

In psychology and social sciences, special terminology can often make the unsurprising seem impressive. As Talcott Parsons, an important sociologist, once said,

> Skills constitute the manipulative techniques of human goal attainment and control in relation to the physical world, so far as artifacts for machines especially designed as tools do not yet supplement them.

I guess that this means that before people used tools and machines, they had to rely on skill to attain their goals. This again illustrates the point that rewriting a sentence so that it has a more concrete subject (*people* rather than *skills* or *artifacts for machines designed as tools*) will usually make it much more comprehensible.

Unfortunately, academic prose is influential in some circles. Educators have been under its undue influence, and the result has sometimes been disastrous for communication between educators and parents.

Lawyers are criticized for using similarly obscure language. It does often seem that the language they use is directed at creating a need for lawyers to interpret it.

There are, however, some very good reasons for lawyers to use language that has been used in the past, where its precise significance has been determined in the courts over a wide range of circumstances. In addition, a good lawyer can use his or her familiarity with past unclarities to make sure that misunderstandings are avoided. If your will says, "I leave my property to my children," it does not provide advice about how to divide things like cars, boats, houses, and antique furniture. It also may not provide properly for the contingency that one of your children dies before you, leaving all of his property to his children. Should these grandchildren get some of your property? And of course it does not say what to do if previously unknown children come forth. More careful (but more complicated) language can make things clearer.

"Loaded" Verbs

Sometimes two verbs that apply to a state or activity differ in the following respect: One term carries the implication that the activity has been successfully completed or that the state or activity has some definite feature, and the other term does not carry that implication. In such a case, the term that does not carry the additional implication is a more neutral description. When people use the more loaded term, they can smuggle in an implication that looks like a part of the description of an action when it really goes beyond describing what has been legitimately established.

"Loaded" Verb	More Neutral Verb
establish, prove, show that X is true	*argue* that X is true
know, realize, recognize that X is true	*believe, think* that X is true
refute a claim	*argue against, dispute* a claim
develop	*change*
rectify a situation	*change, alter* a situation
point out something	*say, claim* something

The extra implication can be smuggled in without argument when the loaded term is used. Saying that the President *realizes* he is in trouble is very different from saying that he *believes* he is in trouble, because the first carries the implication that he is right (i.e., that he is in trouble). To say that a senator's views have *developed* is very different from saying that they have *changed,* because it suggests that they have changed in a positive way and become more mature. In the following pairs of sentences, note what additional claim the speaker implies with the loaded verb.

> On the basis of the witness's testimony, the defendant established that he is innocent.
> On the basis of the witness's testimony, the defendant argued that he is innocent.

> The President recognizes that he will win the election.
> The President thinks that he will win the election.

> The mayor refuted his opponent's charges.
> The mayor disputed his opponent's charges.

The recent congressional action rectified some of the most serious problems in the welfare system.
The recent congressional action changed some of the most significant features of the welfare system.

John pointed out that Alicia could not be trusted.
John claimed that Alicia could not be trusted.

In our own writing, we need to be careful to use the more loaded terms only when they are justified. In judging the work of others, we should be careful to watch out for situations in which these loaded terms are used. Something that looks like a very objective description may carry implications that are not justified by the information actually available.

Context and Emphasis

A well-worn story has it that the captain of a ship once reported in the ship's log that "The first mate was drunk today." Soon after, when the captain was ill, the first mate was in charge of entries in the log. He truly reported, "Today the captain was not drunk."

This story illustrates that the context in which something is said can suggest things that go beyond the bare meaning of what is said. A ship's log must always be true; that is an important rule. But an entry of the sort that the first mate made is appropriate only if it is also noteworthy, usually by standing in contrast to the usual.

Context and placement can undermine a claim. Consider the value of the welcome to college students at the end of this notice:

LANCASTER SQUARE

NEIGHBORHOOD WATCH GROUP

MONTHLY MEETING

THURSDAY, 7 PM

COME AND MEET THE NEW COORDINATOR!

COLLEGE STUDENTS AND CHILDREN

WELCOME

Emphasis within a sentence also helps to indicate contrasts that go beyond the literal meaning of what is said. Though emphasis does not usually change the meaning, you should consider the difference it makes in the example that follows. Read the following sentence aloud, changing the emphasis as indicated. In every case, the emphasis strongly suggests a relevant contrast (which are indicated in brackets).

You should not speak ill of your friends. [But others may.]

You *should* not speak ill of your friends. [But you will.]

You should not *speak* ill of your friends. [You may *act* badly toward them.]

You should not speak *ill* of your friends. [You may speak well of them.]

You should not speak ill *of* your friends. [You may speak ill *to* them.]

You should not speak ill of *your* friends. [Of others' friends, no problem.]

You should not speak ill of your *friends*. [Your enemies or others, go ahead.]

As with words with strong connotations, something beyond the literal meaning is indicated.

Limitations on a claim will also suggest there is a contrast to consider, and that can make a strong suggestion beyond what is actually said. I might not have any idea what John does on weekends, but if I say, "John doesn't wear earrings during the week," that will strongly suggest that he does wear earrings on weekends. If praise is limited, or if a comparison is made, a speaker can make strong suggestions that go beyond the literal content. Although the following statements might be intended as positive statements about John, consider what they suggest about him or his associates:

He is nicer than some of his friends. [This might suggest that some of his friends are not very nice. It might also suggest that John is nicer than only a few of his friends but that most are nicer than he is (especially if *some* is emphasized).]

His recent work shows some promise of success. [Suggests that his past work had no promise and that his recent work is not yet successful.]

He has never robbed any stores with the guys he hangs out with. [Suggests that he hangs out with people who rob stores (or, perhaps, that he robs stores all by himself).]

We can also change the emphasis of a passage by the way in which we relate ideas to each other. Compare these two sentences:

The President signed the welfare reform bill, but he thinks that it has many very bad features.

Although the President thinks that the welfare reform bill has many very bad features, he signed it.

These report the same facts, but the first emphasizes the President's misgivings about the bill; the mention of the misgivings comes last, after *but*, a word that signals that the part that follows is really more important than what goes before. The second sentence emphasizes his responsibility for signing it (in the short, main clause of the sentence).

Writing and Speaking

Picking the right tone is an important part of writing. One should use words with connotations that support the points being made, but one should not use words so loaded that the intended audience will find them inappropriate, offensive, or unintentionally comical.

The problem of a mismatch between tone and content occurs more often in student writing than in most other writing. A wide range of new ideas influence college students, and terminology from some of these sources may be a poor fit for views that the student wishes to express.

I support the administration's fiscal schemes for propping up the social security system.

Here the terminology is a poor fit. With little or no change in content, we could have this:

> I support the government's plans for providing a secure fiscal base for the social security system.

There is no reason to use words that undermine your point when more aptly chosen words cast it in a more favorable light. (You must also keep in mind, though, that a persuasive statement of your point should not be a substitute for reasons that support it. Stating a point clearly and strongly is only a preliminary to justifying it.)

Of course, one must be careful not to go too far in forcefully stating a position. Rhetorical flourishes and strong language used in support of a claim can alienate the audience if the language seems inappropriate to the topic or the occasion.

> Converting the elevator so that it needs a key is just another example of the Nazi mentality of the university administration.

> The President's failure to cut taxes by a larger percentage is a hypocritical betrayal, cheating the American people out of their hard-earned wages in order to prop up an obsolete and pathetic national bureaucracy.

Choosing such strong words makes a ludicrous statement rather than a powerful one. It will alienate your audience rather than convince them.

There is an even more pernicious effect of stretching the use of strong language. If you frequently call people *fascists*, then your charge that someone is a fascist will carry little force. The word *rape* is properly used to apply to sex that is against someone's will. More recently it has sometimes been used much more broadly—for cases in which there is persuasion but not force, for example. A college newspaper editorial suggested that it should apply to any sexual act that a woman regrets; and Andrea Dworkin, a well-known writer and activist, has even said that all heterosexual sex is rape. When these uses are around, we lose the ability to use that powerful word to make a strong charge. If such broader uses become commonplace, the word *rape* will no longer carry with it the idea of sex without consent, and it will lose much of its power.

Gender Bias

When we speak and write English (and many other languages), we are faced with a gender problem. There are many contexts in which we would like to use singular pronouns in general claims about people, but in English, there is no general singular personal pronoun available for use. The pronouns *he, she, him, her, his, hers, himself,* and *herself* are all gendered pronouns and thus not fully general in application.

> Everyone loves *his* mother.

> Every person Alice saw that day was more concerned about *herself* than about Alice.

> Alice knew that each person wanted Alice to reward *him.*

> If someone turns in evidence concerning the crime, *he* will get a reward.

We would really like to have a fully general pronoun for people in place of the gendered pronoun, but none exists. When writing, we can write *his or her* (and corresponding compounds), but that can be cumbersome and oddly formal sounding. (Try it in the sentences above.)

Some people have believed that the masculine pronouns can serve as gender-neutral pronouns, but that does not seem to be the case.

> When a person has breast cancer, he should join a support group.
> (Contrast with: When one has breast cancer, one should join a support group.)

> Each student must park his car in the open lot.
> (Contrast with: If one is a student, one must park one's car in the open lot.)

> Each employee should list the name of his husband or wife.
> Each employee should list the name of his spouse.
> (Contrast with: One should list the name of one's spouse.)

The oddness of these cases (even though a small number of men do get breast cancer) suggests that the use of the masculine pronoun is not neutral. In the examples above, we see that using *one* enables us to produce a gender-neutral version. Using *one* in this way, though, sounds very odd or formal to most American speakers. (It is more normal in British English.) In most cases, we can find a better way to say the same thing.

> Anyone who has breast cancer should join a support group.

Sometimes we can just shift to the plural.

> Students must park their cars in the open lot.

But we are sometimes stuck for an equally good way to do it. For example:

> Employees should list the names of their spouses.

This may leave us wondering how many spouses each employee has and how many names each spouse has.

This deficiency in the English language can mislead if it makes one expect a claim to apply only to males when it really has a broader application. Some research on related issues suggests that the use of masculine terms is not interpreted in a gender-neutral way even when it is intended as gender-neutral. For example, students selecting pictures for a sociology text will select pictures of both men and women to illustrate chapters entitled "Society," "Industry," and "Political Behavior." Yet when the chapter titles are "Social Man," "Industrial Man," or "Political Man," they show a much stronger preference for pictures of males. (Joseph W. Schneider and Sally L. Hacker, "Sex Role Imagery and the Use of the Generic 'Man' in Introductory Texts: A Case in the Sociology of Sociology," *American Sociologist*, February 1973.) When people develop a mental picture that excludes or minimizes female contributions in these areas, they are adopting a stereotype that limits their thinking in ways that are inimical to critical thinking.

A more general discussion occurs in Casey Miller and Kate Swift, *Words and Women* (New York: HarperCollins, 1991). In the following passage, Miller and Swift note the effects of a reversal of the usual situation:

Until a few years ago most publications, writers, and speakers on the subject of primary and secondary education used *she* in referring to teachers.
As the proportion of men in the profession increased, so did their annoy-
ance with the generic use of feminine-gender pronouns. By the mid-1960s,
according to the journal of the National Education Association, some of
the angry young men in teaching were claiming that references to the
teacher as "she" were responsible in part for their poor public image and,
consequently, in part for their low salaries.

EXAMPLE

Rewriting a passage for changed tone. As the following paragraph was rewritten, the
material underlined was replaced. Result: The same facts are presented very differently.

In the upcoming election, <u>many</u> voters will be <u>surprised</u> to find a <u>puzzling,
incomprehensibly technical</u> referendum item on the ballot. <u>Big-money</u> developers have <u>smuggled in</u> a vote on <u>special</u> zoning <u>privileges</u> for <u>their</u> planned
housing development. Studies by local environmental groups <u>have shown in
detail</u> what is <u>obvious to anyone who lives in the area</u>: The number of houses
to be built will <u>overwhelm</u> the sewer system, make <u>our</u> traffic <u>miseries even
worse,</u> and <u>leave us with none of the green areas</u> that we welcome for recre-
ation. Supporters of this <u>aggressive destruction</u> of our town <u>claim</u> that we
need to spark the regional economy, but we should all <u>know</u> that this <u>scheme</u>
only <u>torches</u> our environment.

In the upcoming election, <u>voters will find an interesting</u> referendum item on
the ballot. <u>Major</u> developers have <u>requested</u> a vote on zoning <u>changes that
will make a new</u> housing development <u>possible</u>. Studies by local environmental groups have <u>suggested that</u> the number of houses to be built will <u>put</u> the
sewer system <u>to greater use, increase</u> traffic, and cut down on recreational
areas. <u>While this calls attention to some of the important planning that is
needed</u>, supporters of the <u>development</u> in our town <u>point out</u> that we need to
spark the regional economy.

EXERCISE 3C

1. Rewrite the passage below, reporting the events mentioned here in a way that
   is more neutral or that is opposed to a ban on these video sales. (Don't create
   new events. Report the same events in different language.)

   This week, Citizens for a Clean Community captured the attention of
   many who were trying to keep their heads in the sand. Their demon-
   stration made the general public more aware of the problem of smut in
   our community. The media attention gave the leaders of this organization of concerned citizens an opportunity to point out that the continued sale and rental of so-called "adult" and X-rated videos is part of
   a moral decay that will grow if we let it.

The response was predictable: The usual charges of censorship and violation of free speech from the liberals, who argue against every attempt to maintain moral standards.

Fortunately, this City Council succeeded where those of the past have failed. Their new ordinance banning such sales will clean up our community.

2. Rewrite the passage below, reporting the policies mentioned here in a way that is more neutral or that is unfavorable to those policies. (Don't create new policies. Report the same policies in different language.)

President Clinton's vision for America includes enhanced aid for our poorest citizens, affirmative action measures that advance the cause of social justice, and a stable economy.

For our poorest citizens, he has signed an enhancement of the welfare system that will improve their lives. Instead of encouraging lives of dependency, we will concentrate our aid, giving it for only a few months, while the recipient learns new job skills that will enable him or her to lead a life of independence. This enhanced aid will lead to a more productive, self-supporting populace.

Clinton's America will firmly support continued affirmative action measures. These measures will ensure that African-Americans will be visible in education and in the work force and that Americans from every segment of the population will share in our prosperous economy.

President Clinton will not cave in to the supply-siders who claim that reduced taxes are an easy fix for all of our economic ills; and he will not accept tax plans that aggrandize the rich while doing little or nothing for middle-class Americans. The current course of action is producing the kind of stability that our nation depends on.

ANSWERS FOR SELECTED EXAMPLES IN EXERCISE 3A

10. Trees have a very meaningful language. When they turn up their leaves, that means that it will rain. When they lose their leaves, that means that winter is coming. A language like that tells us something important in a very clear way.

The author is using certain facts about the behavior of trees to justify the conclusion that trees have a very meaningful language. Apparently, the idea is that any changes in the tree that have external meaning must constitute a language. But these changes mean something only as indicators—the same way the first appearance of a robin means that spring is coming—and that has nothing to do with language. A language is meaningful because arbitrarily significant parts (words) are combined in a sentence in a way that conveys a claim about the world, and nothing like this happens with the motions of the trees.

The author, then, is equivocating, confusing two distinct concepts of meaning: A natural indication is confused with the significance that comes from the complex combination of arbitrary signs that constitutes a language.

11. When the President makes his next appointment to the Supreme Court, he should appoint a strict constructionist. Faithful adherence to the text of the Constitution and the intentions of the original framers is really the only defensible principle of Constitutional interpretation. And strictness is what our country needs now. Criminals' rights, minority demands, and individual freedoms have been enhanced at the expense of victims' rights, the will of the majority, and the need to preserve order in the state. That is why the President should appoint someone who will take a strict and narrow view when an individual claims that the state or federal government has infringed on his rights.

   The author uses the word *strict* in three different ways yet acts as if those senses are the same.

   > strict construction (of the constitution): faithful adherence to the text of the Constitution and the intentions of the original framers.

   > strictness: a narrow view of criminals' rights, minority demands, and individual freedoms.

   > strictness: a narrow view when an individual claims that the state or federal government has infringed on his rights.

   The second and third uses of *strict* may be loosely related or overlapping. But both are directly opposed to the concept of a strict constructionist, as defined here. The constitution is clear in requiring a view that is *not* narrow when it comes to criminals' rights, minority demands, individual freedoms, and individuals' claims that the state or federal government has infringed on their rights. Thus this paragraph is presenting opposite views as though they were the same view.

   This example is from Monroe Beardsley's book *Thinking Straight*, 4th ed. (Englewood Cliffs, NJ: Prentice-Hall, 1975). Its continuing relevance shows the persistence of one kind of sloppy thinking.

12. By asking good questions, a student can make his or her professor more able to provide help. Since the professors who are more able to help are the ones who should get tenure, students ultimately determine who should get tenure.

   Here we need to pay attention to the guideline mentioned in this chapter. If you use a comparative, make sure you can clearly identify the things compared. Here we have the comparative phrase *more able to provide help*. You should ask "more than what?" In the first premises, it means "more able than they otherwise would be," and in the second it means "more able than other professors" (presumably). Because these are different comparisons, the two premises do not link together in an appropriate way to make a valid argument.

CHAPTER 4

INFORMAL FALLACIES

SOME PEOPLE SAY THAT SMOKING IS A GRAVE THREAT TO YOUR HEALTH. BUT NO ONE HAS DIED FROM JUST A FEW CIGARETTES, SO THERE IS NO REASON FOR ME TO QUIT.

REPRESENTATIVE HENRY HYDE HAD AN EXTRAMARITAL AFFAIR HIMSELF, SO THERE WAS REALLY NO REASON TO LISTEN TO WHAT HE HAD TO SAY WHEN HE WAS ARGUING FOR REMOVING CLINTON FROM OFFICE.

LOOKING AT PICTURES OF NAKED WOMEN IN *PLAYBOY* IS NO DIFFERENT FROM RAPE. IF YOU GET PLEASURE FROM THESE PICTURES, YOU ARE TREATING WOMEN SOLELY AS SEXUAL OBJECTS; AND IT IS THE SAME AS LOOKING OVER THE BODY OF SOMEONE YOU SEE BUT DON'T KNOW, OR GOING OUT WITH SOMEONE JUST BECAUSE YOU ARE ATTRACTED TO HER BODY, OR FONDLING YOUR DATE WITH- OUT CONCERN FOR WHETHER SHE WANTS THAT OR NOT, OR RAPING SOMEONE.

People get sick in many ways. Often the most casual observer can tell that someone is sick. It usually takes medical training, though, to be able to observe the symptoms and diagnose the illness that is their source. A good doctor will also have another skill: he or she will be able to explain what is wrong to other medical professionals and to patients.

Arguments go wrong in many different ways. If you identified each of the arguments at the head of this chapter as a bad argument, then you already have some ability to detect weakness in arguments. In this chapter, we will look at some of the ways arguments go wrong, so that we can strengthen your ability to see that there is a problem. We want more than that, though. We want to develop your ability to say what is wrong in arguments and your ability to make clear to others just what is wrong in some of the arguments we commonly see. You will need to acquire some vocabulary for diagnosing problems with arguments and some ideas about what to say to others to make your diagnosis clear.

Since Aristotle (384–322 B.C.) founded the first university and introduced the idea of studying logic, the study of *fallacies* of argument has been important. This study encourages the recognition of common types of argument that we should not accept as sound, so that we will have a better chance to avoid being persuaded by such arguments. Once we recognize a fallacious argument, we should also have effective patterns of response, so that we will be able to explain, in a convincing way, what is wrong with the argument.

A sound argument has two important features: It is valid, and all of its premises are true. When these two features occur together, the conclusion must be true as well. The other way to appreciate this is to realize that there are at least two ways in which an argument can go wrong: It can have a false premise (one or more), or it can be invalid.

Two properties make an argument sound: validity and truth. We need to keep these in mind when we consider the rhetorical goal of an argument. Ordinarily we are trying to convince an audience of the conclusion. Considering this, we can then see that an argument can be fallacious—that is, it can fail to fulfill its rhetorical goals—in two main ways:

> It has premises that the intended audience has no reason to accept as true. An argument of this general type involves a fallacy of *unwarranted assumptions* (*unjustifed premises*).

or

> The audience has no reason to believe that the premises support the conclusion. Ordinarily, this is because the argument is not valid. Arguments of this type commit *fallacies of relevance* (*fallacies of unwarranted inference*).

In studying fallacies, our goal is to look at some of the common types of fallacious arguments and to develop some methods for clearly identifying and effectively pointing out the fallacy that is committed. We can learn to do this with just a little study, and we can often do it without a full analysis and reconstruction of the argument. This makes the recognition and diagnosis of fallacies a useful skill. To develop and apply this skill, it is helpful to have some more specific titles that we can use in diagnosing and discussing fallacies. With each type of fallacious argument, we will try to associate a method for presenting a diagnosis of the problem—that is, a way of pointing out that a fallacy has been committed.

UNWARRANTED ASSUMPTIONS

False Dilemma (Black-and-White Thinking)

The most common type of fallacious argument is *false dilemma*. In logic the word *dilemma* refers to an *or* statement, a *disjunction*. The fallacy is that of having a premise that is an unwarranted (unjustified) *or* statement (disjunction).

False dilemma is common because accepting an unwarranted disjunction involves merely overlooking some possibilities that are worth considering; it means focusing on a set of possibilities that is smaller than it should be. Several common human failings can lead us to accept an unwarranted disjunction: Oversimplification, failure of imagination, and overlooking possibilities that make us uncomfortable can all be sources of false dilemma. This fallacy is also known as *black-and-white thinking*, because it often involves focusing on extremes, missing the shades of gray and the chromatic spectrum.

Because the fallacy here is the acceptance of something false, one can make the mistake of accepting a false dilemma even when no argument is present.

CALVIN AND HOBBES. © Watterson. Reprinted with permission of UNIVERSAL PRESS SYNDICATE. All rights reserved.

There are two common types of valid argument with a disjunctive premise: disjunctive syllogism and constructive dilemma. A false dilemma usually involves one of these types of argument:

> Disjunctive syllogism: A or B
>
> not-B
>
> ∴ A

> I'll have to decide between going into debt for this new stereo system or doing without music for a while. But I couldn't go without music, so I guess I'll break out the credit card.

This is a valid argument, but it commits a fallacy because it has an unwarranted assumption. The argument overlooks other ways to satisfy the need for music: a portable CD player, a partial system (with headphones for now and the rest purchased later), etc. As long as these are possibilities worth considering, the argument commits the fallacy of false dilemma. It is a *valid* argument, but it has a questionable disjunctive premise.

> Constructive dilemma: If A, then C
>
> If B, then D
>
> A or B
>
> ∴ C or D

> If you're already logical, then studying logic is unnecessary; but if you're not logical, then you can't understand what it's about anyway, so it's futile. And,

of course, either you're logical or you're not logical. So studying logic is either unnecessary or futile.

One premise here may look like a logical truth: either you're logical or you're not. For the argument's other premises to have any plausibility at all, though, you really need this:

> If you're already *completely* logical, then studying logic is unnecessary; but if you're not logical *at all*, then you can't understand what it's about anyway, so it's futile. And, of course, either you're *completely* logical or you're *not* logical *at all*. So studying logic is either unnecessary or futile.

The first two premises need this paraphrase for plausibility. Of course, it is not very clear what it would be like to be completely logical ("Star Trek's" Mr. Spock?) or not logical at all. Once we have paraphrased the premises to make them more transparent, it is easy to see that the disjunctive premise is obviously a false dilemma, not a logical truth. It overlooks the possibility that you have some logical ability already but could come to understand that ability better and maybe even improve it through the study of logic. Like the example based on disjunctive syllogism, this is a *valid* argument, but it is not sound, because it has a false premise (a false dilemma).

You should associate a clarification procedure with each of the types of fallacy we discuss. This is a method for showing that the fallacy has been committed. In offering a diagnosis of false dilemma, explicitly *point out at least some of the possibilities that the speaker has failed to consider*, if that is possible. That is the best way to make it clear that the disjunctive (*or*) premise is false or at least unwarranted. That is what was done with the two examples just examined.

The diagnosis of false dilemma is also appropriate for claims outside the context of explicit argument. Watch out for headlines that say things like this: "Economics, not biology, may explain male domination." This is not explicitly a disjunction, but the headline seems to assume a disjunction: that either economics or biology is responsible for male domination. This assumption is made without justification, when there are many other possibilities—cultural traditions, religious beliefs, or any combination of these (including combinations that involve economic or biological factors) may be responsible. It is even worth considering the possibility that males are not dominant. As long as any of these are possibilities worthy of consideration, the assumption is a false dilemma. Similar false dilemmas frequently plague the presentation of "nature versus nurture" conflicts, where chronic oversimplification often leads discussions away from serious consideration of the many influences on ability and behavior.

False or Misleading Presuppositions

Sometimes a statement *presupposes* that others are true. This means that the speaker making such a statement already assumes (presupposes) that these other things are true. If I say that Betty has recently quit smoking, then you know that Betty does not smoke now, but you also know that until recently she smoked. To say that she quit presupposes that she once smoked.

Consider how the presuppositions of the following claims say something about John or his associates.

> John doesn't call his fraternity's favorite bookie to bet on the horses. [Presupposed: His fraternity has a favorite bookie.]

> John didn't hide the evidence suggesting that he was involved in criminal activity. [Presupposed: There was such evidence.]

> John doesn't hang out at his favorite bar *every* afternoon. [Presupposed: John has a favorite bar. Contrast suggested by the emphasis: He hangs out there some (or many, or nearly all) afternoons.]

Asking a question with a presupposition can lead to difficulty. Suppose I ask, "Has Betty quit smoking?" If Betty never smoked, then the correct answer is "no." But that simple answer is very misleading, because it seems to accept the presupposition that Betty has smoked. This problem with questions is so common it has a special name: Questions with presuppositions that are unwarranted in the context are called *loaded questions*.

When a question has an unwarranted presupposition (that is, it is a loaded question), a simple answer will be misleading, because offering any simple answer will imply that the respondent accepts the presupposition. If you do not know that the presupposition is true, you must give a more complicated answer, such as "Betty never smoked" or "I don't know whether Betty ever smoked."

Both questions and statements can introduce unwarranted presuppositions into a discussion, but the phenomenon stands out particularly in the case of questions— they put the person answering in a difficult position.

Of course, not all presuppositions are unwarranted. If I ask, "How is your husband today?" I assume that you have a husband. In many cases this may be a true and warranted assumption, and so the question is unproblematic.

EXERCISE 4A

Identify the presuppositions of each of these questions. In some cases, there is more than one important presupposition.

1. Is John still a rigid conservative?

2. Do you still beat your wife?

3. Did your sales increase because of your misleading advertising?

4. Why is capitalism more efficient than socialism?

5. Why are you acting stupid?

6. Where did you hide the evidence?

7. Did you say that because you're deceitful or because you're ignorant?

ANSWERS

1. John was a rigid conservative. (Note that the questioner also *characterizes* John's conservatism, calling it "rigid." It may be important to question the correctness of that characterization.)

2. You have beat your wife. You have a wife. (This is the standard example of a loaded question.)

3. Your advertising was misleading. You sold something. You advertised. (This sentence can be interpreted in at least two ways. One way interprets it as presupposing that your sales increased.)

4. Capitalism is more efficient than socialism.

5. You are acting stupid.

6. You hid some evidence. You had the evidence. There is some evidence (for something).

7. You're deceitful or you're ignorant. Those are the only possible reasons for saying that. You said that.

Loaded questions can "smuggle assumptions into an argument" without explicitly stating them.

> What have the members of this organization done to remedy the effects of past discrimination? Nothing! We need to see action from them.

The call to action is inappropriate if there was no past discrimination. The assumption that there was some discrimination is a presupposition of the question.

The diagnosis just given shows how to criticize a loaded question. Point out that a false or at least unwarranted assumption has been made in asking the question. State what the assumption is.

Formally, a loaded question can often be thought of as a false dilemma, because the unwarranted assumption can usually be formulated as an unwarranted disjunction (though it may take a little stretching at times). Hence the question "Has Betty quit smoking?" presupposes that either Betty still smokes or she has quit. And the question "Where did you hide the evidence?" presupposes that you hid the evidence in place A or in place B, etc. The important thing is to point out the unwarranted assumption in a clear way.

Remember that it is not just questions that have presuppositions. Most of our statements have presuppositions, too; we need to be watchful to prevent these presuppositions from becoming unwarranted premises in our thinking as well. In the example recently discussed, even if the speaker had made the explicit statement "The members of this group have done nothing to remedy the effects of past discrimination," it would still be relevant to bring out the presupposition of the statement (that there has been discrimination) if that presupposition is false or unwarranted. The problem of false or unwarranted presuppositions is especially clear (and has a special name) with questions, but it can exist with statements as well.

Straw Man

Sometimes we argue for a conclusion by showing that it is the only reasonable view; we show that all of the alternatives to that view are untenable. If we have really defeated all of the alternatives to our own view, then this will successfully establish our own position. However, if we have neglected some of the alternatives, then this is not a successful way to establish our own view. In fact, it is a particular kind of false dilemma argument. "Either my view or one of these others is correct; but these others are obviously wrong, so my view is correct." This is a false dilemma when the other views that I mention are not the only alternatives to my view; the disjunctive premise is then not warranted.

When we argue against weak opposing views and ignore the stronger ones, or when we mischaracterize an opponent's position in order to defeat it, we commit the *straw man* fallacy. We have defeated a weak or weakened position (a straw man), but we have not defeated the serious alternatives to our own position. In other words, we have knocked down a straw man, leaving serious opposition untouched. Our argument is fallacious because we have not eliminated all of the alternatives to our own view, yet we act as though we have.

> Senator Napoli has argued for the reduction of defense spending. Apparently he thinks that the instability in the Balkans and in Africa will require no resources from us and will pose no risk to us. But this could not be further from the truth. We must reject this head-in-the-sands approach and maintain our military readiness, and that means no spending reductions!

The view that is criticized here is probably not any senator's view. The view criticized is the view that the instability in the Balkans and in Africa will require no resources from us and will pose no risk to us. Even if Senator Napoli did agree with that, many people who favor defense reductions do not believe it; they just believe that those commitments can be met with a reduced defense budget. That alternative has not been discussed in the argument, so the conclusion that has been offered is not adequately justified.

We can clarify the problem just as we do for any false dilemma argument: by pointing out that there is an important alternative that has not been considered. When someone's view has been mischaracterized, we can point out the misrepresentation.

A two-party political system creates a special invitation to straw man argument. If a politician criticizes a view in order to establish his or her own view, many people will assume that the view criticized is the one the major opponent holds. This is not always the case. Here is an especially nice example, from 1972, when Richard Nixon ran against George McGovern. Nixon made the following remarks:

> Let me illustrate the difference in our philosophies. Because of our free economic system, what we have done is build a great building of economic wealth and might in America. It is by far the tallest building in the world, and we are still adding to it. Now, because some of the windows are broken, they say tear it down and start again. We say, replace the windows and keep building. That's the difference.

The view criticized here—that we should tear down the economy and start again— was certainly never held by McGovern. The only reason for Nixon to criticize it is that he might be able to get some people to associate it with McGovern and thereby see Nixon's policies as the only reasonable choice of the two alternatives offered. We can clarify the problem with such an argument by pointing out what view has been criticized, by pointing out that it is not the view of the most relevant opponent, and by saying exactly what alternative view has been overlooked (if possible).

Slippery Slope

The *slippery slope* fallacy is also a kind of false dilemma. It involves a claim with this structure: "The difference between A and B is really the same as the difference between A and Z, because B is just one step along the road to Z." Sometimes this attempted assimilation is a causal "slope," sometimes it is conceptual, and sometimes it is hard to tell which it is.

In the causal case, it is claimed that the step from A to B *will lead to* further steps, all the way to Z.

> We must not decriminalize marijuana, because that would lead to a casual attitude about drug use, to greater demand for other drugs, and ultimately to a widespread availability of all drugs.

CAUSAL SLIPPERY SLOPE

The actual situation:

A B C D E F G H I J K L M N O P Q R S T U V W X Y Z

MANY DISTINCT IMAGINED EVENTS

The causal slippery slope:

A   B→C→D→E→F→G→H→I→ · · · →X→Y→Z

DISTINGUISHING **A** *FROM EVERYTHING ELSE, WITH EVERYTHING ELSE LEADING TO THE LAST STEP,* **Z.**

In our example, **A** corresponds to maintaining criminal laws against marijuana use, and **Z** corresponds to all drugs being widely available. The questionable disjunction implicit here is the claim that we must either keep criminal penalties for marijuana (**A**) or else (eventually) have all drugs widely available (**Z**). The basis for the claim is an alleged causal connection. Of course, there is nothing wrong with making reasonable predictions about the consequences of an action when deciding whether to undertake that action. The specifics of this causal process are not given here, though, and we should not accept the argument without such plausible specifics. When someone makes a prediction about the consequences of an action, that person should be able to specify the causal processes that produce those consequences. It may be possible to give such specifics in this or other cases, but the causal slippery slope argument is often used even when such specifics are not available.

A conceptual slippery slope is only slightly different. It tries to get us to regard **B** and **Z** as differing from **A** in the same way.

> The current health care plan would make us a socialist country, no different from the countries in which the railroads and major factories are run by the government.

CONCEPTUAL SLIPPERY SLOPE

The actual situation:

A B C D E F G H I J K L M N O P Q R S T U V W X Y Z

MANY DISTINCT ITEMS

The conceptual slippery slope:

A | **BCDEFGHIJKLMNOPQRSTUVWXYZ** |

*DISTINGUISHING **A** FROM EVERYTHING ELSE, AND LUMPING ALL
THE REST TOGETHER, TREATING THEM ALL AS IF THEY WERE
PRETTY MUCH THE SAME AS THE MOST DISTANT ELEMENT, **Z.***

Here it is claimed that it makes no difference how much or what kind of government involvement there is; all differences between **B** (implementing the current health plan, in this example) and **Z** (having a fully socialist state) are said to be insignificant. Such a claim should not be simply accepted—it needs a justification.

Sometimes the "trick" in a conceptual slippery slope is to use the fact that things are similar in one way as a basis for suggesting that they are equally bad, or similar in other ways. At the beginning of this chapter, there was an example of a conceptual slippery slope argument that works in that way:

> Looking at pictures of naked women in *Playboy* is no different from rape. If you get pleasure from these pictures, you are treating women solely as sexual objects; and it is the same as looking over the body of someone you see but don't know, or going out with someone just because you are attracted to her body, or fondling your date without concern for whether she wants that or not, or raping someone.

Even though all of these may be cases of treating women as objects of sexual desire, they are not equally bad and, in fact, have very little else in common. You can break the attempted assimilation by clearly pointing out the things that make raping someone worse than looking at pictures in *Playboy*.

Usually when it is argued that **B** leads down the causal or conceptual slide to **Z**, the arguer wishes to argue against **B** by associating it with a clearer "evil" (**Z**). But this need not be the case. One could always use the assimilation to argue that we might as well go right for **Z** rather than dawdling about.

> Your mother was right. Once you get yourself into shop-lifting you are on your way to (*causal*) [already fully involved in (*conceptual*)] a life of crime. Now that you have helped me get out with the toothpaste we took at the convenience store, you might as well get in on the good action right away and help me rob the bank.

To criticize a slippery slope argument, we must question the assimilation of **B** and **Z**. If it is a causal slippery slope, the strongest response would be to point out a reason why the causal sequence from **B** to **Z** would not occur. [*I would never do anything that might land me in prison.*] That is not always possible, but it is always reasonable to ask for the specific causal mechanisms that lead from **B** to **Z**, if those are not clear. [*Why would I have to go farther just because I helped you this far?*] If the slippery slope is conceptual, then we should point out significant relevant differences between **B** and **Z**. [*Point out a reason why stealing toothpaste from a convenience store is significantly different from robbing a bank.*]

EXERCISE 4B

Here are two examples of arguments against the Brady law, which requires the registration of handguns. Explain what fallacy is committed, and make it clear how these fallacies are different.

> First it's the Brady law, requiring registration of handguns. Pretty soon it will be all guns. Then they can take our guns away at any time. When they do that, there is nothing to prevent the institution of a police state.

> Passing the Brady Law is no different from having a police state. Registered guns are guns that are under the control of the government, and that is the essence of a police state.

Precedents and Slippery Slopes. When we consider the role of precedent and fair treatment in making policy, we can run into some subtle and difficult questions. In applying general policies in a fair way, we are guided by two principles that can conflict.

> Fairness: Relevantly similar cases should be treated in similar ways.

> Distinctness: Cases that are clearly different (in relevant ways) may be treated differently.

The problem is that at the "borderlines," very similar cases may be treated differently. The insanity defense should not apply in all cases, but there will inevitably be some cases of defendants who are "somewhat insane" (their understanding of the consequences of their actions or of the distinction between right and wrong is minimal), so the question of whether the insanity defense can apply is difficult. Their situation is very much like cases in which the insanity defense has applied, and it is also very much like cases in which the insanity defense was not applied, standing between these cases in the degree to which the defendant is legally competent. Precedent makes conflicting requirements, and we must trust to good judgment or make arbitrary decisions when the features relevant to judgment come in continuously varied strengths. In the case of the insanity defense, we are forced to rely on the judgment of judges and juries. In other cases, such as the availability of welfare subsidies, we set arbitrary income guidelines to distinguish the eligible from the ineligible. When there are such arbitrary standards, some very similar cases will be treated differently (people earning $9999 might get full benefits, whereas those earning $10,001 might get some benefits cut, for example), but that is inevitable if the guidelines are to make any distinctions at all. Life is tough for policy makers when there is no clearly identifiable stopping point on a slippery slope.

But even as we acknowledge the difficult position of a policy maker, we should recognize that policy needs to be made. If a student gives serious health problems as the reason for requesting a make-up exam, a professor may feel tempted to make this kind of response:

> I understand your situation and why your health problems have created a special difficulty. But I can't give you a make-up exam, because if I start giving make-ups, I'll end up having to give them to everyone who asks, no matter what the reason.

The student's situation involves a special problem that is relevant, and the professor can distinguish between that case and some others on the basis of that problem. The possibility of borderline cases—cases in which it is not clear whether the student's reason is adequate to justify giving a make-up exam—should not prevent us from making policy. The possibility of borderline cases, though, must lead us to recognize that the principle of fairness (that similar cases are always treated similarly) may need to be breached when the policy is extended to all cases. Some very similar cases must be treated differently if any distinction at all is to be made.

Inconsistency

Another evident fallacy of unwarranted assumptions is *inconsistency*. When a person has inconsistent beliefs, the beliefs cannot all be true. We cannot rely on the policies that follow from those beliefs.

Here are some examples in which a set of beliefs seems inconsistent, and in each case we should be wary of accepting any policies or other conclusions that are based on these beliefs.

> Criminals know what they are doing when they commit crimes. Those who say otherwise are just trying to keep them from being punished. But criminals should be punished, because there is no better way to teach them right from wrong.

> Nuclear power plants represent our main hope in filling future energy needs, and the risk of a serious accident is so negligible that we can ignore it. So Congress must pass the law limiting manufacturers' liability and thus make the construction of such plants possible.

Identify the inconsistency in each of these cases by pointing out that some claim and the contradictory of that very same claim are both involved in the paragraph (the speaker either assumes or explicitly endorses some statement and its contradictory).

Inconsistency is a logical problem even when there is no argument. If a set of claims is inconsistent, we know, for logical reasons, that those claims cannot all be true. Therefore, pointing out that a speaker accepts both some claim and the denial of that very same claim is always a powerful criticism.

Do not confuse the fallacy of inconsistency with the admirable trait of willingness to change one's views in light of new arguments or information. Anyone who accepts a statement and its negation at the same time is making a logical error. Over time, however, a change of mind can be appropriate. In fact, perfect consistency of belief over time is not a virtue. If, by *consistency*, we mean maintaining a belief over time no matter what new information becomes available, then "a foolish consistency is the hobgoblin of little minds," as Ralph Waldo Emerson said.

People often fall into inconsistency because they apply a general principle to others but are unwilling to apply it to themselves. For example, in an interview during the Persian Gulf War, the Iraqi ambassador was interviewed by Larry King. (The interview is cited in Howard Kahane's *Logic and Contemporary Rhetoric*, seventh ed., Wadsworth, 1995, p. 44.)

> *Ambassador:* We deplore Saudi participation with the West in this attack on Iraq, because we hate to see Arabs fighting Arabs.
>
> *King:* You say that you hate to see Arabs fighting Arabs, but you went into Kuwait.
>
> *Ambassador:* But we did not fight when we went into Kuwait!

This exchange illustrates the kind of trouble you get into to when you have inconsistent beliefs. Once King pointed out the inconsistency in the ambassador's position (we always hate to see Arabs fighting Arabs, but sometimes it is OK—when we do it!), the ambassador was led to make an even more evidently absurd claim to try to maintain his view.

Begging the Question (and Circular Argument)

An argument is question-begging if one of its premises is at least as questionable as the conclusion. Of course, whether it is just as questionable will depend on who the audience is, in most cases; but sometimes we can see clearly that the argument will be convincing to very few people.

> Since a fetus cannot have rights, abortion cannot be prohibited.

This assumes that a fetus cannot have rights, but that is very likely to be questioned by anyone who doubts the conclusion. Similarly,

> We must stop the murder of unborn children.

If this is construed as an argument, it relies on the premises that a fetus is a child and that abortion is murder. People who favor a right to abortion will often not accept these premises, so the argument will not convince anyone who does not already believe the conclusion.

Question-begging is easiest to see in the case of *circular argument:* argument in which the conclusion is needed as support for one of the premises, so that there is no independent grounding for the conclusion.

> We know that God exists because the Bible says so.

This argument will be sound only if an unstated premise is true: the premise that whatever the Bible says is true. The only support for that would be, presumably, that God exists and was involved in its authorship. But then we have a circular argument. We would have to assume that God exists before we could prove it.

Sometimes the circle is very small; one of the premises may be the same as the conclusion.

> Anti-government demonstrations must be stopped! There is a simple reason why. Although we support free speech, gatherings in defiance of the government cannot be tolerated.

The statement about free speech does not support the conclusion and is irrelevant. Once you omit it, the argument is this:

> Anti-government demonstrations must be stopped! There is a simple reason why . . . gatherings in defiance of the government cannot be tolerated.

The premise and conclusion are the same (that is, the sentences mean the same thing), so this is a clear case of a question-begging (and circular) argument.

To point out that an argument is question-begging, you must point out that the people who need to be convinced of the conclusion do not accept all of the premises, and you need to indicate what they do not accept. If the argument is circular, you can point out that the only reason for accepting one of the premises is that the conclusion is already accepted.

EXERCISE 4C

Identify the fallacies of unwarranted assumptions in the following examples, and diagnose the problem in each of these examples. (Think of yourself as responding to the author of the passage, and explain what is wrong. You should be able to do so within a few sentences.)

1. You've got to go to dinner with me tonight or you'll be hungry by morning.

2. Tanning parlors are a real danger. People think that they will go just a few times before a vacation. But once they start, they'll get another package deal after vacation to maintain their tans. Eventually they will be going all year, incurring a serious risk of skin cancer.

3. I meant what I said, because I didn't say something I didn't mean.

4. I have seen the benefits of regular exercise on my health. Some people think that these benefits are imaginary, a concoction of Jane Fonda's to sell more tapes; but I can assure you otherwise.

5. If you give women power on the job, they will become even more of a problem. First they'll want special days off for "that time of the month." Next, they'll make excuses for bad decisions by saying they had PMS that day. And when they do have PMS, watch out! They'll persecute every man who disagrees with them. Corporate America will become one big bitch fest, and the United States economy will fall apart.

6. Being persistent and patient brings positive results. So if you stick to your goals and wait long enough, you will get what you want.

EXERCISE 4D

Write three examples of arguments illustrating the fallacies of unwarranted assumptions discussed in the preceding section. For each one, indicate what fallacy it commits.

IRRELEVANT APPEALS

A failure of relevance marks the other major category of fallacious argument. If an argument is not valid and if the premises do not provide any other strong support (inductive support) for the conclusion, then the premises provide no reason to accept the conclusion. These can be called *fallacies of unwarranted inference* or *irrelevant appeals*. (We will discuss inductive support in Chapters 7–9.)

Argument Forms That Are Not Validating

Arguing invalidly captures the general category of irrelevant appeals. In Chapter 2, we recognized two patterns of argument that will not validate an argument: *denying the antecedent* and *affirming the consequent*. People often make the mistake of arguing in these two ways, believing they have argued validly when they have not. This makes denying the antecedent and affirming the consequent particularly important kinds of invalid argument.

Denying the Antecedent	**Affirming the Consequent**
If **A,** then **B**	If **A,** then **B**
not-**A**	**B**
∴ not-**B**	∴ **A**

Denying the Antecedent

If John bought flowers for Valentine's Day, Mary will be happy.

John did not buy flowers for Valentine's Day.

∴ Mary will not be happy.

Affirming the Consequent

If John graduated, then he passed chemistry.

John passed chemistry.

∴ John graduated.

In each of these cases, the arguer is simply arguing invalidly. To show this, it is generally best to describe the kind of situation that would make the premises true with the conclusion false, thus making it clear that the argument is invalid. In the first of our two examples, we might imagine a situation in which John bought something else—maybe a new motorcycle for Mary or a trip to Paris for them—and so Mary was happy anyway. Both premises could be true with the conclusion false in such a case. In the second example, we might imagine that John failed some course other than chemistry, a course that was also needed for graduation, making the premises true with the conclusion false.

We mention these two particular invalid forms because we often see arguments that fit these forms. We can be on the alert for these forms, aware that they will not make the argument valid. Apparently, these forms of argument get their persuasive force from their similarity to the valid argument forms *modus ponens* and *modus tollens* that we discussed in Chapter 2.

Appeal to Irrelevant Authority

Why do advertisers pay big bucks to have famous people endorse their products? There are many attractive, articulate speakers who could present the product's virtues just as well at a much lower cost. If we think of advertising as the presentation of an argument that a certain product should be purchased, then we should be able to evaluate that argument just as well no matter who presents it. A well-paid star has no special knowledge to impart concerning the merits of Gallo wines or Jello. He or she is not a relevant authority.

Why pay the star? Because many advertisements work by developing in us an image of how we want to be, an image that includes the product in question. The advertiser does not want us to evaluate reasons for buying the product. As we noted in the chapter on meaning, rational evaluation is just what the advertiser wants us to avoid. Rational argument is often not the point at all. Inappropriate appeals to authority can often enhance this element of image development because of favorable associations with the star presenting the product.

On the other hand, a wine expert with no paid interest in Gallo wines might be worth listening to; she could have the skills and opportunity to do comparative tasting and comparative pricing that we could never do ourselves. We might value her opinion and use it as a guide in shopping. She is a relevant authority who can cite valid reasons for buying one product rather than another. Still, when we rely on authorities instead of evaluating reasons for ourselves, we are giving up some of the autonomy we exercise in making our own judgments. We should be reluctant to do that, and we should do it only when necessary.

When you must rely on the judgment of authorities because an issue is too difficult or time-consuming for you to make a judgment on your own, you should be sure that the authority fulfills several conditions:

> The person is qualified and reliable when testifying about his or her area of expertise. (Cicero: "Even when speaking the truth, a liar gets no credit.")

> The issue under consideration is within this person's area of expertise.

> The person has no special interest in the outcome of your judgment (no financial interest in Gallo wines, for example).

> The person is not being paid (or otherwise influenced) by someone who has a special interest in the outcome of your judgment.

> Authorities in the field generally agree about the kind of issue under consideration.

If any of these conditions fail, you will need to weigh the evidence yourself; an appeal to this authority will not be a reliable way to make a judgment in such a case. You may use the testimony of such authorities as a part of the basis for your judgment, but there are serious reasons not to rely on it as the sole basis for judgment.

It is also worth keeping in mind that even an irrelevant authority could give you good reasons for buying a product. You just wouldn't have any basis for thinking that this individual's reasons were good except for the quality of the reasons themselves. You would evaluate the argument rather than the individual presenting the argument. There is nothing wrong with that. In criticizing appeals to authority, we are criticizing the reliance on something other than reasons and argument. Evaluation of reasons and arguments in an appropriate way is our ideal, and when we cannot match that ideal, we should give it up and accept authority very reluctantly.

In undermining an appeal to irrelevant authority, you will want to point out that the person fails one (or more) of the five conditions just mentioned. In the case of image-makers, it may be most appropriate to point out that the person in question has given no reasons at all for making a judgment. Mentioning that a person endorsing a product is a paid actor may also support exercising appropriate caution.

Ad Hominem Argument (Attacking the Person)

The flip side of inappropriate appeals to authority is *ad hominem* attack. If you criticize the person presenting an argument rather than evaluating the argument itself, you commit an *ad hominem* fallacy. This is like an appeal to authority in that you evaluate the personal source of the reasons rather than evaluating the quality of the reasons themselves; that is why *ad hominem* argument and appeal to irrelevant authority are often classified together as *genetic fallacies* (fallacies that involve looking at the source of an argument rather than at the argument itself). *Ad hominem* attack is a distressingly common way of avoiding the job of evaluating the reasons for believing something. Whenever someone argues that we should ignore an argument or disbelieve a conclusion because of the argument's source, we have an *ad hominem* attack. It can be a powerful distraction from reasoned consideration of the issues.

> The new health care bill is no good. It was designed by a bunch of people who are mainly interested in enhancing their own political power.

Answering such an *ad hominem* attack means pointing out the need to work harder: We need to evaluate the bill itself, not the people who wrote it. We cannot conclude so easily that it is no good, so the original *ad hominem* attack often has some appeal as the easy way out. The best we can do in pointing out an *ad hominem* attack is to draw attention away from the person being attacked by calling attention to the merits of the position or the argument that he or she had presented.

When you are the object of an *ad hominem* attack, the situation is more difficult. Calling attention to your arguments and positions and ignoring the personal attack carry some dangers. When you ignore the personal attack, it may seem that you are accepting it, or it may seem that you are trying to avoid the substance of the personal attack. This explains why the *ad hominem* attack is a very powerful distraction. You seem to need to do two things at once: defend your argument and defend yourself. The only recourse is to carefully separate the two different things—the issues that were under consideration and the personal charges just made—and offer a separate response to each.

One kind of *ad hominem* attack is more general, providing a psychological analysis of the kind of people that would oppose the speaker's conclusion. For example, someone who was arguing for continuing affirmative action policies in hiring might say, "Affirmative action helps the underprivileged rise to a place of power, and sometimes that's intimidating for the majority group." Such an analysis suggests that psychological weakness rather than reasoned argument is the source of people's support for the opposing view. As in other *ad hominem* arguments, that kind of distraction can lead people not to attend to those opposing views and the reasons for holding them. We are all poorer when we substitute such superficial generalizations for real reasons for our beliefs.

We have spoken about two things that can look very similar: undermining an appeal to irrelevant authority and mounting an *ad hominem* attack. In both situations, a negative evaluation of the source of an argument or opinion is given. In undermining an appeal to authority, we use that negative evaluation as the basis for saying that the person's authority is not an adequate basis for accepting the argument or opinion: We need to evaluate the reasons. In the case of *ad hominem* attack, we fallaciously use the negative evaluation as a basis for disbelieving the opinion or ignoring the reasons for it. If the city councilor who proposes a new sports stadium on the north side of town represents the north side and runs a hot dog business, we should not accept his judgment without looking closely at his reasons; but we also should not conclude that his plan is a bad one until we have looked at the reasons for it (or have at least heard what some more impartial experts have to say about it). In identifying these genetic fallacies, we want to support the evaluation of arguments and avoid replacing it by the evaluation of personality.

Appeal to Force

This is really a substitute for argument. It says, "You should act as though you believe what I say because you will suffer if you don't." This can be good advice about how to act, but it is not a good reason for belief.

> You need to change your ideas about cigarette smoking. Now you may think it should be banned, but the tobacco growers around here can make it pretty uncomfortable for people who think that way.

This provides no argument against banning cigarettes, though it might give you some reason to keep your opinions to yourself. You have been given a motive to change your view or hide it, but you have not been given an argument that your view is incorrect.

Note that when diagnosing an appeal to force, it is very important to keep a clear eye on what the conclusion is. If the conclusion is that cigarette smoking should not be banned, the appeal to force above is fallacious. If the conclusion were instead that you should keep your views to yourself, that is not a fallacious appeal to force; the consequences of expressing your views are certainly a legitimate factor to consider in deciding whether to speak out.

In an appeal to force, the force may be people or institutions that require you to act in a certain way. By extension, it may be the force of circumstance, as it might be for a vegetarian who gives up the idea that killing animals for food is wrong because his girlfriend's family runs a butcher shop.

The unpleasant consequences of holding a belief can be a powerful impetus to change that belief. If the only job you can find involves selling lots of cigarettes, you will feel much better if you believe that smoking is not really so bad for your health. If such factors lead you to believe that smoking is not very harmful, you are accepting this belief despite the good reasons you have against it. This force of circumstance can strongly motivate irrational belief. It may even be that the circumstances of someone's life require irrational belief—belief that runs counter to all of the evidence—for the maintenance of adequate mental health. For example, it may be very disturbing to acknowledge the villainous actions of a spouse, parent, or child, and for that reason, even very extensive evidence may remain unconvincing. Such a life is hard to live.

To point out an appeal to force, indicate the reasons for believing what is true and identify the forces that demand that you not show you have that belief or that demand that you change that belief despite the evidence. Doing so may have its perils.

Appeal to Pity

Like the appeal to force, an appeal to pity is an irrelevant appeal. It gives you no basis for believing a particular opinion; it merely gives you a reason to act as though you believe it. This time, it is asserted that bad consequences will fall on the person making the appeal rather than on the person receiving the appeal.

> *To professor:* My dad will be really angry with me if I don't get at least a B in this course. I know that I haven't earned it, but couldn't you help me out just this one time?

There is no argument that this person deserves a B; rather, the professor is asked to act as though he believes that the student deserves a B.

Not every description of something pitiful is a fallacious appeal to pity. If I tell you about the pitiful situation for homeless cats in Boston, concluding that they need help, there is no fallacious appeal to pity. Helping those poor cats may be a very good thing to do. We use this fallacy diagnosis only when the premises do not appropriately support the conclusion and when the arguer is the intended object of the pity.

As with the appeal to force, you can diagnose the fallacy by citing the reasons to believe what is true and by pointing out the appeal that might lead one to act as though it is not true.

Argument from Ignorance (*ad ignorantiam*)

The general form of an argument from ignorance (*ad ignorantiam*) is this:

> No one has shown that S is true, so S is false.

For example:

> No one has shown that there are black holes [or substitute *ghosts* or *a Loch Ness monster*], so there must not be any.

This is obviously an unreliable form of argument. In cases in which neither S nor its opposite (not-S) has been shown to be true, following this form of argument would lead us to contradictory conclusions: that S and not-S are both false.

We can identify this fallacy easily in these egregious cases. If no one has shown that S is false, then we need only point out that parallel reasoning would support the opposite conclusion.

> No one has shown that S is false, so S is true.

> No one has shown that there are no black holes, so there must be some.

If someone has shown that S is false, then we can point out that there is a much better argument for the conclusion that S is false. Someone has shown that S is false, so S is false. (Someone has shown that there are black holes, so there are some.)

The only subtlety here comes in the case in which we can say that so much investigation had been done that if S were true, then by now someone would have shown it to be true. In other words, the only reasonable explanation for the lack of success in showing that S is true is that S is false. Someone might say that about the Loch Ness monster, for example: So much investigation has been done that the only reasonable explanation for the lack of success in showing that there is a Loch Ness monster is that there is none. (On behalf of the other side, though, the lake is *very* deep.) This may lead us to look for more guidance concerning the evaluation of explanations, a topic we will take up later (Chapters 6–9).

Beside the Point (*ignoratio elenchi*)

Sometimes a speaker's premises are not relevant to the conclusion, but the argument is not one of the specific appeals we have mentioned. In such a situation, we have little choice but to fall back on a general diagnosis: that the premises are not relevant to the conclusion. This general diagnosis of irrelevance has the Latin name *ignoratio elenchi* (roughly, "arguing with ignorance of the goal" and sometimes translated "irrelevant conclusion"). In English, we say that someone's remarks are *beside the point*. Responding to such arguments, we can express our failure to see how the premises are relevant to the conclusion, or, more strongly, we can point out that they are not relevant. A comment such as "That might help to establish X, but it is of no use in establishing Y, the conclusion we are considering" can usually start a relevant discussion.

> *At a trial:* The victim's murder was especially brutal, and so we must make sure that the defendant is convicted, to show our condemnation of such killings.

If the main question is whether the defendant did the crime, then this is irrelevant (*ignoratio elenchi*, beside the point). It is useful for consideration of how to use law enforcement resources and for sentencing those convicted, but it is not relevant to the question of whether to convict.

EXERCISE 4E

Write three examples illustrating fallacies of relevance discussed in the preceding section. For each one, indicate what fallacy it commits.

CHAPTER SUMMARY

Fallacies

There are two steps involved in criticizing a fallacious argument. First, you can try to **identify** a familiar fallacy that has been committed. Then you must **make your criticism clear**. To make your criticism clear, try to associate a standard pattern of criticism with each fallacy. (Consult the chapter for ways to do this. These notes are just a reminder.)

Unwarranted Assumptions (inadequate premises)

False dilemma: Unwarranted "*or* statement" accepted; some possibilities are overlooked; also called *black-and-white thinking*.
Identify at least some possibility that has been neglected.

Straw man: Attack only a very weak opposing position or mischaracterize the opposing position (knock down a "straw man").
Identify other views that should be considered.

Slippery slope: A little bit is the same as a lot (all or nothing at all). Fallacious when steps are ill-defined.
Point out that the "steps" in the slippery slope are unjustified. If possible, make a clear distinction between two adjacent steps on the slippery slope.

Unwarranted presupposition (including **loaded question**): A statement or question has a false or unjustified presupposition.
Identify the presupposition and show that it is false or unjustified.

Inconsistency: The statements (the premises of an argument, in many cases) cannot all be true.
Make the contradictory character of the set of statements clear, preferably by showing that some statement and the negation of that very same statement are both consequences of what has been said.

Begging the question: The premises are just as questionable as the conclusion, and for the same kind of reasons. (Any relevant audience that doubts the conclusion will also doubt the premises.)
> **Circular argument**: The conclusion itself is needed as a basis for justifying one premise of the argument.

Identify the questionable premise and point out that it is no more justified than the conclusion is.

Irrelevant Appeals (no valid argument)

General catch-all diagnosis: *ignoratio elenchi*, arguing "beside the point," irrelevant appeal. Point out that the premise is not relevant to the conclusion.
    Try to use one of these more specific diagnoses if you can.

Ad hominem **(attacking the person)**

Appeal to authority

Appeal to force

Appeal to pity

Arguing from ignorance

Prejudicial language in place of argument (see Chapter 3)

Affirming the consequent

Denying the antecedent

EXERCISE 4F

Read each passage and identify the main problem, if any, in the argument. (In addition to noting occurrences of the fallacies mentioned in this chapter, look for problems discussed in other chapters, such as equivocations, the use of prejudicial language in place of argument, and insufficiently justified *should* conclusions.) [Nearly all of these are based on examples constructed by my students to illustrate the various fallacies. I thank the many students who contributed.]

1. Either God exists or we are just biological organisms reacting to stimuli. Clearly we think of ourselves and others as more than that.

2. Eighteen-year-olds shouldn't have the right to vote, because if they aren't old enough to drink at that age, they aren't responsible enough to vote.

3. At first she will study in the evening, after cleaning the kitchen, when the children are sleeping. But as exams approach and papers are due, she will gradually neglect more and more of the housework: She will not cook, the shopping won't be done, and she will even forget to check her daughter's homework and take her son to his doctor's appointment. Eventually the whole family will be in immense chaos. Nobody should try to finish a degree and care for small children at the same time.

4. We need more government regulation of the media. TV news becomes more and more influential every year, and as the Sesame Street generation comes of age, it is coming to be their sole source of information. If the situation is not brought in check, the news anchors on the major networks will have more influence than the President.

5. If you did well on that test, you're smart. But you didn't do well on that test, so you're not smart.

6. Finishing my degree is important for my self-esteem, because graduating is essential for my own sense of worth.

7. Never let your neighbor borrow anything. First it's a cup of sugar, then your favorite scarf, and the next thing you know she'll want to borrow your spouse to do some "jobs" around the house.

8. Everyone in the room thinks that John stole the money, so I wouldn't speak out on his behalf if I were you.

9. We can go out to dinner tonight and have a thick, juicy steak at the Scotch and Sirloin Restaurant, or we can have a thin, dry one at the Big Sky Steak House.

10. Those who support abortion believe that a woman has the right to kill another human being. We know that nobody has that right, though, so abortion should not be legal.

11. If the President signs the bill, then it will become a law. The President will sign the bill, so it will become a law.

12. If I spend a good portion of my time learning the computer, then I will learn to work efficiently. I have not spent much time on the computer, so I do not work efficiently.

13. Despite the fact that he had several relationships with other women during his marriage, he was never disloyal to his wife, because he always told her the truth about his affairs.

14. All survivors are strong, because only the strong survive.

15. If I don't go to class, then I won't pass the course. But I attend regularly, so I'm sure to pass.

16. In one of his songs, jazz and blues singer Mose Allison describes someone by saying, "Your mind is on vacation, but your mouth is workin' overtime." Apparently some people oppose campus speech codes because they believe that the condition described in the song is perfectly all right for college students. We should expect more, though. Campus speech codes require you to think before you speak, and everyone should favor such a standard in a university community.

17. The welfare system gives every low-life the kind of life that others have had to work hard for. People who pull themselves up by their bootstraps and work to make an economic contribution deserve what they earn; but the welfare system just rewards the undeserving.

18. You can insult me all you want, but we'll see who is right when I tell your girlfriend what you did.

19. As a politician you should recognize that older people have a strong voice and use it; and they turn out at the polls. Any changes in social security will cost you votes. Don't you agree that the social security system is best left the way it is?

20. I do not mind working long hours to produce the results that you requested, but I hope that you appreciate the personal time I have devoted to this project. I look forward to your appraisal.

21. We need better controls on guns. The other side opposes controls because registering guns is inconvenient. But without more controls on guns, violence in the cities will continue to escalate. A little inconvenience in filling out a few forms or in waiting for a background check is not too high a price to pay for safer cities.

22. [Based on a letter to the editor of the Syracuse *Post-Standard*, February 19, 1996. Reprinted with permission of the *Post-Standard*.]

    Scott Renshaw, member of CHANGE-NY, wants to eliminate tax subsidies for "symphonies, social programs (and) zoos." Change indeed. His letter chills us with visions of a new century in which people waste away from avoidable suffering, in which wrecking balls smash down concert halls where the hearts of thousands once soared with music, in which the only intimate sight of animals is provided by the gun sight of the hunter's rifle. . . .

    Renshaw should ask himself how it is that the wealthiest country in the world can imagine change only as a deepening winter, without the community of song, without the dignity of passion, without places to share our pleasure in nature.

23. We should not have just one final letter grade for a course. Although some students like to have such simple evaluations, a single, final evaluation on a set letter scale is undesirable.

24. Forbes wants a flat tax, but he is a billionaire, and so we can be sure that his proposals are going to work against the great majority, whose yearly hard-earned incomes are less than his average hourly income from investments.

25. John doesn't really respect free speech. Even though he voted in favor of allowing the astrologer to make a presentation on campus, he said that astrology was super-silly superstition, and he didn't think that it would be worth anyone's time. That doesn't show much respect.

26. Some people think that the Big Mike hamburger has too many grams of fat in it. They say if they eat it, they're going to be fat. Actually, the Big Mike has three fewer grams of fat than the Monsterburger, so eat up, America!

27. Tax incentives for the ultra-rich. Though they are a nightmare for the majority of taxpayers, they are still the sweet dreams of the candidates in the Republican primaries. They can't shake off the outdated, Reaganite, "trickle-down" mentality that infects all of their tax proposals. Every plan they come up with includes a regressive system of taxation that would make the rich better off.

28. [The paragraph that follows is from a letter to the editor of the Syracuse *Post-Standard* published June 10, 1992.]

    There is something wrong with people who oppose executing murderers of innocent people but would allow the killing of innocent babies through abortions. I favor the death penalty. Liberal wimps favor the criminals, not the victims.

29. If Mark buys a boat, he's bound to run out of money. First he'll buy the boat and then he'll need to spend money for gas and engine repairs. He will pay for dockage and new gadgets for his "little baby," and eventually he'll outgrow that boat and have to get a bigger one. Then he'll start buying new things for that boat and taking it on expensive trips. Very soon he'll be bankrupt!

30. If Saddam Hussein had agreed to pull his forces out of Kuwait with no prior conditions, then the best course of action would have been for U.S. forces to stop their attacks. But he didn't agree to that, so stopping the attacks was not the best course of action for the United States forces.

31. The idea of raising the age for licensed drivers is ludicrous. It is supported by unstable people. These are people who are biased from losing loved ones in situations that involved young drivers, and they need counseling.

EXERCISE 4G

Find examples of three of the fallacies mentioned in this chapter. Look in newspapers, books, or magazines (or on television or the Internet). Clearly indicate the source (with date and page number or URL), and diagnose the fallacy that has been committed. (Letters to the editor are often a fruitful source of examples; advertisements are sometimes good.)

CHAPTER 5

ANALOGY

An analogy is a comparison, especially a comparison of things of very different sorts. Analogies are used sometimes to clarify, sometimes to persuade without argument, and sometimes to persuade in connection with an argument. They are especially useful when we want to call attention to similarities that are easier to visualize than to describe or that resist easy description for other reasons.

DESCRIPTIVE (NON-ARGUMENTATIVE) USES OF ANALOGY

An analogy can be meant merely as a way to state a point without argument.

> The galaxies are receding from one another like raisins in a pudding that is spreading out over the floor.

This tells us that the spread is a general one and suggests that it is a part of the general spread of the stuff in which the galaxies are embedded. The analogy is a particularly useful, concrete way to get this across, and the point is more difficult to make and less vivid if we merely state it without using an analogy. Without further context, however, the analogy may suffer from the main problem that afflicts analogies; it is not clear what the scope of the comparison is. It is clear that the analogy is intended to illustrate vividly the idea that the galaxies are receding from one another; it is not clear whether the analogy is also intended to illustrate the idea that they are receding as a part of a general spreading out of some stuff that contains them. That latter idea may be a feature of the raisins in the pudding (the *analogue*) that is not intended to be extended to the galaxies (the principal subject matter). With almost every analogy, there is some uncertainty about the extent of the comparison being made. An analogy invites us to look for similarities, but we cannot always tell where to stop.

Even when a descriptive analogy is not the basis for any argument, it may persuade us of more than it should. An analogy invites us to compare the analogue and the principal subject, looking for a family of similarities. Because an analogy invites us to "cast about" for similarities, an analogy often suggests similarities that are not related to the main comparison being made. In addition, we have attitudes toward the analogue, and the analogy invites us to transfer those to the principal subject. In 1998, the Senate was debating the status of medical savings accounts, favored by many Republicans. Republican Senator Phil Gramm said in Senate debate that the people who favored the "Kennedy bureaucracy bill" hate the idea of medical savings accounts.

> They draw back from it like a vampire does from a cross.

The explicit analogy concerns the reaction to medical savings accounts, but the comparison also has the power to suggest that there are other important similarities, even though nothing is said to justify any further comparison. It is clear who Gramm thinks the bad guys are and where he thinks virtue lies. We need to note that this is a way in which someone may suggest comparisons without making them explicit and without giving any grounds for them. We should not let inexplicit and unjustified comparisons mislead us into uncritical acceptance of any view.

A good writer knows how to take advantage of this ability of analogies to get us thinking in many ways about the two things compared.

> Cora was like a tree—once rooted, she stood in spite of storms and strife, winds and rocks in the earth. —From Langston Hughes, "Cora Unashamed," in *The Ways of White Folks* (New York: A. A. Knopf, 1934).

Sometimes we even use the language of analogy to compare things when the only real similarity is in our reactions to them. This can be a vivid way to express a reaction, but it says little or nothing about the objective features of the things under consideration.

> Love is like a flower-filled spring day.

> Lawyers are like skunks. When I am around them, I just think about how much I want to be somewhere else.

ARGUMENTS EMPLOYING ANALOGY

Often an analogy will be an important part of the presentation of an argument. In the best and clearest cases, however, it is not actually a necessary part of the argument.

The following analogy, which C. S. Lewis once presented, has several features that are important for us to consider. (C. S. Lewis, *Mere Christianity*, Macmillan, 1952, p. 75.)

You can get a large audience together for a strip-tease act—that is, to watch a girl undress on the stage. Now suppose that you came to a country where you could fill a theatre simply by bringing a covered plate onto the stage and then slowly lifting the cover so as to let everyone else see, just before the lights went out, that it contained a mutton chop or a bit of bacon, would you not think that in that country something had gone wrong with the appetite for food?

The suggested conclusion is clear: Something is seriously wrong with the appetite for sex in those cultures that have striptease shows. The primary subject, then, is striptease shows and the appetite for sex. The *analogue* is the unveiled mutton chop and the appetite for food. This analogue is imaginary, but that doesn't matter. The analogue illustrates a general principle that is the basis for the argument. This general principle is a premise in an argument that draws a conclusion about the primary subject matter.

The general principle in this case can be stated explicitly: *If people will pay to have an appetite teased by a theatrically unveiled peek at an example of the object of that appetite, then the appetite itself is not operating in a healthful way.* This principle is illustrated by the (imagined) audience for the mutton chop and then applied to those who watch the striptease. The statement of the analogy involves a direct comparison of two particular cases, but to evaluate the argument, we will need to state the general principle that applies to the two cases. Note that our statement of the general principle does not explicitly mention either mutton chops or striptease shows; rather, it is general enough to apply in both cases.

This is the pattern for an ideal use of an analogy in an argument: The analogy makes a general principle clear, and the general principle is the basis for drawing a conclusion in the case that is of interest (the primary subject matter—in this case, striptease shows). The analogy is not really a necessary part of the argument at all; the presentation of the analogy is a way to get the audience to see what the general principle is by appealing to it in a case in which its application is especially clear and persuasive (mutton chops). In evaluating the argument based on this analogy, we can ask whether the general principle that seems to apply so clearly to our appetite for mutton chops really applies to all appetites, and especially whether it applies to sexual appetites. We should consider whether the general principle is really true, or whether something special about the case of the mutton chops has led us to a principle that we should not apply to other cases.

Ideal Use of Analogy

In the ideal case of an argument based on an analogy, the analogy will be only a way of making a general principle clear. The general principle is then used in an argument.

Case A illustrates this principle: All things that have properties $F_1 \cdots F_n$ also have property G.

Case B has $F_1 \cdots F_n$.

∴ Case B has G.

B is the *primary subject matter,* A is the ***analogue*** of B, and $F_1 \cdots F_n$ are the **similarities** on which the comparison is based. Here the general principle is

All things that have properties $F_1 \cdots F_n$ also have property G.

We will call this general principle the ***connecting principle***. (This principle connects the similarities mentioned in the premises with the property attributed in the conclusion.) Note that the argument based on the connecting principle and the second premise is a simple valid argument.

All things that have properties $F_1 \cdots F_n$ also have property G.

Case B has properties $F_1 \cdots F_n$.

∴ Case B has G.

After the connecting principle is made explicit, the analogy is not a necessary part of the argument; the analogy is merely a way of making the connecting principle clear and vivid (usually without explicitly stating it). (The Universal Syllogism is the most common and simplest type of argument involving a general claim and its application to a specific case. An analogy could be used to illustrate a general principle that is then used in some other type of argument as well.)

An analogy will be especially useful if the connecting principle it illustrates is difficult to state—for example, when many different properties are involved or when the connection between $F_1 \cdots F_n$ and G is more easily visualized than stated. Even in such cases, however, when we want to evaluate critically an argument connected with an analogy, that evaluation will benefit from the clearest possible explicit statement of the connecting principle that the analogy supports.

CALVIN AND HOBBES. © Watterson. Reprinted with permission of UNIVERSAL PRESS SYNDICATE. All rights reserved.

Design Argument

Probably the most famous case of the use of analogy in presenting an argument is the so-called "argument from design" for the existence of an intelligent designer of things that are not designed by people (that is, for the existence of God). William Paley's statement of this argument is the most important one. (William Paley, *Natural* Theology, 1802. Punctuation and spelling follow the Bobbs-Merrill edition, 1963, edited by Frederick Ferré. The passages are from the opening paragraphs of Chapters One and Three.)

In crossing a heath, suppose I pitched my foot against a stone, and were asked how the stone came to be there, I might possibly answer, that, for anything I knew to the contrary, it had lain there forever; nor would it, perhaps, be very easy to show the absurdity of this answer. But suppose I found a *watch* upon the ground, and it should be inquired how the watch happened to be in that place, I should hardly think of the answer which I had given, that for anything I knew, the watch might have always been there. Yet why should not this answer serve for the watch as well as for the stone? Why is it not as admissible in that second case as in the first? For this reason, and for no other, *viz.*, that when we come to inspect the watch, we perceive (what we could not discover in the stone) that its several parts are framed and put together for a purpose, e.g. that they are so formed and adjusted as to produce motion, and that motion so regulated as to point out the hour of the day; that if the different parts had been differently shaped from what they are, if a different size from what they are, or placed after any other manner, or in any other order than that in which they are placed, either no motion at all would have been carried on in the machine, or none which would have answered the use that is now served by it.

. . .

Every indication of contrivance, every manifestation of design, which existed in the watch, exists in the works of nature; with the difference, on the side of nature, of being greater and more, and that in a degree which exceeds all computation. I mean that the contrivances of nature surpass the contrivances of art, in the complexity, subtility, and curiosity of the mechanism; and still more, if possible, do they go beyond them in number and variety; yet in a multitude of cases, are not less evidently mechanical, not less evidently contrivances, not less evidently accommodated to their end, or suited to their office, than are the most perfect productions of human ingenuity.

The analogy of the watch makes a certain principle clear:

> Whenever an object (or system) has parts ordered, arranged, and interrelated in a complex, delicately balanced way, so as to achieve a certain purpose, the object (or system) is the product of an intelligent designer.

Then that principle is applied to the primary subject matter of the argument, natural objects ("the contrivances of nature") that have no human designer. The eye of humans and other animals is the example he discusses most, so the argument centered on that example is this:

1. Whenever an object (or system) has parts ordered, arranged, and interrelated in a complex, delicately balanced way, so as to achieve a certain purpose, the object (or system) is the product of an intelligent designer. (*connecting principle*)

2. Many natural contrivances—the eyes of humans and other animals, for example—have parts that are ordered, arranged, and interrelated in a complex, delicately balanced way, so as to achieve a certain purpose (vision).

3. So, many natural contrivances, such as the eyes of humans and other animals, are the product of an intelligent designer.

Paley's discussion fits the form of our ideal standard. The analogy (focusing on the consideration of the watch) makes a general principle clear, without explicitly stating it. The argument is an application of that general principle.

Note that when we make that principle explicit, we do not mention watches or eyes in the principle. That is typical. The connecting principle is general enough to cover both cases, the analogue and the primary subject matter; both cases are examples of things that exemplify the properties $F_1 \cdots F_n$ mentioned in the connecting principle (All things that have properties $F_1 \cdots F_n$ also have property G). Neither the analogue nor the primary subject needs to be explicitly mentioned. In this case, the properties that the watch and the eye are said to have in common are that they have parts that are ordered, arranged, and interrelated in a complex, delicately balanced way, so as to achieve a certain purpose. Those properties play a role in the statement of the general principle, but neither of the particular examples, watches or eyes, is individually mentioned.

The argument we have presented is a simple, deductively valid argument, so questions about its soundness must focus on the evaluation of the premises. The best criticism of Paley is to undermine the connecting principle of the argument by explaining how such things could come into existence without a designer. Charles Darwin did this about half a century after Paley presented his version of this argument, when he explained how animals and their organs can evolve to fulfill a particular purpose without a designer.

Inductive Model

If the connecting principle is weakened, then the premises may give some inductive support to the conclusion, but even if the premises are true, the argument will not guarantee that the conclusion is true. Arguments like the following are not deductively valid.

Case A illustrates the principle that nearly all (80%; most) things that have properties $F_1 \cdots F_n$ also have property G.

Case B has $F_1 \cdots F_n$.

∴ Case B has G.

The strength of the support given to the conclusion will depend on how much the connecting principle has been weakened. For example:

I have enjoyed nearly all of the mystery shows from Britain that I have seen on PBS.

Tonight there is another mystery show from Britain on PBS.

So I will enjoy the mystery show that is on tonight if I see it.

The conclusion gets some support from the premises, even though this is not a deductively valid argument. Clearly, however, the strength of the support in arguments like this depends on the strength of the connecting principle. If I say "most" or "many" or "70%" instead of "nearly all," then there is much less reason to accept the conclusion.

Less Articulate Uses of Analogy

Often when an analogy is used, it is very difficult to say exactly what the connecting principle is. In such a case, the analogue becomes a more integral part of the argument, and the argument becomes more difficult to evaluate.

> Case A has property G.
>
> Case B is like case A in many ways that are evidently relevant to having property G.
>
> ∴ Case B has G.

Such cases can be persuasive if we are certain that when things share the noticed similarities between A and B, they must also share property G. We might say that the similarities between A and B must be sufficient to make A a good *model* of B, as far as property G is concerned.

> The endocrine systems of rats and people have much in common—they have the same organs, and they secrete the same or similar hormones.
>
> Drug addiction significantly alters hormone secretion in rats.
>
> So drug addiction (probably) significantly alters human hormone secretions in similar ways.

The rat's endocrine system is a good *model* for the human system. Precise similarities are not specified here. However, such an argument will be much clearer and easier to evaluate if we can make the similarities between A and B explicit and formulate the general claim: Those similarities (enumerate them) are enough to guarantee similarity with respect to property G (in this case, similarity with respect to the effect of drug addiction on hormone secretion).

If we explicitly enumerate the endocrine similarities of rats and humans in the general principle, the analogy will then be in the ideal form discussed above. The general principle would say, "Any organism with an endocrine system with features $F_1 \cdots F_n$ will have its hormone secretions significantly altered by drug addiction." (Here, $F_1 \cdots F_n$ would be replaced by some specific description of the properties that the endocrine systems have in common.)

The following example from Plato's *Republic* will serve to illustrate further the less articulate uses of analogy. Socrates says the following, in order to draw a conclusion about what is involved in being a lover of learning (a philosopher):

> As for one who is choosy about what he learns, . . . we shall not call him a lover of learning or a philosopher, just as we shall not say that a man who is difficult about his food is hungry or has an appetite for food. We shall not call him a lover of food but a poor eater. . . . But we shall call a philosopher the man who is easily willing to learn every kind of knowledge, gladly turns to learning things, and is insatiable in this respect.

Here Socrates indicates a number of points of comparison between the lover of learning (the philosopher) and the lover of food. The connecting principle suggested seems to be this:

To be properly called a "lover of" X (where X is any very general kind of thing, like food or learning), a person must love every kind of X (and accept it when offered).

This principle seems quite implausible once we make it explicit. (It doesn't even apply to food, the illustrative analogue.) The points of comparison do not seem to support the conclusion. These criticisms become evident when we make the connecting principle explicit. (Plato may be joking in this passage.)

Usual (Even Less Articulate) Uses of Analogy

In many perfectly normal cases, the analogy is presented in a way that suggests that the argument has the following structure.

Case B is like case A in many ways.

Case A has G.

∴ Case B has G.

This is a perfectly mad form of argument, however, so you should never rest with this as the final analysis of an argument.

Rats and people are alike in many ways: They have very similar systems of enzymes and hormones, they adapt well to a wide variety of environments, and so on.

People carry umbrellas.

∴ Rats carry umbrellas.

It is easy to think of other counter-examples to this general form of argument (just think of two things that are similar in many ways but different in at least one way), and one should not present such an argument unless one also believes that the ways in which A and B are similar are at least relevant to whether or not A and B have property G. In interpreting the examples drawn from C. S. Lewis and Plato, for example, I assumed that the similarities cited (between unveiling a mutton chop and a striptease; between loving food and loving learning) were thought to be relevant to the conclusion drawn. Otherwise, the argument would make no sense. But if such connections among properties are necessary to make the inference reasonable (or even sane), then we should regard the statement that there is an appropriate relation among the properties as an unstated premise of the argument. As we have learned, one important step in evaluating an argument is to make the unstated premises as clear and explicit as possible.

Many presentations of arguments will look like the "less articulate" and the even less articulate "usual" forms of the argument. In evaluating an analogy, you should try to make the connecting principle as explicit as possible. Often analogy is used just because it is very difficult to do this, but you will find it valuable to articulate the connecting principle as well as you can when you are trying to identity an analogy, understand it, or explain its limitations.

By emphasizing the role of the connecting principle, we have destroyed a distinction that is often seen as the key to classifying arguments that employ analogies.

Sometimes these are seen as "case-to-case" arguments, as opposed to arguments involving general claims. This looks plausible, because usually only the analogue and the primary subject matter are mentioned, without any explicit statement of the connecting principle. This is misleading, however, because such arguments are only as strong as the connecting principle, and the evaluation of such arguments will ordinarily be illuminated by an explicit statement of the connecting principle.

CRITICISMS OF ARGUMENTS BASED ON ANALOGIES

When an analogy is used in connection with an argument, there are many ways in which problems can occur. Suppose that we have an argument that individual B (principal subject matter) must have property G because it is relevantly similar to individual A (analogue) and A has property G. Then the argument might be criticized in some of the following ways.

1. Point out that A (the analogue) doesn't have property G.
   Rather than illustrating a general principle that applies to both A and B, the analogue is actually a counter-example to that principle. (The analogy from Plato seemed to have this problem.)

2. Point out that B (the primary subject) is not relevantly similar to A (the analogue). B does not have properties $F_1 \cdots F_n$ (the properties said to be relevant to having G), so even if the general principle is clear and true, it does not apply to the case in question.

Consider this from an article by Michael Kinsley, "Keep Trade Free," *The New Republic,* vol. 188, no. 14 (April 11, 1983), p. 11:

> The balance of payments is a measure of economic health, not a cause of it; restricting imports to reduce that deficit is like sticking the thermometer in ice water to bring down a feverish temperature.

He uses the example of the thermometer in ice water to illustrate a connecting principle:

> One cannot change a measurable quantity by manipulating its indicators.

But one is most likely to take issue with this on the grounds that the balance of payments is not merely an indicator of economic health, so that it does not share the relevant similarity to a thermometer reading.

Usually, though, the best criticism of an analogy is this:

3. Point out that the connecting principle (that all things that have properties $F_1 \cdots F_n$ also have property G) is false or at least questionable. (In other words, we note that $F_1 \cdots F_n$ may be genuine similarities between A and B, but that the presence of $F_1 \cdots F_n$ is not enough to guarantee the presence of G.) To point this out effectively:

3A. Give a counter-example (something that has $F_1 \cdots F_n$ but not G) that shows the falsity of the connecting principle.

This is the usual way to show that an analogy is misleading. State the general principle that is needed to support the conclusion, then show that it is false. The Darwinian response to Paley's argument presents examples that show the falsity of the general principle that is employed in the argument.

3B. Extend the analogy, suggesting that the similarity ($F_1 \cdots F_n$) equally supports the attribution of other properties, H, J, etc., that are obviously unacceptable (even absurd). This calls into question the significance of $F_1 \cdots F_n$ in predicting properties of B.

This criticism is weak if the argument is in ideal form. In that case, a counter-example is more appropriate. But if the argument is in one of the less-than-ideal formats, then it may be more appropriate to undermine the significance of $F_1 \cdots F_n$ in this way. For example, if someone merely says that the complexity of people is like the complexity of watches, so people, like watches, must have a maker, then one might ask whether people must be assembled in a factory, like watches. This approach forces the person giving the analogy to clarify the relevant similarities, and it can be used when the connecting principle is not clear.

3C. Show that the conclusion is false.

Show that there are independent grounds for holding that B does not have property G. If the analogy is not in ideal form, then the conclusion that B has property G may be false even though the claims about the analogue are true.

ANALOGY IN LAW

In legal argument, precedent plays an important role. Precedents are the basis for people's expectations about the application of the law, and considerations of fairness require that relevantly similar cases be treated in the same way. What we have already said about analogy applies to the process of identifying and applying precedents. In the ideal situation, we would identify and state a principle that was applied in the past, we would note that the principle applies in the case at hand, and we would apply it. Going from a precedent case to a current case can look like "case-to-case" argument, but the argument is successful only when there is an acceptable principle that applies to the two cases. Evaluating judgments is best done in the light of an explicit statement of the general principle that applies to the precedent case and to the particular case under consideration.

The legal principles that apply in a precedent case might not be fully articulated, however. We have to compare the new case to older ones and ask (1) whether the similarities between them are the features that served as a basis for judgment in the old cases and (2) whether the similarities between them are the features that can serve as a basis for a decision in the new case. If we do not explicitly state the general principle that applies alike to the two cases, then we are using analogy in the less articulate way that we already discussed. When one person is found "not guilty by reason of insanity," exactly what precedent does that set for other cases? Must the person be unable to control himself? Must he be unable to understand what he is doing? Must he have lost contact with what is right and what is wrong? These kinds of questions are often unanswered by the action in a single case or even a number of cases, because that case (or those cases) has (or have) many features, and it may not be evident which features are the basis of the decision. The fair treatment of new cases is difficult when it is difficult to determine what counts as a relevant similarity to past cases. Such judgments are much easier when the standards of insanity have been made clear, because then we have an explicit connecting principle that we know how to apply to a wider range of cases.

ANALOGY IN LOGIC (REFUTATION BY ANALOGY)

Suppose that I want to show that this argument is invalid:

Argument A1

> If Bill Clinton is from Toronto, then Bill Clinton is from Canada.
>
> Bill Clinton is from Canada.
>
> ∴ Bill Clinton is from Toronto.

Here one of the premises is false, so we know right away that the argument is not sound. But knowing that it is invalid means knowing that even if the premises were true, that would not be enough to guarantee the truth of the conclusion. That might not be so obvious. To show this, we try to identify a general pattern of argument that preserves all of the logically relevant features of the argument we are considering, and then we show that this pattern does not guarantee validity. Pattern A seems to preserve all of the logical structure of argument A1:

Pattern A (affirming the consequent)

> If S1, then S2
>
> S2
>
> ∴ S1

Pattern A is not a validating argument pattern, so it will not validate argument A1. We can show that a general form of argument (like pattern A) is invalid by giving a counter-example—that is, an argument of that form that is obviously invalid. For example, we can show that pattern A is not a validating argument form by presenting the following argument:

Argument A2

> If Bill Clinton is from Ohio, then Bill Clinton is from the U.S.A.
>
> Bill Clinton is from the U.S.A.
>
> ∴ Bill Clinton is from Ohio.

We can all see that this fits pattern A and that it is not a valid argument. We know that this argument has true premises and a false conclusion, so we know that pattern A does not guarantee validity.

Formulating pattern A enables us to make the invalidity of argument A1 clear. Argument A2 is used in showing that pattern A is not a validating pattern. Unless we see other features of A1 that might make it valid, we can be sure that it is not valid. (Its fitting pattern A was the only basis for suspecting that A1 might be valid, and we have seen that fitting pattern A does not suffice to guarantee validity.)

Sometimes we can show invalidity without explicitly formulating any general pattern.

Argument B1

Some doctors are rich.

All female surgeons are doctors.

∴ Some female surgeons are rich.

We could effectively show invalidity by presenting the following argument.

Argument B2

Some doctors are males.

All female surgeons are doctors.

∴ Some female surgeons are males.

It is obvious that argument B2 is invalid: The premises are true but the conclusion is false, and we all know that. It is also obvious that argument B2 has all of the logical properties of argument B1 that are relevant to validity, so we now know that those properties are not sufficient to guarantee validity. Hence Argument B1 is invalid.

In this case we have formulated an analogous argument without ever explicitly noting the general form of argument B1. B2 is so similar to B1 in all of its logical features that we are sure that B2 has all of the logical features of B1 that might make B1 valid, and we see that those features are not enough to guarantee validity. As in other "less articulate" cases of analogy, we compare two particular cases without explicitly formulating any general principle that states the relevant features they have in common. This is all right as long as we are confident that we are working with the appropriate common features of the two cases, even though we have not said specifically what those features are.

CHAPTER SUMMARY

Arguments and Analogies

Ideal use of analogy in connection with argument:

Case A illustrates the principle: Things that have properties $F_1 \cdots F_n$ also have property G.

Case B has $F_1 \cdots F_n$.

∴ Case B has G.

The analogy illustrates a general principle, but the analogy is not an essential element of the argument.

Normal, but inadequate, presentation:

> Case A has G.
>
> Case B is like case A in many ways.
>
> ∴ Case B has G.

This is a clearly invalid form of argument. To try to make out of it something that can be more sensibly discussed, try to identify a general principle that case A illustrates. This general principle should apply to both A and B (but should not mention either specifically). In other words, try to turn this into the ideal form of argument.

Criticism:

1. Case A doesn't have G.
2. Case B is not relevantly similar to A. B does not have properties $F_1 \cdots F_n$.
3. The principle that things that have properties $F_1 \cdots F_n$ also have property G is false.

   3A. Give a counter-example (a clear case of something that is $F_1 \cdots F_n$ but not G) to show falsity.

   3B. Show that the ways in which A and B are alike (listed as $F_1 \cdots F_n$ in the ideal case) are not relevant to G. Extend the analogy, suggesting that the similarity of A and B equally supports the attribution of other properties, H, J, etc., that are obviously unacceptable (even absurd). (This does not work if the analogy is in ideal form.)

   3C. Show directly that B does not have G. (If the analogy is not in ideal form, then the conclusion may be false even if the premises are true, because the general principle connecting the stated premises to the conclusion will not be there.)

EXERCISE 5A

Evaluate the following analogies. If the analogy is used in connection with an argument, identify the primary subject, the analogue, and any general principles (connecting principles) that are intended to apply to them.

1. Children are like slaves. Their parents can make their major decisions for them—where they go to school, where they live, what clothes they will have, whom they will associate with, and what they will have available to eat. Children are not even allowed to vote, presumably because it is thought that their parents' votes will adequately represent them. It is time for us to recognize that a new era of emancipation should be before us! Just as we freed the slaves, we should free our children from this tyranny, allowing them to make their own choices and control their own lives.

2. Politicians are like doctors. They are there to cure the ills of the economy. When you go to a doctor, you acknowledge that he or she knows more about your health than you do, and you pay for the advice you get. There is no point in going to a doctor if you are not prepared to follow that advice. Similarly, there is no point in electing politicians if you are not going to give them free

rein to act after they are in office. Criticizing politicians defeats them and defeats yourself, and it's just as silly as going to the doctor and then refusing to follow the advice you get.

3. It takes pressure from parents and teachers to motivate kids to study and learn to solve mathematical problems. With similar pressure, kids could learn to solve *emotional* problems as well. They get almost no training in this important skill now.

4. A presidential campaign is like a marathon race. You have to be in it for the long haul, able to keep going against every challenge, even when there are others ahead of you. Just as we are glad when the best runner wins a marathon race, we should be glad when the person who runs the best campaign becomes President.

5. The way I look at it, the liver is like a muscle. Just as you keep a muscle in shape by exercising it, you need to exercise your liver by drinking an ample quantity of alcoholic beverages.

6. Censoring dangerous material and taking antibiotics have a lot in common. Antibiotics will usually kill the harmful bacteria in your body, but at the same time, they will kill good bacteria, because the medicine does not distinguish between the good and the bad. Although censorship may eliminate unwanted speech and writing, when we impose it we also risk losing valuable information and ideas.

7. A good criminal trial is like a boxing match. The defense must respond to each punch the prosecutor throws, and the trial judge, like a referee, must make sure that the contest stays within the rules. The process of allowing appeals of a verdict, with a new judge and a new set of arguments, is like having a new fight to decide who *really* won the first one. This process would be absurd in the case of boxing, and it is equally absurd in a criminal trial.

8. The courts have ruled that a woman has a legal right to an abortion. Some people have jumped to the conclusion that because of this, the government has to pay for abortions for Medicaid patients. There is a constitutional right to privacy, but the government has no obligation to pay for anyone's window shades.

9. I think censorship is good and I believe that the government should be careful in how it applies censorship. When I was young, we had cable TV in the house. My parents, however, did not let me go and watch whatever I wanted. I wasn't ready to discern what was good and what was bad. Because I was very impressionable, my parents didn't want wrong ideas filling my mind. Instead, they encouraged me to watch shows like "Sesame Street" and "Mr. Rogers' Neighborhood." They allowed me to watch TV, but they wanted me watching programs that would help me to learn. Sure, those violent TV shows and movies were being produced and broadcast. But I simply wasn't allowed to watch them. The government should use censorship in the same way: not to disallow people from expressing themselves, but to keep the free expression of people's own beliefs in the right context.

10. Love is like wine. Before you have it, you don't know what you are missing. When you do have it, it can be one of the greatest enjoyments in life. But if it is a bad year, the experience can be awful. So before you fall in love, make sure you check the label.

11. Computers are like drugs. Before you try one out, you don't need one, but after you use it a couple of times, you can't live without it. Computers can, like drugs, ruin your social life. So before buying a computer, make sure you are aware of the possible hazards that can occur with its use.

12. Men are like dogs. Women prepare their meals and do everything to keep them content. Men count on women like dogs count on their owners. Like dogs, men are not satisfied with this good treatment. They get fidgety and begin to sniff out new territory and eventually find someone new dishing out the bones.

13. Talking about health insurance coverage for Viagra: "You can bet men, not women, were behind the ill-advised decision to underwrite this insurance coverage. If ego enhancement is an insurable expense, why not cover cosmetic surgery?"

14. It is time for our city to get new police cars, and replacing the fleet of cars is like getting a new suit. You wouldn't want to buy the pants one year, then the jacket another year, then the vest another year. You won't get a good match that way, and so you will end up with a mismatched suit. Besides that, by the time the suit is complete, it will already be out of style. We want a fleet of cars in which everything works and is up to date, so we need to replace our old fleet with a completely new one.

15. The purpose of language is the expression of thought. Because of this, censoring speech or written work is like allowing people to have cars but not allowing them to drive those cars where they want to go. It defeats the purpose of having a car, and censorship defeats the purpose of having a language.

CHAPTER 6

UNDERSTANDING AND EXPLANATION

The development of a system of beliefs relies on more than deductively valid argument. One aspect of this is obvious. Valid arguments need premises, and we can always ask what justifies those premises. Just as important, what we directly observe in the world cannot justify all of our further beliefs by valid argument alone. Many beliefs are justified because they contribute to our attainment of the best *understanding* of what we observe. We want a system of beliefs and ideas that *explains* our experience. This desire for understanding—for explanations of what we observe—can motivate and justify significant changes of belief.

In Chapters 6–8, we will consider what explanations are and what makes some explanations better than others, and we will begin to develop a clearer set of standards for evaluating explanations. We will come to see that this is a key to understanding the non-deductive justification of beliefs.

Why

There are many types of explanation *why* things are true.

1. Why did Bill set four plates? Because four people will be at dinner.
2. Why do some stars go dark? Because they burn up all of the hydrogen that fuels their reactions.
3. Why haven't I ever seen a red crow? Because all crows are black.
4. Why does this window have a mechanical arm attached to it? Because the window is designed to open when there is a fire alarm. The arm is hooked into the alarm system, and it opens the window in the event of an alarm.
5. Why is the window open? Because there was a fire alarm, and the automatic system activated the arm that opens it.

Sometimes we explain by giving the purpose of a thing or saying how it fits into some plan that fulfills a purpose (explanations 1 and 4). At other times we give the causes of an event (as in explanations 2 and 5). Still other times we simply fit it in as a consequence of some more general facts (explanation 3). Most often we are explaining something we have observed in terms of something that is less immediately observable: a plan, a cause, or a general pattern. These different kinds of explanations are answers to *why* questions, the principal kind of question that calls for an explanation.

How and *Why*

Not everything called an explanation is an answer to a *why* question. Answers to *how* questions are often called explanations too, but sometimes a question about how something happened (or how something works) is just a request for a narrative account of a particular situation.

> How did you cook this? We fried it in olive oil with some garlic.

Although the answer to these simple *how* questions could lead us to claim that we understand how something was cooked, it is not this kind of understanding that we wish to consider here. Similarly, accounts of *what* you are doing or what something means are not the kinds of explanations we want to consider. In talking about explanations, we will be considering explanations that can be thought of as answering *why* questions (giving us an understanding of why something is true).

The *how* questions just discussed required only simple narrative answers, but the answers to some other *how* questions provide more than just a narrative. They provide an account of the causes of something.

> How do the planets maintain elliptical orbits? The gravitational pull of the sun modifies their paths, which would otherwise be straight.

This question about the planets can be rephrased as a *why* question (Why do the planets maintain elliptical orbits?), and the answer given here involves a causal explanation. We appeal to general principles of gravitational attraction and motion. Attempts to understand why things happen lead us to many of our beliefs, and developing standards for good answers to *why* questions will help us to make judgments about the success of such attempts and about the acceptability of the beliefs acquired. When a *how* question requires an answer that includes general causal principles, as the one just considered does, it is equivalent to a *why* question, and the answer provides the kind of explanatory understanding we are considering here.

Because

We often give explanations without any explicit question that requests it. We all recognize the word *because* as a correlative of *why*. The word *because* often introduces explanatory material. We can look for *because* statements as frequent indicators that an explanation is being given.

> John drank the squid-ink because he wanted to show how macho he was.
>
> The car stopped because it had burned all of its fuel.
>
> The paint is chipping off your house because paint always chips off after seven years.

explanans and *explanandum*

Two technical terms often occur in the discussion of explanation. When someone gives an explanation, what is explained is called the *explanandum,* and the explanatory material is the *explanans.*

> Judith is getting red spots because she was exposed to the measles virus.

Something is observed (Judith's red spots), and an explanation is given. The occurrence of the red spots is the *explanandum*, the event explained; the exposure to the virus is the *explanans*, the explanatory fact.

KINDS OF EXPLANATION: A DEEPER LOOK

Explanations Involving General Claims

Sometimes an explanation can involve a general claim that applies to the case under consideration.

> The piston goes up and down because pistons do that when the engine is running normally, and this engine is running normally.

Here we have a specific fact, that this engine is running normally, and a general fact, that in normal engines the pistons go up and down. There is even a related valid argument here:

> Specific fact: This engine is running normally.
>
> General fact: In engines that are running normally, the pistons go up and down.
>
> ∴ The pistons are going up and down in this engine.

This related valid argument *exists*, but it is not being used here to convince us of the truth of the conclusion. We started out knowing that the conclusion was true, and we wanted to understand why it was true. The argument shows that this particular observation follows from some other facts, specific and general. In fact, an argument of this general pattern often exists when we have an explanation:

> Specific fact: This is a case of type A.
>
> General fact: All A are B.
>
> ∴ This is a case of type B (the fact to be explained).

Some philosophers have even said that some pattern like this is always available when we have an explanation. It is important to emphasize, though, that when there is an explanation, this argument is not ordinarily being presented, and usually no one is trying to justify a belief in the conclusion of this argument. A person who is explaining the up-and-down motion of the pistons is not ordinarily presenting an argument to convince us that the pistons are going up and down. Rather, we started with knowledge of the conclusion (the *explanandum*), and the facts that imply it are an explanation for why it is true (the *explanans*).

This explanation of the pistons' motion is not very "deep." If you are looking to understand the causes or purposes of pistons' motion, it will probably be unsatisfying to be told that the pistons are going up and down because that is what happens in normal engines. This is a very shallow explanation, because it does not give you any more general account of the causal processes in engines or the purposes of those processes. It is not totally empty, however, because it does tell us that the motion of the piston is an instance of a particular type. (It is an instance of motion in an engine that is running normally. There is nothing unusual happening in your car.) Connecting it with some property in this way is sometimes explanation enough, without the presentation of any particular causes or purposes. However, we often want something deeper.

Argument and explanation

Consideration of another example may help us explore the relationship between explanation and argument. Consider this argument:

It is very hazy out tonight.

Whenever it is very hazy out, no one can see comets in the night sky.

So John cannot see comets tonight.

When an argument like this is valid, people can present an explanation of why the conclusion is true, citing the premises as *explanans*; they can also present the argument to convince us of the conclusion; and they can do both together.

If John has looked up in the sky to see a comet that is supposed to be passing over, and he has not seen it, then someone might *explain* his lack of success:

John can't see the comet tonight because the sky is too hazy.

The other part of the explanation (the general claim that whenever it is very hazy out, no one can see comets in the night sky) would probably be left unstated, because it is fairly obvious. We would have an explanation, but the speaker would not be presenting an argument to try to justify a belief that John cannot see the comet. The speaker is not trying to convince us that John can't see the comet—we already know that.

In a different kind of situation, a speaker might present the argument that is under consideration here. Suppose that someone who is not with John knows that John is outside trying to see the comet tonight. She might infer that John cannot see the comet, if she already knows that it is too hazy.

Look how hazy it is. John sure can't see the comet tonight!

Then the argument has been employed to justify a belief in the conclusion that John can't see the comet.

In still another kind of situation, someone could present both the argument and the explanation.

John can't be seeing the comet tonight, because it is too hazy.

In all three of these cases, the argument is sound and the explanation is correct. Whether someone will be interested in the argument or the explanation will depend on what that person already knows.

Causal Explanations

Often we seek causal explanations for what we observe.

> The cactus looks pale because it has had too much water.
>
> The window broke because a rock hit it.
>
> The earth is warming because of the increase in atmospheric carbon dioxide.
>
> The phone rang because Carla dialed our number.

This can ordinarily be seen to fit the pattern we cited for arguments with general premises. Although we often cite only the specific fact that is involved in the explanation, it is easy to see that each of these explanations also relies on some general claim if the explanation is to be adequate.

> Providing too much water can cause a cactus to look pale.
>
> A rock hitting a window (at an appropriate angle and with sufficient force) will break the window.
>
> (Sufficiently) increasing atmospheric carbon dioxide can cause the earth to warm.
>
> Dialing our number from another phone causes our phone to ring.

Causal explanation is widespread both within and outside of science, and it will be helpful to look more closely at its features.

Necessary and sufficient conditions

Causal claims often seem to express the concept of *necessary conditions* or the concept of *sufficient conditions*:

> She got the measles because she was exposed to the measles virus. A person cannot have measles without the presence of a measles virus: the presence of the virus is a necessary condition for having measles. (If the virus is not there, then there is no measles.) However, the presence of the virus is not a sufficient condition for having measles, because antibodies can prevent development of the disease.
>
> The marigold plants died because we deprived them of water for several weeks.
> Depriving a marigold plant of water for several weeks is a *sufficient condition* for its death. But that is *not a necessary condition* for its death, because there are many other ways to kill it (stomping it, poisoning it, flooding it, burning it, etc.).

Our use of the word *cause* sometimes seems indiscriminate, because we seem to use it for both necessary and sufficient conditions. The virus causes the measles, and depriving the plant of water causes its death.

There is, however, an understanding of causal claims that connects them more uniformly with the concepts of necessary and sufficient conditions. *For something to be a cause, it must be a necessary part of some sufficient set of conditions.* When Amy killed Bernie, she caused his death by pointing the gun at his head and pulling the trigger. In this case, her act of pointing and pulling by itself is *not necessary* for his death—she could have used poison, an ax, or a car bomb, or someone else could even have killed him instead. But by itself, pointing and pulling is also *not sufficient* for his death; other circumstances needed to be in order as well—the gun was loaded and working properly, Bernie was only three feet away, he didn't move out of the way, nothing else caused his death earlier, etc. A whole set of conditions, taking all of these circumstances together, is causally sufficient for Bernie's death, and Alice's pointing the gun and pulling the trigger is a part of what makes this set sufficient; it is a necessary part of a sufficient set of conditions.

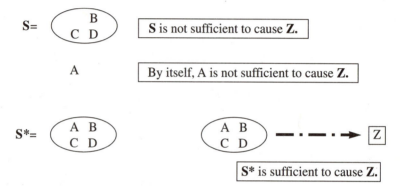

A is a necessary part of a set of conditions (S*), that is sufficient to cause Z. It is a necessary part, because without A, the set is not sufficient (i.e., **S** is not sufficient) to cause **Z**. So we can say that A is a cause of **Z**.

This idea seems to apply to all causal claims. If **A** causes **Z**, then **A** must be a necessary part of some sufficient set of conditions for **Z**. Sometimes we focus on the necessity of a cause: Given that there was no poison, no ax, and no car bomb or the like, then the act of pointing and pulling was necessary. (No set of actual conditions was sufficient without this). At other times we focus on the sufficiency of a cause: If other circumstances were in order (the gun was loaded, and so on), then the act of pointing and pulling was sufficient (i.e., it completed a sufficient set of conditions).

Once we sort it out, we can see more clearly how causal explanations work. The *explanans* will be a cause, some event that is a necessary part of some sufficient set of conditions. Whenever we have an adequate causal explanation, a causal *explanans* (cause) C occurred, causing an event of type E (the effect or *explanandum*). Thus C is a part of some sufficient set of conditions for E and the following argument will be sound:

Some set of conditions K, including C as a part, occurs (or occurred or will occur).

K is sufficient to guarantee that an event of type E occurs. That is, whenever conditions like K occur, an event of type E occurs.

∴   An event of type E occurs (or has occurred or will occur).

K would then be a full explanation of why E occurred (if we could identify all of its components). C will be a part of the full explanation if C is a necessary part of K (i.e., the set K – {C} is not sufficient to cause E).

It is worth noting that a full set of circumstances K that is sufficient for E's occurrence explains E by fitting E into a general pattern (whenever conditions of type K occur, an event like E occurs), the type of explanation we first discussed. But in giving causal explanations, we ordinarily focus on some fact C that is a necessary part of K, not on a full set of sufficient conditions K.

We usually cite as the cause an element of K that is important to us. Usually, if I let go of my pen and someone asks, "Why did his pen drop?," it is perfectly suitable to answer, "Because he let go of it." However, in a basic physics class, most of the students are likely to guess that if the teacher asks why the pen dropped, she is more likely to be looking for an answer that says something about the existence of a gravitational force or that calls attention to the fact that the pen has mass. The letting go, the gravitational force, and the mass of the pen are necessary parts of a set of actual conditions that was sufficient to guarantee that the pen would drop, and which one we are interested in depends on the context.

If a fire inspector is holding a news conference and a reporter asks why a warehouse fire started, the fire inspector will surprise everyone if he says that the fire started because of the presence of oxygen in and around the building. That is a necessary part of a sufficient set of conditions for a fire, but it is not the one that we are ordinarily interested in. The fire inspector would be making a joke or evading the question—probably both. We are looking for the specific unusual events that led to *this* fire, not just for the usual conditions that contribute to fires. We want to know whether it was arson or accident, for instance, and that determines what sort of condition we are looking for.

Teleological Explanations

Often an explanation leads to our understanding something by enabling us to see how it contributes to the attainment of a goal.

> There is a wire along that wall because there is a telephone in the next room.

Here the explanation enables us to understand why the wire is there because the explanation makes the purpose of the wire clear. Explanations that fit things into a plan that leads to the fulfillment of a goal are called *teleological* explanations. (The Greek word *telos* means (roughly) "goal.")

> Alice bought telephone wire because she is planning to install a telephone in her study.

> The wire on that wall is transmitting electricity because that will make the phone ring.

We can often understand activities and events by seeing how they contribute to the fulfillment of goals. When something plays a role in a plan that fulfills a goal, we can often speak of its function (its role in fulfilling the goal). For example, we can say that a wire's transmission of electricity has the function of causing the phone to ring. Such *functional* explanations are a kind of teleological explanation, because they explain something in terms of its contribution to the attainment of some goal.

Some *why* questions can be answered with either causal or teleological explanations. These explanations do not conflict; they simply provide distinct sorts of understanding of the events to be understood.

Why did the phone ring?

> *Teleological*: To indicate that we should pick it up.
>
> *Causal*: Because Carla dialed our number.

Why does the piston go down?

> *Teleological*: Because its going down compresses the gas, making the gas burn explosively, so that the piston will go back up. This up-and-down motion is ultimately transmitted to the wheels, making the car go.
>
> *Causal*: Because the arm this piston is attached to causes this piston to go down when the other piston goes up, and the other piston went up.

Why do many Africans carry the sickle-cell trait?

> *Teleological*: Because those who carry this trait can avoid serious malaria, and consequently they can stay healthier in Africa, where malaria is common.
>
> *Causal*: Because past epidemics of malaria killed or weakened those who did not carry the trait. The population has come to consist mainly of people who inherited the trait from those who were better able to have children and care for them, and those with the sickle-cell trait were better able to have children and care for them.

We can explain the phone's ring in terms of its general function or in terms of its precipitating causes. In the case of the piston, each explanation provides an understanding of the piston's motion—one in terms of its contribution to a goal (making the car run), the other in terms of other motions that bring it about. In the case of the sickle-cell trait, the teleological explanation enables us to understand the connection of this trait with its effect, the well-being of individuals. The causal explanation, on the other hand, enables us to understand how the trait's contribution to health causes the trait to be common.

One of the most usual sorts of explanation, the explanation of people's actions, can be thought of as both teleological and causal.

> Why did Jennifer buy those flowers? Because she believed that Alicia would like them, and she wanted to get something that Alicia would like.

Jennifer's action of buying the flowers fits into a plan to fulfill a goal (pleasing Alicia), so the explanation is teleological. But note also that the explanation mentions two states of Jennifer: her believing that Alicia would like the flowers and her wanting to buy something that Alicia would like. Those states of belief and desire can be thought of as causal factors in Jennifer's action. Having a thought is a state of a person, and the thought can be about a particular goal. Therefore, when we explain people's actions by saying what beliefs and desires they have, we combine teleological and causal explanations.

CHAPTER SUMMARY

Some standard terminology of explanations

Explanandum: what is explained.

Explanans: what does the explaining.

John broke his leg (*explanandum*) **because** *he had a bad skiing accident* (*explanans*).

Types of explanations

Fitting into a **general pattern**
My dog's nose is cold because healthy dogs are always like that and mine is healthy.

Causal
My dog limps because a car hit him.

Teleological (goal or **design)**
Explanation of something in terms of its role in contributing to the attainment of a goal.
I give my dog candy to reward him.
My dog has long canine teeth because they enable him to tear meat apart.

A cause is a necessary part of some set of conditions that is sufficient to bring about the effect.

The car's hitting my dog was a necessary part of a set of conditions that was sufficient for his limping.

EXERCISE 6A

In each of the following examples, identify the *explanans* and the *explanandum* of any explanations presented or mentioned. If the explanation is a causal explanation or a teleological explanation, identify it as such.

1. Bob Dole spent most of his campaign budget in the early primaries in order to eliminate other candidates and consolidate his position as the front-runner.

2. Some birds eat small stones because the stones help in grinding up their food.

3. They raised the cockpit electronics and wiring out of the ocean because they thought that it would help them to understand why the plane had exploded.

4. On the day of the women's marathon, many people were tense. A bomb had exploded at a park the day before.

5. At the beginning of the history of the United States, only free men who owned property were allowed to vote. Gradually the restrictions were lifted. The requirement that voters own property was repealed, slavery was abolished, and women got the right to vote. In addition, the voting rights law passed in the 1960s prohibited practices that produced racial discrimination. The nation survives only because the voting population was steadily expanded in these ways.

6. Bush had raised taxes after promising that he would not do so. This resulted in a considerable loss in credibility, and thus Clinton was able to win in 1992.

7. Looking at the Milky Way, one sees a band of faint light encircling the sky. This light comes from an enormous number of faint stars at great distances, as was first shown by Galileo in 1610 when he turned his crude telescope toward the heavens. But . . . [there are] various dark regions, called rifts, crossing the Milky Way. These dark regions cannot be places where there simply are no stars, because they would then have to be enormously long, skinny tunnels that cross through our stellar system, all pointing toward the Sun. . . . The explanation of these rifts is that there are clouds of interstellar dust particles—small, solid grains of matter floating in the space of the stars— that block the light from distant stars in certain directions. [From R. Robert Robbins and William H. Jeffereys, *Discovering Astronomy*, 2nd ed. (New York: John Wiley, 1988), pp. 22–23.]

EXERCISE 6B

In August, 1996, *The Journal of the American Medical Association* published an article with some interesting findings concerning United States Navy pilots who had been prisoners of war in Vietnam. ("Long-term Health Outcomes and Medical Effects of Torture Among US Navy Prisoners of War in Vietnam," D. S. Nice, C. F. Garland, S. M. Hilton, J. C. Baggett, R. E. Mitchell, Vol. 276, No. 5 (pp. 345–426). An abstract is available at *http://www.ama-assn.org./sci-pubs/journals/archive/jama/ vol_276/no_5/oc5a31a.htm.*) In the following report of that article, more than one explanation is indicated. Identify the *explanandum* (the thing observed) and the *explanans* (what explains the observation) for each of the explanations suggested here.

Physical and Psychological Problems Still Show up in Vietnam Era POWs

According to a study in *The Journal of the American Medical Association*, United States Navy pilots who were POWs in North Vietnam continue to have an unusual number of nerve problems in their arms and legs. Researchers say that this is probably due to the leg irons, handcuffs and other restraints used by their captors.

Arthritis and back problems are also developing now in the prisoners of war, much more than in other pilots who weren't taken captive, according to the study.

The POWs, however, show no higher rate of psychological problems than pilots who were not imprisoned. These findings probably do not mean that torture was less traumatic than previously believed. Being a pilot who wasn't captured was traumatic as well. Dr. Joseph Westermeyer, chief of psychiatry at the Minneapolis Veterans Affairs Medical Center, points out, "These pilots who weren't POWs underwent a lot of stress. There were people trying to kill them day in and day out." [Based on a report in the Syracuse *Post Standard*, August 7, 1996]

EXERCISE 6C

In each of these passages, something is observed. In each case, try to think of two or more possible explanations for what is observed. (Your explanations do not need to be the correct explanations, but they should consist of something that, if it were true, would explain what is observed.)

1. Although they had no physical evidence linking him to the bomb at Centennial Olympic Park (Atlanta Olympics, 1996), the FBI made sure that the news media were aware of who their principal suspect was. Why might they release his name when they had no solid physical evidence?

2. Some word that sounds similar to *mama* is a common word for *mother* in many languages from all around the world. Why?

3. Many restaurants are in business only a short time (less than three years) before they close down, yet there always seem to be plenty of new restaurants opening to take the place of those that close. What could explain these two facts?

4. In courses in mathematics, students who fall behind in their work generally don't pay attention in class after that, so they end up doing worse and worse as the semester goes on. Why don't they start paying attention so that they can do better in the later part of the course?

5. When I go to an appointment with my doctor, I often have to wait a long time if my appointment is in the afternoon, but I rarely wait very long if the appointment is in the morning. Why?

EVALUATING EXPLANATIONS

INFERENCE TO THE BEST EXPLANATION

In Chapter 6, we discussed how explanations help us to understand what we observe by fitting those observations into general patterns, by indicating their causal origins, or by indicating how the events observed fit into a plan. When I see my ivy plants drooping, I may come to understand this immediately because I know some relevant explanatory facts: that I haven't watered them for several weeks and that these plants droop if they are not watered often.

At other times we are in a different situation, however. We have a problem to solve, we can think of more than one explanation for what we observe, and we need to figure out which explanation is best. I may see my cactus drooping, and I may wonder what the explanation of its droop is. Maybe it has had too little water, maybe it has had too much, or maybe there is an insect infestation, for example. We must now deal with the general question of how we justify the beliefs that play a role in the *explanans* of an explanation: We have made an observation (the cactus wilting), and we will know more when we identify the correct explanation (*explanans*) for it.

Much of what we believe is justified because it is part of the best explanation for what we observe. When the telephone rings, I answer it because I believe that there is an incoming call. My belief is justified because there being an incoming call is part of the best explanation of my hearing a ring. In general, I am at least somewhat justified in accepting an explanation **E** if the premises of the following argument are true.

> I observe **O**.
>
> **E** is part of the best explanation I can find for why I observe **O**.
>
> ∴ **E**.

Note that this is not a deductively valid argument. The best explanation I can find may be wrong. My intellect, my creative ability, and my investigative resources are all very limited, so even when the premises are true, the conclusion can be false. In addition, if I have not tried hard enough to find a good explanation, then my belief

in the conclusion **E** (the best explanation I can find) will not even be justified. A study of this type of argument, however, is a key to comprehending the standards of justification that apply when deductive standards are not applicable. We can call this pattern *inference to the best explanation* (IBE).

Much of our thought is involved in finding explanations for what we observe. When I noticed tiles falling off the bathroom wall, I immediately became interested in finding the explanation for it. A number of alternatives came to mind:

> Carpenter ants have weakened the wood under the tiles.
>
> The adhesive is old, and it is normal to have to replace it at this age.
>
> The tiles had the wrong kind of adhesive for this situation.
>
> The adhesive was poorly applied.
>
> There is excessive moisture because of insufficient ventilation.
>
> There is excessive moisture because of leaks from the outside.

I want to know which explanation is right, because knowing this will provide me with a better understanding of the world I live in. In this case, that understanding is also likely to provide me with the best information about how to repair the wall in a way that will prevent such problems from arising in the future. I have identified several different explanatory *hypotheses* or *theories* (we will use these words largely interchangeably), and I need to decide what the right explanation is. (The right explanation might be some combination of these or some theory that I did not think of in advance of my exploration, of course.)

We seek explanations all the time. Recently, I have wanted to explain why my garage door won't stay down, why my sinuses are stuffed up, why my bird-feeder was emptying so quickly, and why there was unusually heavy traffic on my way home. In each case, I could think of several possible explanations, and so I was faced with trying to determine which was correct.

If we are to use inference to the best explanation as a standard for evaluating beliefs, then we will need to develop standards for making the judgment that one explanation is better than another, so that we can decide which is best. In Chapter 9, we will also consider the ways in which we can try to test explanatory theories. Because the goal of explanation is to develop an understanding of our experience, we will be able to use that goal as a guide in developing standards for the evaluation of explanations.

It is useful to consider cases in which we draw conclusions non-deductively, in order to develop an appreciation of how we can think of such conclusions as being justified because they are the best explanation of what we observe.

A Mystery

When we find Vincent lying still on the floor of his house, and touching him reveals that he is very cold, we may conclude that he is dead. Such a conclusion is justified when it is the best explanation of what is observed, and no other explanation of his cold, still state may be available. But how do we determine the cause of his death? Perhaps the death was natural, but we may know that his nephew Irving will inherit a fortune, and this gives Irving a motive for murder. Perhaps Vincent's business partners will benefit if Vincent is out of the way. How do we recognize the truth when we find it? How do we determine which of these is the best explanation of Vincent's death?

In looking for a cause of death, we try to use independently justified generalizations to locate the causal factors. If we observe that there is a large hole containing a bullet in Vincent's body, the best explanation of this would probably be that the bullet was fired from a gun into Vincent, making the hole and stopping. Of course, someone could make a hole and then insert a bullet, but such an event would be quite extraordinary, and without special reason to suspect that particular kind of unusual occurrence, we are justified in assuming that the hole with the bullet in it is explained in the usual way. Forensic examiners can often make much more subtle judgments than this one, connecting the marks on the bullet with a particular gun, showing that the bullet had been fired from that gun. The marks show this because having been fired from that gun is the best explanation of the bullet's bearing those marks. Each gun makes marks that cannot be made in any other way (or are at least extremely difficult to make in any other way). We are justified in accepting these claims because there are established theories that explain the marks on the bullet in ways that fit into an integrated understanding of what happened. The beliefs about the marks on the bullet are justified as long as no reasonable alternative explanation exists.

We can connect Vincent's nephew with the death because of the motive he has for murder. But this motive alone will not establish that he did it. There will always be the possibility of alternative explanations—it was natural, someone else did it, etc. To connect Irving with the death in a more convincing way, we need to find something that is explained by Irving's murdering Vincent, but not by anything else. If Irving's fingerprints are on the gun, and if Irving has no alternative explanation of how they got there, then we may be justified in explaining their presence as a result of Irving's touching it in the process of murdering Vincent. If Irving's fingerprints cannot get there except by his touching it, and if there is no other adequate explanation for why he touched it, then we are likely to be convinced.

Note that his fingerprints make us very sure of one thing: He touched the gun—or at least those parts of it that have his fingerprints. The theory that supports this is well established, and facts about the particular case we are considering will not affect our beliefs about the uniqueness of fingerprints or about how they can get on things. As long as nothing except Irving's touching the gun can explain the fingerprints, we will be sure that he touched it. The further claim that Irving touched the gun in the process of murdering Vincent is much more questionable. Here we need to know that nothing else could explain why Irving touched the gun. But that requires looking at particular facts that are special to this case. Would Irving have another reason to use the gun? Might someone have tricked him into holding the relevant part of the gun without his realizing it? We need to look at particular motives and scenarios, and we have no clear, well-established general theories of motives that will so definitely rule out all alternative possibilities. There are many people in the world, and we need to rule out the possibility that one of these others murdered Vincent. To rule out the other relevant possibilities, we must show that the gun was the murder weapon (i.e., that the only explanation of the death is the bullet from this gun) and also that no one except Irving could have used the gun.

All of this illustrates how our discoveries are justified because they explain what we already know and because alternative explanations can be eliminated. When in doubt, we try to find facts that can be explained in only one possible way. Our well-established causal theories play an especially important role in helping to establish facts firmly when they explain the observations and limit the explanatory alternatives. The evaluation of explanations and explanatory theories is central to understanding the conditions under which our beliefs are justified.

Explanatory Theories

An explanation is usually further from observation than is the *explanandum*. We start from some data or observation, and we use something that is less directly observed to explain the observation or data. There may be many levels of data and explanations, where what counts as an explanation at one level is part of the data for further explanation.

We seem to feel a coldness when we touch Vincent.

> **Possible explanations:** He is cold. We are hallucinating.

Vincent is cold.

> **Possible explanations:** He is dead. He is undergoing a novel medical procedure. He never was human anyway.

Vincent is dead.

> **Possible explanations**: He was killed by a bullet. He died of natural causes. He was poisoned.

Vincent was killed by a bullet.

> **Possible causal explanations**: His nephew shot him. He shot himself. A burglar shot him.

> **Possible teleological explanations**: He was shot for his money. He was shot to relieve his suffering from a painful disease.

The explanation at one level becomes the data to be explained as we move away from more basic observations. In this case, teleological explanations become interesting when we reach events (his being killed) that might play a role in carrying out some plan.

In the kind of sequence we just mentioned, several different levels could be called either observational or explanatory, depending on how much we are willing to take for granted. Rather than thinking of our claim that Vincent is dead as an explanation for why he is so cold, we are likely to regard it as a direct observation, for example. The alternative explanations for his coldness are not ones we would ordinarily consider.

In most observations, we can identify a sequence of statements that could, in varying circumstances, be considered as observations.

I seem to see a purple blob.

A small purple blob is magnified under the microscope.

A dyed amoeba is on the slide.

Amoebas have developed in the fluid on the slide.

Exposure to air introduced amoebas into the fluid.

I seem to see a white sky.

I see a white sky.

It is snowing.

A moisture-laden cold front has moved in.

The jet stream shifted, bringing air from the north.

In each of these sequences, each statement before the last is explained by the ones below it. Even the last statement in each sequence might be considered an observation in a context in which we are taking for granted all of the other explanatory connections in the sequence above it.

Finding the Best Explanation

When our explanations rely on stable, independently established theories, we often feel that we have reached the best explanation possible. In our mystery story, we could be especially sure that Vincent was dead, that Irving touched (parts of) the gun, and that the bullet came from that gun. Although cryogenic preservation exists, cold bodies on the floor in an ordinary room must always be dead. The general truth that human life in an ordinary room requires continued warmth is well established. We can express this point in terms of *inference to the best explanation*: The best (the only) explanation for Vincent's coldness, stillness, and lack of pulse is that he is dead. Similarly, unless someone has a way of faking fingerprints, Irving's touching a spot can be the only explanation of his fingerprints' being there. And the particular marks on the bullet can be explained only by its having come from that gun. These general facts might be altered by future technologies, but for now they stand as general facts that are established independently of the case at hand, and they eliminate alternative explanations (that something other than death can account for Vincent's coldness, that something other than Irving's fingers could make these marks on the gun, that something other than being fired from this gun could make these marks on the bullet).

To understand something is to fit it into what we believe. We understand something when we see it as an instance of a general pattern, when we know where it came from (what caused it), or when we can see it as contributing to a plan that achieves some goal. Our understanding of a phenomenon is deeper when it fits a pattern that applies to a wider range of cases. Explanations are better the more they contribute to this understanding. Theories are better the more they enable us to develop satisfying explanations and rule out alternative explanations. We are most secure when we can rely on well-established regularities.

Justifying New Explanatory Theories

Times come when we must give up old theories and adopt new ones. We always want to select the best explanatory theory, and sometimes we find that familiar explanatory resources no longer provide the coherent understanding they once did. New discoveries and new attempts to integrate our insights can lead us to adopt new theories.

When Galileo first observed the moons of Jupiter in a telescope that he had designed and constructed, he came to believe the following:

> I am observing a particular pattern of light spots in the telescope.
>
> This pattern is caused by moons revolving around Jupiter.

This causal explanation would be established as a part of a new theory that conflicted with the astronomical theory that was dominant at that time. The theory that was dominant had developed from Aristotle's theory of celestial motion. According to Aristotle,

> The earth is the only center of celestial revolution.

Because this geocentric theory was part of a developed understanding of the place of humans in the universe and of the nature of celestial motion, people were very reluctant to accept Galileo's account of what he saw. Before Galileo, the Aristotelian idea had been modified to fit observations. Accepting Galileo's claims would be a much more radical change, though; it would mean giving up this developed theory and losing the understanding of the universe that it seemed to provide.

Nevertheless, with the new telescope there appeared to be celestial objects that revolved around Jupiter, not the earth, so that there was more than one center of celestial motion. The observations that Galileo made seemed to conflict with established theory. Although reasons could be found in favor of each of these theories, at least one of the theories had to be wrong.

Because the geocentric theory had considerable explanatory value, people were reluctant to accept Galileo's theory about the source of the spots in his telescope: Could they be reflections, lens distortions, or distant stars? In this case, however, it was eventually necessary to set aside the dominant astronomical theory; reasons that had long been accepted for thinking that the earth was the center of everything were overturned. A new understanding of the planets—and even a new understanding of the position of humans in the universe—had to be developed. Later we will look at this case in more detail to see what it shows us about the conditions under which the adoption of a new theory can be justified.

In brief, we can say now that Galileo's suggestion that Jupiter had moons became widely accepted when it was seen as a part of a view that provided a better overall explanation of observations of planetary motion and thus a better understanding of planetary motion. It became even more firmly established when it was shown to fit into a more general theory that provided a deeper understanding of all motion and of gravitation.

Such revolutionary changes in belief occur when people come to see the need for a shift in their explanatory theories in order to have better explanations of what is observed. We must look in more detail at the kinds of features that make one explanation better than another if we are to evaluate cases of inference to the best explanation.

EVALUATING THEORIES

In evaluating theories, we look for five things:

1. The theory should have definite *content*. This is sometimes stated as the condition that the theory should be *falsifiable in principle* or that the theory is *testable*.

2. The theory should have scope. It should involve truly general patterns, so that it "economizes" and organizes our beliefs.

3. The theory should integrate with other beliefs.

4. The theory should be unfalsified.

5. Alternative explanations should be ruled out.

Content

The theory should have definite *content*. This really just means that the theory should have some consequences that could be imagined to be false. If the theory is correct, though, these consequences will be correct. The theory will be *falsifiable in principle, but unfalsified* in fact. We can test the theory because we can imagine what kind of situation would show it to be false, and (in many cases, at least) we can then try to produce that kind of situation. The theory is *testable*.

Having content is a fundamental requirement of explanatory adequacy. A theory must be able to tell us what to expect, predicting some things and ruling out other possibilities. A theory is best established when it has some true consequence p that differs from what would be expected on the basis of any different theory. This makes the theory uniquely able to explain the truth of p; it gives the theory a "surprise value" that is important in establishing that it is a better theory than others.

When we combine our knowledge of fingerprints with the hypothesis that Irving touched the gun, we can explain something that no other available theory can explain. The particular details of the marks on the gun would be explained by Irving's touching that part of the gun and not by anything else. Our theory says that Irving's touch can leave those particular marks and that nothing else makes exactly those marks. Our hypothesis that these marks are caused by Irving's touch is very easy to falsify: If the fingerprint pattern does not match Irving's fingerprints, then we know that the marks are caused by someone else's touch. We can also easily imagine what would falsify our general theory of fingerprints: It would be easily falsified by showing that many people have the same fingerprints, that people's fingerprints vary from day to day, or that it is easy to duplicate someone's fingerprints wherever one wants to do so. But none of these things is true (as far as I know, at least), and so the theory is falsifiable in principle (we can easily imagine what would show it to be false), and yet it is unfalsified. Thus our theory of fingerprints has some definite content, it explains the marks (if they do match Irving's fingerprints), and no other theory explains the marks in such detail. If we find those marks, that gives us very good reason to believe the hypothesis that Irving touched it.

Several factors can weaken the content of a theory and thus make it less powerful. Some of these weakenings can be important in adapting a theory to new data, but they can also destroy it by stripping it of content, if they are carried too far.

Lack of clarity

A theory can be weak in content if it so lacks sufficient clarity that it is not clear what would count as a test of the theory. If it is not clear what counts as a test, it is not clear how to apply the theory to particular cases.

Suppose your friend says that smart women are never attractive. You might then propose your anthropology teacher and the winner of the college math award as falsifying data: smart women who are very attractive. If the friend says that the anthropology teacher doesn't count because she is not really smart in quite the way your friend means, and if he also says that the award winner doesn't really meet the standards of attractiveness that he had in mind, you should begin to wonder whether the theory has any real content. Unless we can independently say what counts as smart and what counts as attractive, the theory has no explanatory or predictive value. As long as your friend can reject all proposed falsifying examples on vague, uncheckable grounds, the theory is being held as *unfalsifiable* or *untestable,* and that is the death knell for explanatory content.

Astrological predictions often rely on vagueness to provide an appearance of real predictive power where there is none. Some very general traits of personality apply at least approximately to almost everyone, and people share many similar beliefs about themselves, and when those traits or beliefs are presented vaguely enough, they provide a personality profile that most people will feel is a very close match.

> Some variety is important for you.
>
> Independent thought is sometimes one of your characteristics.
>
> You are sometimes uncertain about your decisions.
>
> Sexual issues have presented problems for you.
>
> You have abilities that you have not used fully.
>
> At times you are outgoing and friendly, but at other times you are cautious and reserved.

Most people find that nearly all of these descriptions fit them. This produces an appearance of content. The use of terms like *some, often, sometimes,* and *at times* helps to make these claims safe enough so that almost everyone will "see themselves" therein. Broad terms like *sexual issues, problems, outgoing,* and *reserved* also encourage a reader to find an interpretation that fits. But the claims don't conflict with any theory, so the astrological prediction is not contributing any content of importance. An astrological theory that made striking, easily checked, and uniformly correct predictions like these would be very impressive:

> This Thursday, you will be fired from your job.
>
> You will win the lottery on Friday of this week.
>
> You will suffer in a sudden, major ecological disaster on Saturday of this week.
>
> You will fall in love on Sunday of this week.

We do not have such theories.

Lack of precision

Precision generally increases the content of a theory and thus makes it a better theory. Suppose two theories make predictions that are consistent with each other, but one theory is more precise. For example, suppose that in three cases theory A predicts values of 10.77, 14.83, and 17.54, and theory B predicts values between 9 and 11, between 14 an 16, and between 17 and 19 in the same three cases. And suppose that we can measure outcomes accurately enough to see that theory A has predicted exactly the right values. Then, if the theories are otherwise on a par, it is much better to adopt theory A, because it will explain more. It can explain why the first value is 10.77 instead of 10.51, but theory B cannot do that. Theory A is more precise, so it is more likely to be falsified (a larger class of possible observations will falsify it), and hence its successes are more significant.

We have already noted the value of precision in the case of fingerprints. Because fingerprinting tells us in great detail what to expect in a clear fingerprint, it enables us to make many distinctions. This way we can eliminate a large class of possibilities.

ad hoc devices

Often theories start their histories as strong hypotheses with a clear, testable content but then are altered to accommodate data that falsify the original version of the theory. These alterations may be appropriate at first, but cumulatively they can erode the theory until there is no content left.

The ancient Greek astronomical theorist Eudoxus held that the stars and planets were attached to spheres, with the earth at the center, and that the rotation of these spheres accounted for the motions we observe in the sky. This theory had definite predictive content, and it turned out to be false—there was no way to fit the theory to the actual observations. Subsequent geocentric theories, such as Ptolemy's, developed some built-in way of accommodating data so that the theory fit a wide range of outcomes: They allowed for the possibility of *epicycles* on an orbit, circular additions to the principal motion around Earth. By the addition of epicycles (and the use of some other special techniques of measurement), Ptolemy was able to produce a more complicated table of planetary motion that fit the observations. When such devices for accommodating data are too flexible, however, the fundamental principles of the theory no longer make definite predictions. And Ptolemy's devices for building astronomical theory on circular motions became too flexible; his fundamental theory did not provide clear predictions because it allowed for too many possibilities. Epicycles could be added in an unlimited number of different ways, and they could thus be tailored to fit too many different observations.

This erosion of content can be linked to the use of *ad hoc* devices. If the way of accommodating data allows for the introduction of *ad hoc* devices like epicycles, then it also introduces a number of new things that are not explained:

Why is there an epicycle in that place rather than another?

Why does the epicycle have that size rather than some other size?

Nothing in the Ptolemaic system explains these things. Thus *ad hoc* devices are associated with two kinds of problems in theories. (1) When *ad hoc* devices are needed, the fundamental principles of the theory are not making specific prediction and explanation possible, and (2) each use of an *ad hoc* device introduces a number of new things that need to be explained. Sometimes an *ad hoc* addition can be an important way to preserve the best theory we have, but the cumulative effect of many such additions is to erode the explanatory efficacy of the theory.

A need for *ad hoc* devices shows a weakness in a theory's predictive and explanatory content, and *ad hoc* devices introduce a number of new, unexplained phenomena.

Vacuous explanations

Sometimes a theory is weak because it is the same as the data and consequently provides no explanation and no real understanding. Moliére's example remains the most famous. The learned doctor explains why opium causes sleep by pointing out its *virtus dormitiva*; but to say that something has a *virtus dormitiva* is the same thing as saying that it causes sleep. Technical terms are often necessary in theories, but we should make sure that they are not merely empty substitutes for real theory. When you hear an economist on TV "explain" the decline in stock prices by citing a slump in the market (and I have heard this pseudo-explanation more than once), it is time to turn off the television.

Scope

A theory should have scope. It should involve truly general patterns, so that it "economizes" and organizes our beliefs. A wide range of phenomena can be understood as instances of a single general principle if the theory has sufficient scope. Understanding in general involves organizing and linking beliefs, and this requires some principles with broad scope that can make such connections possible.

The power of Isaac Newton's fundamental ideas concerning gravity and motion becomes evident when we see how they explain the motion of both ordinary, terrestrial objects and planets and note that they can play a role in explaining the

CALVIN AND HOBBES. © Watterson. Reprinted with permission of UNIVERSAL PRESS SYNDICATE.

way temperature, volume, and pressure are related in gases. Increased scope also means increased content, which means increased liability to falsification. This is valuable, especially if the theory remains unfalsified. (Of course, Newton's theory eventually succumbed to falsification.)

Even a particular explanatory hypothesis can be more convincing if it plays a role in explaining several otherwise unconnected observations.

Theoretical Integration

A theory should mesh with other beliefs. The ultimate test of a theory is whether it plays a role in the best overall theory of everything. That means that it needs to be consistent with the other things one believes. It means that a theory is better if it can be seen as a consequence of some deeper theories, in the way that the laws governing the relationship of volume, pressure, and temperature in gases can be understood as consequences of theories of motion and molecular composition.

CALVIN AND HOBBES. © Watterson. Reprinted with permission of UNIVERSAL PRESS SYNDICATE.

We should be very skeptical of explanations that appeal to bizarre forces. When someone claims to bend spoons telepathically or to read minds, we should expect a trick, not a novel force. In these cases, it is difficult to see how to integrate these alleged powers into an understanding of how minds (or spoons) work. In the case of the spoons, we have no idea how mental activity could have a distant effect on matter of this kind. How would the thoughts connect with something material that could cause bending? What would carry this material change to the spoon? In the case of mind reading, it is difficult to see how the "mind reader" could have access to the neuronal activity of another individual and difficult to see how that neuronal activity could be "read" even if there were access. On the other hand, if something other than neuronal activity were to be transmitted, it would be by a very extraordinary force. Fortunately, we have people like the magician James Randi to provide us with an understanding of such phenomena by showing us how a magician can use ordinary forces to duplicate the tricks that look like spoon bending or mind reading.

"THE AMAZING RANDI"

The magician James Randi has duplicated the feats of many well-known "psychics." Uri Geller had made quite a reputation for himself, but James Randi was able to duplicate his feats, such as spoon bending and cup rattling, by ordinary tricks. (An excellent 1994 episode of the PBS program "Nova" shows some of James Randi's work in exposing such claims.)

This advice about theoretical integration must be taken with some caution, however. We do not wish to exclude all major theoretical developments on the ground that they do not mesh well with the theories we already have. Major change in theories must be possible. These issues are explored, through the extended consideration of an example, in the section on major change in astronomical theory. There you can get a fuller sense of the interplay between openness to theory change and the need to maintain theoretical integration.

The Theory Should Be Unfalsified

A theory is falsified when it makes a definite prediction and that prediction turns out to be false; and if a theory is falsified, we should not accept it. At least that is the simple version of the story.

If a theory is fairly specific, this simple version of the story works pretty well. If I believe that Mr. X is the biological father of baby Y, then I can predict that there will be a close genetic match. Observations that can now be done can sometimes falsify such a prediction by showing that there is no appropriate match between Mr. X and baby Y.

With very general theories, however, falsification is usually much less clearcut than this picture suggests. When Galileo observed the rough surface of the moon through his telescope, that observation seemed to falsify the older theory that claimed that celestial matter (such as the moon was thought to be made of) must always exist in the form of a perfect sphere. Questions of a kind that nearly always arise came up here.

> Was the observation really a result of features of the observer or features of the apparatus?
>
> What facts might explain the observation without a change in theory?
>
> Can the observation be accommodated by a small change in theory rather than a full abandonment of the theory?

Because of suspicion of the telescope and of Galileo, and because of people's desire to retain theories that seemed to provide them with an understanding of phenomena, many sought alternative explanations. It was suggested that celestial matter might have both some dark portions and some transparent portions and that therefore, what appeared to be mountains and valleys could be just the dark stuff mixed in with the transparent stuff within a perfect sphere. Such a revision could preserve the "perfect celestial sphere" aspect of the older theory, enabling people to hold on to the larger (geocentric) theory of which it was a part. Thus Galileo's observations did not definitively falsify the older theory.

Clear falsification via some small amount of data may be very difficult when a theory is very general. As in the case of the moon's matter, it is very often possible to come up with a way to accommodate a small amount of potentially troublesome data. Even if we can't accommodate such data immediately, we should be reluctant to give up a theory too quickly, before an adequate substitute is available. Thus, when a theory makes a prediction that turns out to be false, we need to consider what to do. In such cases, we should consider the ways in which the data can be accommodated, but we should always be ready to give up the theory when the data are sufficiently against it. We must avoid the temptation of adding excessive *ad hoc* hypotheses that accommodate the data but erode the predictive content of the theory.

In 1997 and 1998, astronomers were grappling with some troublesome findings. Their best theories and their best data about the evolution of the universe seemed to yield the conclusion that the universe is about ten billion years old. However, their best theories about the processes within stars indicated that some stars are about fifteen billion years old. Something was wrong. The astronomers needed to find a way to resolve this conflict by finding some extra factor that made the data fit better, by introducing some changes in existing theory, or by developing some entirely novel astronomical theories. In such a situation, we know that something in our theories is false, but often we cannot be sure how to revise our theories to fit our data. Ultimately, the theories that emerge from these processes are judged by their having the virtues we have discussed: They must explain observations in a way that is clear, general, and well integrated with other theories that we retain.

Scientific testing of theories, discussed in Chapter 9, is specifically designed to try to produce situations in which some theory is falsified. The problem of identifying the clear observational consequences of a theory is discussed again in connection with the consideration of scientific testing in that chapter. To justify acceptance of a theory, we must rule out alternative explanations of relevant phenomena by critical tests, if possible. This means it is necessary to identify alternative possible explanations and to devise tests that will distinguish among them. Critical tests—tests that can show a theory to be false—are not easy to devise; they involve many assumptions about the experimental situation. Hence, in deciding what theories are better, we also look for theories that are optimal in the other ways already mentioned. A theory with these other desirable features must still stand up to the best tests we can devise.

Alternatives Should Be Ruled Out

In our discussion of content, we mentioned the importance of "surprise value" in a theory we are considering. The surprise value of a theory can also be understood as a failure of the theories that are explanatory alternatives: Though these alternatives may explain many of the same things as the candidate theory, someone relying on those theories will be surprised. Our candidate theory predicts something that conflicts with expectations based on any of the explanatory alternatives, and the prediction turns out to be right. Sometimes this occurs in a critical experiment that yields an observation that is predicted by the candidate theory and that conflicts with the alternative theories. (We mentioned surprise value when discussing the need for *content* in a theory, because clear prediction requires clear content.)

A scientific theory becomes much more credible when (1) it makes a prediction that conflicts with predictions made by other theories, and (2) that prediction turns out to be right. The scientific theory then has valuable content. Einstein proposed a theory that predicted that the light from distant stars would bend in the strong gravitational field of the sun (or, to put it another way, that the space through which light travels would bend in the vicinity of the sun). This meant that an observation of those stars would show a predictable deviation when the sun was at or near the path of light from the star to us. This deviation existed and was not explained at all by the principal alternatives to Einstein's theory, thus providing strong reason to accept Einstein's account. The clear content gives the theory predictive and explanatory power that helps to establish the theory, and that content makes the theory useful once it is accepted. The more precise the predictions of a theory are, the more this power is enhanced, as long as some of those predictions conflict with alternative theories and turn out to be true. Einstein's theory and Newton's theory predict similar values over a wide range of circumstances, so it was necessary to look to the extreme situations, in which they diverged in an observable way, to show that Einstein's theory made better predictions. The strong gravitational field of the sun provided one such extreme situation.

Of course in our discussion of the need for a theory to be unfalsified, we considered the problem in finding and accepting simple falsifying evidence. We rarely have ideal cases of falsification but, rather, a question of balancing considerations of content, scope, and theoretical integration as we revise our theories to fit the data (i.e., as we alter our theories so that the revised theory is not falsified by observations). Theories are often *ruled out* because they have become cumbersome, loaded with *ad hoc* devices needed to make the theory fit observation, rather than because there is a critical falsifying experiment. This is explored in more detail in the section at the end of this chapter on the Copernican revolution, to provide a better idea of how such balancing can proceed.

EXERCISE 7A

In July 1996, TWA Flight 800 exploded near Long Island. In November 1996, officials of the National Traffic Safety Board released information about the state of the investigation. Read the following report and answer the questions that follow (adapted from a *New York Times* report).

Investigations Inconclusive in Flight 800 Explosion

November 4, 1996—Nearly all of the remains of TWA Flight 800 have now been recovered from the ocean floor. Investigators say that they still cannot determine what caused the plane to explode and plummet into the sea.

Senior National Transportation Safety Board investigators have recovered so much of the aircraft that they can no longer run a metal rod through the reassembled wreckage. This means they cannot find a plausible path for a missile through the aircraft. It now appears much less likely that a missile caused the explosion.

Investigators also have no direct evidence of either a bomb blast or mechanical failure. If no other cause is found, they indicate that they will have to conclude that mechanical failure is the source of the explosion.

The idea that a rocket attack caused the explosion had been one of the working theories because more than twenty credible eyewitnesses reported seeing streaks of light rising in the sky moments before the Boeing 747 exploded and crashed. Nevertheless, a senior criminal investigator indicates that if a rocket attack had occurred, "we would have found something, some indicator, that would carry us on in that belief. At this point, now that 95 percent of the plane has been recovered and analyzed and we haven't found anything pointing to a missile, you have to start wondering and seriously doubt that this is the cause."

What are the three theories of how the plane exploded? The missile theory has consequences that are thought to be false. What are the false consequences that undermine that theory?

There is lack of direct evidence for the theory that there was a bomb blast, and there is a lack of direct evidence for the theory that there was a mechanical failure. On the basis of this, the investigators seem to conclude that there was no bomb blast, but they do not conclude that there was no mechanical failure. Why?

Criticism of an Inference to the Best Explanation

We can apply our evaluative criteria for theories in a way that will yield more specific guidelines about how to criticize theories. First let's take a look at a general pattern for inference to the best explanation (IBE).

P1   I observe **O**.

P2   **E** is [part of] the best explanation I can find for why I observe **O** (i.e., for why P1 is true).

∴   **E**.

One explanation is better than another insofar as it contributes to a system of beliefs that is better able to provide an understanding of what we observe. But we can break that down into specific components that can be criticized in the evaluation of an explanation.

To criticize a particular case of IBE:

> Criticize P1 in one of these ways:
>
>> P1 is false. You didn't observe **O**. (*P1 is incorrect.*)
>>
>> There is additional evidence **O'**, and **E** is not [part of] the best explanation for observing **O** + **O'**. (*P1 is inadequate.*)
>
> Criticize **E** directly in one of these ways:
>
>> If **E** is a general claim, give a counter-example to **E**.
>>
>> Derive consequences of **E**, and show that those consequences do not obtain. (Do an experiment, make more observations, or use information you already have to show that the consequences are false.) That is, falsify **E** by devising a critical test of **E**.
>
> Criticize P2.
>
> Show that there is *a better explanation* than **E**, or at least show that **E** has many explanatory weaknesses, so that alternatives should be sought out and considered. Possible weaknesses (though none is decisive):
>
>> **E** *is not well integrated* with beliefs we already have; **E** appeals to special forces or bizarre processes, or it conflicts with particular facts that we are sure of.
>>
>> **E** *does not have explanatory scope.* An explanation with greater generality explains more in a unified way. The goal of explanation is a unified understanding, and bringing many phenomena under a single generalization makes a unified understanding possible.
>>
>> **E** *lacks explanatory content.* More specifically, look for these characteristics:
>>
>>> **E** is unclear.
>>>
>>> **E** is untestable (unfalsifiable).
>>>
>>> **E** needs to be supplemented by too many *ad hoc* devices in explaining or predicting particular observations.
>>>
>>> **E** is not as precise as alternative explanations.
>>>
>>> **E** is vacuous. (Vacuity can also be seen as the ultimate failure of scope: The "explanation" is merely a restatement of the thing "explained.")

Examples

Criticize P1 (the observational premise).

> Example: *I just saw Stanley carrying a whole bunch of my books into his room. He must be stealing stuff from my room.*
>
> P1 is false. You didn't observe **O**.
>
> *Stanley wasn't carrying your books. Remember that Stanley is taking exactly the same courses that you are. He was carrying* his *books, but he is using the same texts that you are using.*
>
> There is additional evidence **O'**, and **E** is not [part of] the best explanation for observing **O + O'**. (P1 is inadequate.)
>
> *Come and look in your room. The pipes have burst and your bookshelf is getting flooded. Stanley was rescuing your books, not stealing them.*

Criticize **E** directly.

> Example: *Whenever I go to the grocery store, all of the sale items are sold out. They must never really stock the things that they put into their ads.*
>
> If **E** is a general claim, give a counter-example to **E**.
>
> *When I was there on Tuesday, I found plenty of the potato chips that were advertised at a special sale price.*
>
> Derive consequences of **E**, and show that those consequences do not obtain. (Do an experiment, make more observations, or use information you already have to show that the consequences are false.) That is, falsify **E**.
>
> *If your theory is right, then we should be able to go to the grocery store on the first morning of the sale period and find that it does not have the items that it has advertised. So we will go on Sunday morning to check on what the store has advertised as specials in the Sunday paper. If it has the sale items, that will falsify the theory that it doesn't even stock the sale items.*

Show that there is *a better explanation* than **E**, or at least show that **E** has many explanatory weaknesses, so that alternatives should be sought out and considered.

> Example: *The other night, I dreamed that my sister was walking down a long aisle in a white dress. The next day she called to tell me that she was engaged. I'm convinced that there is a telepathic connection between us.*
>
> **E** *is not well integrated* with beliefs we already have; **E** appeals to special forces or bizarre processes, or it conflicts with particular facts that we are sure of.
>
> *The apparently prophetic dream can be explained in some more mundane ways. The dreamer may have many dreams, and each of those is subject to many interpretations. The fact that one interpretation of one dream is related in some way to something that happens some time soon afterward could be just a coincidence. Of course, if the dreamer knows his sister well, this dream may also be due to the dreamer's having recognized (or at least*

responded to) real signs that an engagement was about to occur. An explanation in terms of coincidence or ordinary processes is always preferable to one that posits a bizarre and incomprehensible force, if there is a more mundane explanation available.

Example: *When I was walking across the Quad, a strange thing happened. A trash can just a few feet ahead of me shook, even though no one else was around. There must be some special force associated with that trash can that can make it shake without any external cause.*

E *does not have explanatory scope.* An explanation with greater generality explains more in a unified way. The goal of explanation is a unified understanding, and bringing many phenomena under a single generalization makes a unified understanding possible.

There are many common processes that might make a trash can shake: a squirrel inside, its resting on a paving block that shakes when someone steps on another, nearby paving block, etc. These other explanations connect with processes that can be used to explain many ordinary events, so they are to be preferred over an explanation that appeals to very special, local processes.

E *lacks explanatory content.* More specifically, look for these characteristics:

E is unclear.

Example: *Men and women differ in their mental abilities.*

This lacks explanatory content because it does not make it clear whether the difference is a difference in averages, a universal difference, or what, and there is no specification of what mental abilities are being tested or how those abilities might be connected with testable performance. As a result, we do not know how to apply this to particular cases to get a real explanation of any observation.

E is untestable (unfalsifiable).

Example: *There is a major conspiracy among software companies to keep their prices up. Every attempt to find evidence of collusion has failed, showing just how clever they are at covering their trail.*

This theory has built in a way to nullify all possible counter-evidence.

E needs to be supplemented by too many *ad hoc* devices in explaining or predicting particular observations.

Example: *Near the beginning of the twentieth century, Hendrik Lorentz found some mathematical transformations that could be added to Newton's theory to accommodate some observations that did not fit the theory. There was no adequate accompanying explanation for why these transformations applied.*

Without a theory, these are ad hoc *devices that need explanation. Why these values? Why any transformations at all? These new questions needed answering if the theory was to continue to be acceptable. (Einstein's theory explained the new observations in a way that was theoretically integrated.)*

E is not as precise as alternative explanations.

Example: *God created each species of animal.*

This theory does not in itself explain the limitations on the historical sequence of animals that is observed. Evolution predicts that you will not find that one species comes into existence without there being any similar species in existence before that time. According to evolutionary theory, we should be very surprised by a situation in which some canines came into existence at the time of dinosaurs, and then all canines died out, then wolves came into existence hundreds of millions of years later (with no more immediate canine predecessors). No prediction as precise as this comes from the theory of special creation, so evolutionary theory explains much more.

E is vacuous. (Vacuity is the ultimate failure of scope: The "explanation" is merely a restatement of the thing "explained.")

Example: *The economic upturn in the United States explains American businesses' success this year.*

EXERCISE 7B

Evaluate the explanations offered in these short passages. If there is an argument, indicate what the conclusion is. If there is an explanation that is not a vacuous explanation, indicate what alternative explanations should be considered. Why might the alternative explanation be a better explanation?

1. Most men who have never been married are obsessed with sex. This is explained by the fact that that's the way bachelors are.

2. All of my friends taking PHI 107 or PHI 191 are getting bad grades. That should convince anyone that philosophy is a very difficult subject.

3. [For this example, assume that the first sentence is true.] Psychiatrists have a higher suicide rate than any other occupational group. It must be that many emotionally unstable individuals are attracted to psychiatry.

4. Professor Benson is an excellent teacher. When we look at the evaluations from his students, we can see this clearly. The students say that his class presentations are difficult to follow, and they never get really interested in class discussion. Consequently, they give him a low rating. But we know that this means that they have to work on their own to learn the material, and getting students to work on their own is one of the most important goals of college teaching, even if students don't appreciate it. Looking through the other teaching evaluations, we can see many different ways in which our faculty excel in their teaching.

5. According to a leading economic analyst, stock prices went up earlier this year because of a surge in the market. This phenomenon is well known among stock analysts, and it can be identified with considerable precision.

THE COPERNICAN REVOLUTION

In this section we will explore a major theoretical change in a way that will illustrate the operation of some of the criteria we developed for the evaluation of theories. Criteria such as *coherence with other theories* and *contribution to overall explanatory power* are difficult to illustrate in the context of brief examples. Consideration of a major change in theory, a change of the sort that Thomas S. Kuhn has called a "paradigm shift" (see his book *The Structure of Scientific Revolutions*), shows much better how we must integrate many theories in an overall view that optimizes explanatory power.

Consideration of a major theoretical change also provides us with some ideas about what kinds of things can motivate major changes in belief. When our beliefs don't fit together, we can be led to revise fundamental beliefs when doing so becomes the only reasonable basis for an integrated system of beliefs.

Background

Aristotle (384–322 B.C.) was guided by a simple and elegant ideal account of natural motion on earth and in the skies, derived largely from **Plato**'s ideas. It begins with the idea that the earth lies at the center of the universe. Sublunar material, the stuff we see here on earth, was thought to have a natural resting place, the center of the universe. The tendency to go toward this natural resting place was assumed to explain why ordinary matter falls to earth. The matter of the heavens, on the other hand, was said to be unchanging and perfect. Such unchanging stuff has no natural destination where its motion will cease, and nothing can externally influence its motion. It moves in a circle, a shape that is perfectly understandable because there are no eccentricities—no curves, corners, or pivots—and "every destination is a fresh starting point." Thus every heavenly body must go in a perfect circle around the earth.

But even in Aristotle's day, it was known that things could not be so simple. The planets deviate from the uniform path followed by the stars. (The word *planet* itself is derived from a Greek word meaning "wanderer.") This deviation falsifies the simple theory; it needs an account, and accounting for the motion of the planets is one of the fundamental problems of astronomy. **Eudoxus**, like Aristotle a student of Plato, elaborated the theory to explain the wandering of the planets. In this more developed view (adopted by Aristotle), the heavenly bodies are fixed to transparent spheres, the stars being on the outermost of these. The inner spheres have their own rotational motions, added to the motions caused by the influence of the rotation of the outer spheres. The planets, attached to inner spheres, show this composite motion.

The theory proposed by Eudoxus has a number of virtues. It provides a nice model of nested spheres to enable us to picture and understand the celestial arrangement. It preserves the fundamental Aristotelian principles concerning motion, while at the same time fitting the actual observations more adequately. There are now more motions to explain: We might well wonder why each sphere is where it is and why it has the particular motion it has. More such questions are raised in the new theory, but the added complexity is not great, and it is needed to fit the data. We could still preserve the fundamental account of motion (circular motion) by allowing now that the motions of celestial spheres influence each other.

Over subsequent centuries, difficulties were found in fitting the observations even to Eudoxus's system of spheres, and **Ptolemy** (A.D. 85–165) proposed a more flexible system for accounting for the observed motions. The planets followed circular orbits, but with some modifications from the original view. Orbits could have epicycles, smaller circular motions around points lying on the basic orbit. In addition, the center of the main orbit might not be precisely at the center of the earth. And the planetary speed might not be uniform around the center of its orbit. By locating the epicycles, the orbital center, and the variation in velocity, an astronomer could develop an account of a planet's motion. There was no way to fit all of this into a nice picture, like the system of embedded spheres that Eudoxus proposed, but one could get the data to come out right. In 1252, in Toledo (Spain), a new set of tables based on the Ptolemaic methods was published, continuing a long tradition of fine-tuning theory to account for ever more observations.

Elements of the Pre-Copernican Consensus

Stellar

The earth is at the center of all stellar motion. (People are at the center of the universe.) All stellar motion is based on circular motion.

The stars are on a fixed sphere that rotates around the earth.

The earth does not move. It neither rotates, nor moves out of the center of the universe.

There is no change among the stars.

Planetary, solar, lunar

The planets have the earth at the "center" of their orbits.

The orbits are constructed on Ptolemaic principles—circles with epicycles (and other devices for accommodating calculations).

There is no change within the planetary–solar–lunar environment.

Earthly

Account of why things fall to earth.

Comets are meteorological (atmospheric) phenomena.

Human

People are at the center of a universe that was designed for them.

Copernicus

In the 1500s, **Copernicus** (1473–1543) criticized the Ptolemaic methods and proposed a radical alternative. His criticism is very instructive, because he did not rely on data that conflicted with the prior accounts. Rather, he criticized the Ptolemaic astronomy because it did not provide a realizable model by which to understand the planetary motions.

> It is as though, in his pictures, an artist were to bring together hands, feet, head and other limbs from quite different models, each part being admirably drawn in itself, but without any common relation to a single body; since they would in no way match one another, the result would be a monster rather than a man. (From the preface of Copernicus' *De Revolutionibus Orbium Caelestium* (1543), as translated in *The Fabric of the Heavens,* Stephen Toulmin and June Goodfield, New York: Harper and Row, 1965, p. 170.)

The Ptolemaic system had got so far from the original simple model that it could no longer provide a unified model at all. In addition, the Ptolemaic system required a large number of deviations from perfect circularity, with no way to explain why the deviations occurred in just the places they did and with just the magnitude they had. Thus its tables provided a bag of tricks for calculating where celestial bodies could be sighted, but it had lost its explanatory power because there was no way to integrate the calculating tricks into a real account of how the celestial bodies were moving and why they moved in this way. The Ptolemaic model had lost its ability to provide a real understanding of celestial phenomena; it offered only an accounting tool.

Copernicus proposed a different system, based on circular motion. He proposed that the sun was at the center of the universe, with most other bodies, *including the earth,* circling around it. The moon was said to orbit the earth. This remarkable new view had precedents: Some ancient Greeks had believed that the earth moved, and just a century earlier, Nicholas of Cusa had suggested this possibilty. But this was not a common view, and there were a number of reasons for resisting Copernican theory.

1. If the earth moves, why can't we feel it?

    Although the idea that the earth moves had been proposed before, and the ancient Greek Aristarchos and others had answered this question, the idea that there is this unfelt motion is certainly an obstacle to accepting views that are not geocentric. The absence of a feeling of motion and contemplation of the very idea that the earth is not stable work together to make the Copernican idea difficult to accept.

2. The Copernican system has no single center of motion. Why would there be two centers of motion, the sun and the earth? What purpose could that serve? How could it be explained?

    Asking for a purpose for the celestial arrangement may seem very out of place to us now. But if you see the universe as a place designed for people, then this question makes much more sense.

3. There is a problem of stellar parallax.

    Tycho Brahe, a remarkable astronomer who lived just after Copernicus, noted that the Copernican claim that the earth moves leads to a problematic prediction. If the earth travels a distance of more than 100 million miles around the sun, then it seems that the angle of observation on the stars should change, so that the constellations would change shape at least a little as our angle for viewing them changed, just as our perspective on a building changes as we go past it. But no such change could be observed, even by the best of methods. Thus it would seem that there must be a fixed spatial relationship to the stars, requiring a fixed earth, and this would refute the Copernican theory.

4. If Venus and the earth are going around the sun as Copernicus claims, then sometimes Venus is approximately four times farther away than it is at other times. But then we should observe some variation in brightness if Venus is producing its own light, but we do not experience that much change.

5. If it is reflecting light from the sun, Venus should have phases like the moon. Sometimes the side that is lit by the sun faces us, and sometimes it faces away. But Venus always looks (more or less) like a bright, round star.

6. If Copernicus is right about the planetary relationships, then the apparent disk size of Mars should vary by a significant factor also. (According to Copernicus, sometimes it is, relatively speaking, close, and sometimes it is very far away.) But the observed disk size doesn't vary.

7. Calculations based on the Copernican system are no better than those based on the Ptolemaic. No great advantage in predictive precision can be gained, and in fact the Copernican system is really less accurate in many cases.

8. We would need a new theory of why things fall to earth. Once we adopt the Copernican view, we can no longer use Aristotle's account of why things fall to earth. In fact, it seems that a Copernican should expect things to fall toward the sun when we drop them, but that is obviously not what we observe. Thus a Copernican is left with no explanation at all of why things fall to earth, and with no understanding of earthly matter, its motions, or its goals.

9. The geocentric theory is also anthropocentric, and if we lose that feature of our theory, we lose a great deal in our understanding of the world. Why would God put people somewhere other than at the center of the universe? This needs explanation. If people are not at the center of God's plan, then what are we and why do we exist?

10. The Holy Scripture says that, in an extraordinary event, the sun stood still; and it says that the earth is stable in its place in the heavens, and other, similar things. These claims would make no sense if the sun is ordinarily still and the earth is always moving.

Although some of these concerns may seem a bit odd to us now, they are all real problems that require some sort of answer before the heliocentric theory can be accepted. And because the Copernican theory offered no obvious advantage, it should not seem too odd that there was a strong resistance to it.

But Copernicus's powerful misgivings about the Ptolemaic system motivated him to look for a more satisfying explanatory theory. (Copernicus also had some mystical motivations for heliocentrism, the centrality of the sun.) The Ptolemaic system did not provide a unified model of planetary motion. In addition, its flexibility in making predictions undermined its explanatory value. The system of epicycles and other devices could be manipulated to account for almost anything that might be observed in the skies. This may seem like a strength at first, but some reflection should make it clear that this is a serious defect in an explanatory theory. Ordinarily, if it is to have some value in explaining why A happened rather than B, a theory must be able to tell us that A *will* happen rather than B. But for almost any possible observations A and B, the Ptolemaic system had resources for fitting either observation, A or B, into its system by marshaling a suitable system of epicycles (and other devices). Because of this, the Ptolemaic system could no longer *explain* why A happened rather than B. It was losing explanatory content as it elaborated the devices that made it possible to accommodate all of the data. Although Plato and Aristotle had proposed a simple, unifying idea of circular paths around the earth, that model could not be made to fit the data. The theory was clear and testable, and it failed the test, because the planetary motions did not conform. The elaborations needed to accommodate the planetary motions ultimately undermined the theory by making almost any observation consistent with it. The theory had lost its content because it no longer ruled out very many possibilities.

In the last half of the 1500s, two great scientists responded to Copernicus.

Tycho Brahe (1546–1601) was an extraordinary astronomical observer. His meticulous investigations found no stellar parallax, so he was responsible for keeping this problem for the Copernican view in the forefront. He also established some things that were inconsistent with the more traditional view. The followers of Aristotle viewed the celestial bodies as unchanging objects made of a perfect material (unlike the material of earthly objects that change and degenerate). Observations of a comet and a supernova shook this idea, because these bodies demonstrated an unanticipated changeablity in the heavens. Brahe's observations and calculations established that both of these were indeed celestial and not meteorological phenomena. (That is, they were farther away than the moon, rather than being atmospheric phenomena.)

Brahe also contributed his own geocentric theory, with the earth at the center of the orbits of the sun and the moon, but with Venus orbiting the sun. This theory had multiple centers of motion, so it shared some of the problems of the Copernican view, but it managed to avoid most of those difficulties while positing a realizable explanatory model for planetary motion.

Johannes Kepler was a student of Brahe, but he was willing to follow Copernicus's conjecture that the earth moved around the sun. Using Brahe's data, Kepler was able to find a variation that fit the data better than the Copernican account could. Kepler proposed that the planetary orbits were *ellipses* rather than circles. By doing so, he was able to accommodate the data about as well as the Ptolemaic system could. In fact, Kepler was able to uncover three significant mathematical regularities in the planetary orbits.

1. The orbits are ellipses with the sun at one focus of the ellipse.

2. Let Y_X stand for the length of time it takes a planet X to orbit the sun (the length of its year). Let R_X stand for the average radius of its orbit. Then

   Y_X^2 is proportional to R_X^3.

   In other words, if we consider any two planets, say Venus and Mars, then

   $Y_V^2/R_V^3 = Y_M^2/R_M^3$.

3. If we look at the (pie wedge) area swept out by a planet as it orbits part of the way around the sun, we will find that the planet sweeps out equal areas in equal times, even though the orbit is elliptical and the distance from the sun varies greatly. This means that the planet's orbital velocity is less when it is farther from the sun.

We will return later to assess the significance of these generalizations, which are usually called **Kepler's laws**.

Galileo

In the early 1600s, **Galileo Galilei** (1564–1642) constructed a vigorous defense of the Copernican system and developed the resources for answering the objections to Copernicus's view that we mentioned earlier. The major resource was the telescope, a device that Galileo probably invented for himself in 1609. (Others invented it independently at about the same time.) Galileo turned the telescope to the skies and made several discoveries.

1. There are many more stars in the sky than are observable with the unaided eye. The Milky Way observed in the sky is (as many suspected) a great number of stars that are not individually distinguishable with the unaided eye.

   These discoveries had some significance that might not be immediately obvious. The traditional view included the idea that the universe is made for people and the idea that the stars are on a fixed sphere that rotates around the earth.

   a. Stars that are observable only with a telescope raise the question of what purpose they could serve in a universe made for people.

   b. In addition, the observation of additional stars suggests (though it does not prove) that the stars extend out from the earth at various distances rather than being on a fixed sphere. This is a very different picture from the more traditional one.

   c. In particular, if the stars extend out infinitely, then the whole idea of the earth's being at the center of the universe collapses. There is no center if the universe extends infinitely in all directions.

   d. The earth *could* still be the center of all of the universe's motions. But Galileo also noted that if the stars are very distant from us, then their daily revolutions around the earth must take place at an astonishing speed. If they extend out infinitely, the idea that there is a daily revolution of the stars makes little sense; it would then seem that the earth must rotate.

2. When observed through Galileo's telescope, a star's diameter was not magnified.

   This seems to mean that the apparent diameter is no indication of the real diameter. We are not really viewing the disk size of the star but only a spot (or smear) of light that comes from the star. This tells us that the stars may be very bright and very, very far away. (If we were seeing the true disk size and they were so far away, then they would have to be extraordinarily huge to produce the disk we see. But if we are not seeing the true disk size anyway, then great distances are possible.)

Great distance for the stars will solve the problem of stellar parallax. If the stars are so far away that the distance the earth moves is insignificant compared to their distance from the earth, then the parallax would be too slight to be observable. The stars' great distance also suggests that the Earth must rotate; otherwise, the daily motion of stars at such a great distance would be imponderably fast.

3. The moon has craters and mountains. (Galileo showed this by actually measuring the heights of shadows and noting their shift as the angle of the sun changed.)

    This discovery undermined the idea that all heavenly bodies are perfect spheres made of an unchanging, perfect matter. The moon now seemed much more like the earth in its material composition.

4. Sunspots.

    Like the craters on the moon, these show that the heavenly bodies are not made of the kind of matter previously thought. Like the supernovas and comets (documented by Brahe), sunspots exemplify *change* in the heavens.

5. Four moons of Jupiter.

    The fact that moons orbit Jupiter shows that the earth is not the only center of celestial motion. Again, this reinforces the idea that the earth is not a unique place in the universe but, rather, shares various characteristics with other places. In particular, it is only one of many centers of revolution.

6. Venus has phases.

    The pattern of these phases shows pretty convincingly that Venus circles the sun, reflecting the sun's light. This resolves two of the problems mentioned before. Venus has phases, and it is a crescent when it is closest to us and a full face when farthest away. That is why it always has approximately the same brightness, even though its distance varies considerably.

Note that no single discovery here requires total abandonment of the view previously held. For each, one has several choices. One can question the discovery. ("Do those little dots of light in that funny device really mean that?!") One can modify the older theory slightly, to accommodate that discovery. Or one can write off the discovery as an anomaly that will be explained later.

Let's look at the moons of Jupiter as a particular case. What basis would one have for accepting what Galileo claimed about the moons of Jupiter?

As we have already noted, when Galileo first observed the moons of Jupiter in his telescope, he saw a pattern of spots around Jupiter that he thought was due to moons orbiting Jupiter. The prevailing geocentric theory included the conflicting principle that the earth is the only center of celestial revolution. Because the geocentric theory was part of a developed understanding of the place of people in the universe and the nature of celestial motion, people were very reluctant to accept Galileo's account of what he saw. Accepting Galileo's claims would mean giving up this developed theory and losing the understanding of the universe that it seemed to provide.

The earlier, geocentric theory had seemed to provide a way of understanding the apparent motion of the planets and stars. A claim that conflicts with such a general theory needs careful examination, and it is not likely to be accepted if accepting it means abandoning the principal means of understanding some significant range of phenomena. Some people doubted that Galileo saw the spots, assuming that he was mistaken, or even lying, about what appeared through the telescope. Many doubted Galileo's claim about the cause of his telescopic observations, suspecting that the telescope was misleading and that the pattern of light spots might be produced by something other than moons around Jupiter (stars behind Jupiter, atmospheric phenomena, reflections on the lens, and so on). Some denied that evidence gathered through a telescope was significant, noting the reflections, distortions, and other factors that interfere with telescopic observation. A few observations are not enough to overthrow a powerfully explanatory theory.

Of course, it was also possible to modify the older theory without completely abandoning it. Tycho Brahe had proposed a system with two centers of motion. In his system, the earth was still at the center of the universe, with the sun and stars going around it. But the sun was also a center of motion for the planets. Adding one more center of motion (Jupiter) is not such a drastic change from this, and it preserves all of the rest of the understanding that goes with the geocentric picture. We would have the problem of understanding why there are three centers of motion in the universe, but we would retain the view of people's primacy in the universe, our understanding of the stars, and the Aristotelian theory of motion.

Each of Galileo's discoveries could be accommodated by making such changes in the geocentric theory, but taken together, they significantly weaken the unified understanding that had been the merit of the original geocentric picture. Nevertheless, this does not conclusively overthrow the geocentric picture. Only when the astronomical problems with heliocentrism were answered could we really replace the geocentric view, and the problems of understanding motion and understanding people's place in the universe remained even then. Astronomical discoveries advanced the heliocentric case with increasing accuracy, but Newton's laws really settled the matter. They give a general account of motion, they explain why Kepler's laws of planetary motion hold, and they even explain other, very different phenomena, such as the relationship of temperature, pressure, and volume in confined gases. They enable us to make very precise (highly falsifiable, yet unfalsified—for a while at least) predictions.

Thus in this case, it was eventually necessary to set aside the dominant astronomical theory: Reasons that had long been accepted for thinking that the earth was the center of everything were overturned by a wide range of problematic observations and, more important, by an explanatory theory that combines great generality (with predictions involving many seemingly disparate phenomena) with very specific explanatory and predictive precision. As a consequence, a new understanding of the position of people in the universe had to be developed along with a new understanding of the planets.

In brief, we can say now that Galileo's suggestion that Jupiter had moons became more compelling when it could be seen as a part of a view that provided a better overall explanation of observations of celestial motion and thus a better understanding of celestial motion. It became even more firmly established when it was shown to fit into a theory with broader scope that provided a deeper understanding of motion and gravitation.

CHAPTER SUMMARY

Evaluating Explanations, Hypotheses, and Theories

To the greatest extent possible, an explanatory hypothesis or theory should exceed rival explanations in its possession of these virtues:

> Having **content**, being testable (being falsifiable in principle)
>> having adequately clear terms
>> we can imagine what observation would show it false (though we won't observe that if the theory is true)—that is, it is falsifiable in principle, and thus testable
>> explaining without the help of *ad hoc* aids that dilute content and that would require further explanation of their own (avoiding epicycles or the attribution of other special features that accommodate observation but are not otherwise theoretically motivated)
>> having precision (increasing testability)
>
> Being **unfalsified**, fitting with observations
>
> Having **scope**, generality; explains more cases, is more testable
>
> Being **integrated** with the developed system of beliefs, conservative
>
> **Alternative explanations** of the phenomena should be **ruled out** (or be weaker with respect to the other virtues)

EXERCISE 7C

In each of these examples, an explanation is offered or reported. Respond to these items:

(a) What is being explained, and what is being offered as an explanation?
(b) What alternative explanations should be considered? (Try to give at least one.)
(c) What additional information (if any) would help us decide which explanation is correct? Indicate briefly how we could get the information.
(d) Give an explanation that is clearly *worse* than the one offered here. Explain why it is worse.

1. Americans show low voter turnout for elections, so Americans must not be very concerned about the welfare of their nation.

2. Late one sunny afternoon, police came upon a one-car accident near a rural road. The car had run off the road on a gentle curve and turned over into a

ditch. A man inside the car was dead, and a woman was lying dead about fifteen yards from the car. Police theorized that the woman had been injured in the car but then had walked away until she collapsed from her injuries and died.

3. On a certain South Pacific island, nearly all of the natives have lice. In fact, the people who do not have lice are all very unhealthy. The natives believe that lice are a source of good health.

4. People often take some of the consequences of evolutionary theory for granted, and because of this, they neglect some of its virtues. Why don't we find cases in which two closely related species whose periods of existence are separated by a long interval of time? For example, why don't we find some animal like zebras existing with the dinosaurs and dying off millions of years before other horse-like animals appear? As far as I can see, creationists have no way of explaining this, but it is a straightforward consequence of evolutionary theory that such cases would have to be extraordinarily rare.

5. [From a "person-on-the-street" interview in the *San Francisco Chronicle,* February 25, 1990] When a baby is born and you spank it on the bottom, it cries. How would it know to cry if it didn't know about pain from another life? How would it know how to react to the feeling of pain? To me that's some kind of proof that a person has lived before. Crying is a natural reaction because of previous lives where the person learned to cry.

CHAPTER 8

GENERALIZATION AND CAUSAL INFERENCE

This chapter will consider the justification of some common types of beliefs: generalizations based on observation of individual instances, and causal claims. We will see that the best way to evaluate the justification of such beliefs is to use the model of inference to the best explanation (IBE), which we have already developed. In the case of causal claims, we often use statistical information in justifying the claim, so it will also be useful to look at some of the problems that commonly arise in evaluating statistical justifications for causal claims.

ARGUMENTS THAT GENERALIZE

Inference to the best explanation justifies belief in a theory or hypothesis on the grounds that it is part of the best explanation of what is observed. In many cases of claims that we would not ordinarily think of as theories, the claims are also justified because they are part of the best explanation of what is observed. Consider the belief in a general claim that has held for all observed cases—for example, that all cats meow. On a preliminary basis, the argument for this belief could be represented in this way:

> P1   All observed A are B.   All observed cats meow (are meowers).
>
> ∴ C   All A are B.   ∴ All cats meow.

This inference seems reasonable when the conclusion is that all cats meow. This process, extrapolating from limited experience to general beliefs that go beyond our experience, is certainly an important part of the development of our system of beliefs. These general beliefs can then serve as a basis for our expectations about cats yet to be observed.

The argument pattern is evidently not deductively valid, however, and in some cases it is even a foolish inference.

> Every doctor I have seen has been a graduate of an American medical school. So every doctor is a graduate of an American medical school.

Every observed moment of my life has been followed by further living.
So I am immortal.

Every observed moment of my life has been before 2020.
So every moment of my life will be before 2020.

Every person I have seen so far today has been female.
So every person I see today will be female.

The best way to understand when this kind of inference is justified is to evaluate it as a case of IBE in which the premise about the explanation has been left implicit. The argument to evaluate is this:

P1   All observed A are B.

P2   C is [part of] the best explanation for P1.

∴   C   All A are B.

At first this may seem an odd way to think about such cases. *Don't we just generalize on the basis of what we observe? What does explanation have to do with it?* We may form habits and expectations based on prior experience without reflecting on the justification of our expectations. Yet once we begin to focus on the question of what *justifies* the generalizations that express these expectations, the criteria for evaluating cases of IBE come to the fore, providing just the right standards of evaluation. In each of the "foolish" cases above, there is a plausible alternative explanation for the truth of the premise, and so we are not inclined to accept the indicated conclusion. The indicated conclusion is not the best explanation for why the premise is true.

For example, suppose that I observe a few birds of a new species—call them "florks"—and I find that all of them that I observe are white and have livers. Now consider two conclusions:

All florks are white.

All florks have livers.

The first of these conclusions is not very well supported by the observations made, but the second is virtually certain to be true, given my observations. Why should these cases be different if the number of observed florks is the same in both cases? The conclusion that all florks are white is not well supported, because there are many other plausible explanations of why all of the observed florks are white, explanations that would allow the possibility of non-white florks. Perhaps

All florks around here are white (but not all florks are white).

All mature florks are white (but not all florks are white), and I observed only mature florks.

It is just a coincidence that the florks I found were all white. There is actually considerable variation in flork color.

These hypotheses are all plausible explanations of the uniformity in my observations. Thus the explanation that all florks are white is not well justified because it is not clear that it is the best explanation of the observed uniformity. Note, however, that no such plausible alternatives exist in the case of the hypothesis that all florks have livers. Because this is a feature of deeper anatomy, it is not very plausible to think that there will be regional variation within a species, or that only mature florks have livers, or that the uniformity among the observed florks is just a coincidence. Just one flork liver is pretty convincing evidence that all florks have livers (and it even offers evidence that all birds have livers, so strong is our theoretically grounded expectation of uniformity). We can rule out alternative hypotheses right away in the case of the conclusion that all florks have livers.

We are here discussing the *justification* of beliefs. We are not saying that people must actively consider alternative hypotheses in coming to have such beliefs. People may have these beliefs because they develop habits or expectations after they observe a number of similar cases. After observing several white florks, I may come to expect the next florks I see to be white. This expectation is not self-justifying, however, and if we ask when such beliefs are justified, then we are led to evaluate the belief by the standards of inference to the best explanation. A general belief is justified if it is part of the best explanation of what is observed, and a particular belief (for example, that the next flork I observe will be white) is justifiable if it follows from some justified general belief.

When speaking of drawing general conclusions from regularities in our observations, we often speak of *sampling* from a *target population*. In the example we are considering, the target population is all florks; we are considering the conclusion that all florks are white. The sample is the observed florks. Judging the inference by the standard of IBE provides a guide for deciding when a sample is too small to justify generalizing about the target population. The sample of florks I imagined is too small to support the generalization that all florks are white, because other explanations of what I observed have merit. In particular, if I observed only a few florks, it could be just a coincidence that all the florks I observed were white. Thus it is not clear that the best explanation of the regularity among observed florks is that this same regularity (whiteness) exists among all florks. When we consider the question of whether all florks have livers, however, the very same sample is large enough to support strongly a positive answer, because alternative explanations can be ruled out on other grounds. It cannot be a coincidence that the individuals in the sample I observed all had livers, because we are quite sure on independent grounds that if some florks have livers, then they all do. It is a deep anatomical feature that is not at all likely to vary within the species.

We can say the same thing about *biases* in our sample. A sample is relevantly biased if it does not enable us to rule out some alternative explanations that we ought to consider. If our sample of florks is regionally biased, that is relevant to the question of whether all florks are white, because it is plausible to believe that the whiteness of the observed florks may be a regional peculiarity. It is not so plausible to believe that their having livers is a regional peculiarity, because this is a feature that we expect to be uniform within a species.

Criticizing Arguments That Generalize

Once we have recognized that the standards of IBE should be applied to arguments that generalize from observation, we know how to criticize such an inference. We can apply the same ideas that we considered in a general way for IBE.

P1   All observed A are B.

P2   C is [part of] the best explanation for P1.

∴ C   All A are B.

Criticize P1

1. P1 is false. Not all observed A are B.

   You actually saw some green florks, but you didn't recognize that they were of the same species as the white florks.

2. There is additional evidence **O'**, and C is not [part of] the best explanation for observing P1 + **O'**.

   There is a bias in the cases (the sample) already observed, and further examples, selected in an unbiased way, would change your view about what is the best explanation: A regional bias in observing florks, for example, can be overcome with further evidence.

Criticize C

1. Give a counter-example to C: Find an A that is not B (a flork that is not white).

2. Derive consequences of C, and show that those consequences do not obtain. (Do an experiment, make more observations, or use information you already have to show that some consequences of C are false or at least questionable.)

   Even though all directly observed reptiles are cold-blooded, the assumption that dinosaurs are cold-blooded would lead to conclusions that conflict with other things we know about them. For example, it would seem that there could not be large, active predators of the kind that we know existed among the dinosaurs.

Criticize P2

Show that there is *a better explanation* (for P1) than C, or at least show that C has many explanatory weaknesses, so that alternatives should be sought out and considered. Possible weaknesses (though none is decisive):

1. C *is not well integrated* with beliefs we already have; we have independent, better reasons to think that C is (or at least might be) false, so the observed cases are misleading.

   If the number of observed A is small, then the observed regularity may just be a coincidence; that is, the sample may be too small to rule out coincidence as a possible explanation for P1. Other beliefs should not be altered in such cases.

   Other theoretical beliefs may stop us from drawing conclusions even when the sample is large. Consider the man who falls from the top of a 120-story building. He would not be justified in reasoning that because he has passed over 100 stories and is still OK, he will still be OK after he passes every story of the building. Other beliefs should intervene. Also, if we observed many black crows, we would still have some reason to doubt the conclusion that all crows are black if we know that albinism is a rare occurrence that has been observed in nearly all bird species. Another generalization, based on observations among nearly all bird species, casts doubt on the simple generalization that all crows are black.

2. Some other explanation of the observed regularity has greater *explanatory scope.*

Observation suggested to Aristotle that all ordinary objects fall toward the center of the earth. The theory of universal gravitation, however, is a more general theory that makes some predictions that conflict with Aristotle's view. It predicts that if you take an ordinary object to the moon and let go of it, it will fall toward the center of the moon, not toward the center of the earth. The theory of universal gravitation also has much more explanatory scope, because it tells us about the motion of planets with respect to each other.

3. C *lacks explanatory content.* More specifically, look for these properties:

A or B is unclear.

C is untestable (unfalsifiable) beyond the cases already observed.

(Cases like these were discussed in Chapter 7.)

ARGUMENTS WITH CAUSAL CONCLUSIONS

Causal beliefs about the world are central to our being able to operate in the world and to our general understanding of it. We believe that eating food makes us feel less hungry, that the presence of a gravitational force (or field) will eventually cause a thrown ball to drop, that some viruses cause disease, and that smoking sometimes causes cancer or heart disease. Our general understanding of how the world works consists, at least in large part, in beliefs about causal connections.

In evaluating the legitimacy of general causal conclusions, it is best to view the conclusions as being inferred in two or more steps from observations.

P1   Observed events of kind A and events of kind B have been correlated (in a certain way).

C1   ∴ A and B are generally correlated (in that way).

C2   ∴ Events of kind A cause events of kind B.

(When I have placed a kettle of water over a hot flame on the stove, the water has heated. I conclude that this is a more general regularity, going beyond my experience: that water in kettles over flames will heat. I further conclude that putting a kettle over a flame *causes* the kettle to heat.) C2 is a general claim about the causal connection of two kinds of events. Often we are interested in applying this to a particular case.

C3   ∴ This particular event of kind A caused that particular event of kind B.

(If I put this kettle over this flame now it will heat.) The last of these steps, the application of a general causal principle to a particular situation, depends on details of the particular situation, and we will set it out of our consideration right now, as we try to get clear about the justification for the inferences with conclusions C1 and C2.

The inferential steps justifying C1 and C2 are best understood as arguments to the best explanation. For these to succeed, each conclusion must be the best explanation of the truth of the statement used as evidence for it. Hence the fuller argument is this:

P1   Observed A and B have been correlated (in a certain way).

P2   C1 is [part of] the best explanation for P1.

C1   ∴ A and B are generally correlated.

P3   C2 is [part of] the best explanation for C1.

C2   ∴ Events of kind A cause events of kind B.

Causal claims are often based on the observation of regular correlation in experience. The claim of causal connection implies that the observed correlation will extend to similar cases that we did not experience. Even more, in making causal claims, we go beyond the claim of a correlation. We are claiming that the causal factor is a necessary part of a set of factors that produces the effect.

Scientists found that there was a correlation between the presence of a certain virus and the presence of a certain rash (and other measles symptoms). This leads first to some general claims of correlation: Anyone with this kind of rash (and other associated symptoms) has the measles virus, and almost everyone who is exposed to this virus for the first time gets these symptoms shortly thereafter. In justifying such claims, we can apply all that we have already said about generalizing from observed cases to all cases. Beyond these general claims, we are further led to causal claims: The presence of the measles virus causes the red rash, but the reverse does not hold; the rash does not cause the virus to be present. The events are correlated with each other, but we make the causal claim in only one direction.

Whenever my knee hurts, it soon starts to rain. I do not conclude that my knee's hurting causes rain, even though they are strongly correlated and the pain in the knee comes first. No plausible theory says that my knee's hurting causes the rain. Moving from correlation to cause requires that we fit the general claims into a larger theory. In this particular case, we might theorize that the low barometric pressure and high humidity that precede the rain cause my knee to hurt. If we are to make a causal claim, we need to go beyond mere correlation to find a theory that accounts for the observations.

When we make a causal claim, we are committed to a causal theory about what we observe. We generally accept the idea that if *all* the relevant conditions were exactly the same, the same effect would occur (though we do not usually know what all of the relevant additional conditions are). That causal theory must be integrated with the other beliefs we have.

We often make causal claims on the basis of a statistical correlation rather than on the basis of an observation of a universal association. To see why that is the case, consider what we said about causal claims in Chapter 6, where we first discussed causal explanation. When we say that A caused B, we are saying that A is a necessary part of a set of conditions that are sufficient to guarantee that B occurs. The measles virus causes the rash in some people but not in others, because a lack of immunity to the virus is also a part of the set of conditions sufficient to guarantee the occurrence of the disease. In most cases we are not in a position to check whether all of the other conditions are in place; in fact, we usually do not even know what all of the other conditions are. We support our belief in a causal connection by noticing a strong statistical association; then we produce a causal hypothesis that explains that statistical association.

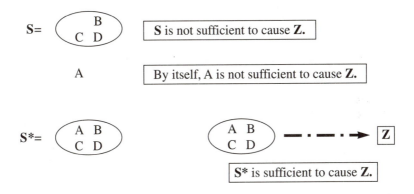

A is a necessary part of a set of conditions (**S***) that is sufficient to cause **Z**. It is a necessary part, because without A, the set is not sufficient (that is, **S** is not sufficient) to cause **Z**. So we can say that A is a cause of **Z**.

On the basis of a statistical correlation, we have been able to establish that smoking causes lung cancer, even though not all people who smoke get lung cancer. The increased prevalence of lung cancer among smokers is explained by the fact that many people fulfill all of the other conditions that are needed for getting lung cancer. They are constitutionally susceptible, we might say, but without adding the one additional factor, smoking, they will not get lung cancer. Some of those people smoke and some do not. Those among this group (of constitutionally susceptible people) who smoke enough get lung cancer, and those among this group who do not smoke do not get lung cancer. As a result, the incidence of cancer among smokers is higher than the incidence among non-smokers. Even though we do not have enough information to separate the part of the population that is constitutionally susceptible to cancer, and observe that within this population smoking always causes cancer, we can observe the statistical effect on the general population. The hypothesis that smoking causes lung cancer in some people explains the statistical difference between the smokers and the non-smokers.

We do not know what all of the other factors are that contribute to cancer, but the statistical correlation between smoking and cancer makes it clear that in some people, smoking will complete a set of conditions sufficient to guarantee the presence of lung cancer. That is the kind of observation we have as the basis for many causal conclusions. When we try to show that C causes E, we usually do not know what all of the contributing factors are. In many cases, though, we can be pretty certain that those other contributing factors are equally distributed in the two groups, those in which C is present (smokers) and those in which C is absent (non-smokers). Thus it is C (smoking) that accounts for the difference in the incidence of E (lung cancer). It is a universally effective cause among those who fulfill other conditions (the "constitutionally susceptible"), but because we do not know what all of those other conditions are, we can observe only the statistical effect on the general population.

Knowing that the proportion of smokers who get lung cancer is much higher than the proportion of non-smokers who get lung cancer enables us to connect the two, as long as there are no other significant, relevant differences between the smokers and the non-smokers. That kind of inference is very important in drawing conclusions about causal processes and in devising tests of causal hypotheses.

We will discuss this connection between statistics and causes in more detail when, in Chapter 9, we consider what is needed to test a theory.

Criticizing Arguments With Causal Conclusions

Once we have recognized that two separate arguments are needed to justify causal claims on the basis of observation, and that each of these is an instance of IBE, we can use our general guidelines for IBE as a basis for outlining some possible criticisms of causal generalizations. Here is an outline of steps in justifying a causal conclusion:

P1   Observed A and B have been correlated.

P2   C1 is [part of] the best explanation for P1.

C1   ∴ A and B are generally correlated.

P3   C2 is [part of] the best explanation for C1.

C2   ∴ A causes B.

This gives us a general conclusion: Things of kind A cause things of kind B. Often we are then interested in drawing a conclusion about a particular case: This instance of A caused this instance of B. Even such a particular case must be an instance of a general claim if there is a causal connection. If there is a causal connection, then the full set of conditions, including an instance of A, that produced the effect B in this case would produce a similar effect whenever those conditions were duplicated. For example, consider a singular causal statement:

The stabbing caused William's death.

That will be true only if there is a general connection between stabbings and death in these circumstances. Anyone with exactly William's physical condition, stabbed in exactly this way, with a weapon exactly like this, and then treated the same way afterwards would die. This is a necessary part of a set of conditions such that, whenever those conditions are duplicated, they will lead to the same result. Thus even the singular causal statement involves a commitment to a more general causal claim— a more general theory of causal histories. We really need to consider the justification of general claims as the basis for any causal conclusion.

Criticize P1: No such correlation exists.

Although it may seem like it never rains when you have your umbrella, a closer study of the data will make it evident that there is no significant correlation of that kind.

Criticize P2: The claim that C1 is the best explanation of P1.

There is additional data D, and when D is added to P1, some explanation other than C1 is the best explanation for P1 & D.

I did a study. I had Scotch and soda on Monday evening, and I got drunk. I had bourbon and soda on Tuesday, and I got drunk. I had tequila and soda on Wednesday, and I got drunk. Soda makes me drunk.

Bill: Almost every time I dream about my sister, I see her the next day. Alice: But you see your sister almost every day, whether or not you dream about her.

When all the information is there, we see that the alleged effect is just what we would expect even without the alleged cause. No special correlation exists.

Accidental correlation (The sample is too small for coincidence to be ruled out as an explanation.)

I wanted to know whether studying late at night interferes with sleep. I studied hard on each of three nights last week, and each night I woke up in the middle of the night and could not get back to sleep. I'm convinced.

Another account for uniformity of observed cases (bias of sample)

I wanted to know whether studying late would interfere with sleep. I know that most of my friends study harder than usual the night before a major exam. So I had all of my friends write down their sleep experience on the night before an exam. Nearly all of them had some trouble sleeping.

Worry about the exam itself or concern about recording their experiences could be the cause of the friends' sleep problems. It is also possible that their sleep was normal but that recording the details made them more aware of unevenness in their normal sleep patterns. Thus there are several ways in which this group's reports of unusual sleep before exams might not be representative of the experience of the general population.

Criticize P3: The claim that C2 is the best explanation of C1.

Non-causal accounts of regularity

My friend has noticed an intriguing relationship. There were several students in his class who had been to Paris. He found out that they all had visited Europe. He concluded that people who visit Paris must all develop a desire to visit Europe.

A weakness in geographical knowledge has led this person to look for a causal connection when there is another kind of connection between the relevant facts.

Other causal accounts

B causes A.

These pains in my knee must cause it to rain, because they always occur right before the rain starts.

The rain is a part of a more general change in the weather conditions, and other aspects (humidity and barometric pressure) precede the rain and cause the pain.

On a certain island, all of the native people believe that lice are necessary for good health, because people without lice are very unhealthy.

Lice desert a sinking ship. Poor health causes licelessness, not the other way around.

Common cause

Many people die while they are in hospitals, so being in a hospital must cause death in many cases.

Being severely ill often causes people to go to hospitals, and it is also a frequent cause of death. The correlation between being in hospitals and dying may be accounted for by their having a common cause.

High school graduates who have watched a lot of TV throughout their lives generally get lower SAT and ACT scores than those who have watched less TV. So watching more TV leads to lower scores.

Perhaps there is a common cause for excessive TV watching and lower scores: lack of interest in school subjects or lack of parental supervision, for example.

Complex causal relation

Emile Durkheim found that in a certain area, there was a smaller percentage of reported suicides among Catholics than among Protestants. He concluded that some features of the Catholics—a deeper religious commitment or closer family ties—accounted for the difference.

Because Catholicism forbids suicide, the statistics may reflect some false reporting. Instead of bringing down the number of suicides, Catholicism may merely reduce the number of suicide reports.

As sex education has increased, the prevalence of venereal disease has increased. So sex education increases the spread of the disease.

A much more complex relationship involving increased awareness, increased activity, the presence of new methods of birth control, and perhaps other factors seems plausible.

A causes B in only an insignificant number of situations. (Other causal factors are much more significant.)

The correlation between high coffee consumption and heart attacks suggests that drinking coffee may cause heart attacks.

Coffee may be a minor factor, with some common cause, such as a certain lifestyle, playing a much more significant role in causing heart attacks.

SOME THINGS TO LOOK AT WHEN EVALUATING STATISTICAL INFORMATION

Because a cause is a necessary part of some set of sufficient conditions, and because the other factors in the set of sufficient conditions are not always (in fact, not usually) known, we often use statistical information to justify causal claims. This may be a good time for us to make note of some difficulties that arise in the use, presentation, or evaluation of statistical information. There is much more to be learned from a fuller study of statistics, but these notes will alert you to some problems that we frequently encounter in drawing conclusions from statistical data.

Our key guideline in all of this is familiar: Ask what was observed, and then consider whether the conclusion offered is really the best explanation for what was observed.

Correlation of Broad Trends

Statistical trends that are fairly uniform over a long period of time are all correlated with each other. Thus, over the last 25 years, increased computer use, increase in the proportion of color TVs to others, increased Asian immigration, and the decline of the pileated woodpecker are all correlated. By itself, this kind of relationship should never be used to justify a causal claim, though occasionally such broad correlations are cited, as in the following examples that I have seen:

Increased food additives over the last 50 years have caused increased violence.

Increased TV watching over the last 50 years has caused increased violence.

These claims can look a little bit plausible if there is some independent reason to suspect a causal connection. The independent reason, however, not this correlation, must do all of the justificatory work. A lack of a correlation would be a problem for a theory that claimed a causal connection, but the presence of a long-term correlation of trends that always continue in the same direction can *never* be significant evidence in favor of a claim of causal connection.

Sometimes one can also undermine conclusions drawn from broad trends by pointing out that the alleged effect began before the cause. For example, the welfare system that began in the 1960s and continued into the 1990s was often blamed for steadily increasing unemployment among young African-American males and for increased teenage pregnancy among African-American females. However, the trend toward increasing unemployment is a steady trend that began in the middle of the 1950s, well before this welfare system was in place; and the percentage of teenage African-Americans getting pregnant has been unchanged (at around 4%) since the statistics were first collected much earlier in the twentieth century. It is possible that there is a causal connection—maybe things would have changed in the other direction if there had been no welfare system. That idea, however, gets no support from the statistical information, because no real statistical change can be connected with the introduction or continuation of this welfare system.

Compared to What?

We mentioned in Chapter 3 that comparisons need a careful look. The claim that Colgate kids get fewer cavities should lead you first to ask, "Fewer than whom?" The suggested causal conclusion, that Colgate toothpaste is better than others for cavity reduction, is legitimate only if Colgate kids get significantly fewer cavities than kids who use other toothpastes. If the comparison was instead to kids who don't brush their teeth, then it cannot support the most relevant conclusion (that we should purchase Colgate rather than some other toothpaste).

Regression to the Mean

The phenomenon of regression to the mean is one to watch out for in contexts in which there is a significant random or otherwise uncontrolled element. Any unusual outcome is likely to be followed by something more ordinary, simply because the ordinary *is* ordinary. (The *mean* is the *average,* so the idea here is that an unusual occurrence is likely to be followed by one that is more average.) To see the phenomenon clearly, consider a purely random activity, such as tossing a pair of dice. If you toss a high number, 11 or 12, it is very likely that your next toss will be lower, simply because the odds of getting 11 or 12 on any throw are very low, and the odds of throwing a lower number than that on any throw are correspondingly high. Clearly, it would be a mistake to think that throwing a high number causes you to throw a lower number on the next throw, even though throwing a high number is nearly always followed by throwing a lower number.

There is evidence, however, that people make mistakes very much like that. For example, all evidence developed by psychologists suggests that praise is much more important than criticism in the positive development of athletes, musicians, and the like. But coaches nearly always believe otherwise. After all, nearly every time they conspicuously praise an athlete, the athlete does worse on the next performance, and nearly every time they conspicuously criticize, the athlete does better!

The phenomenon of regression to the mean may be the source of the coaches' view. When they praise unusually good performances, those are nearly always followed by more ordinary performances, simply because the ordinary is more likely to occur. Similarly, criticism of unusually bad performances is likely to be followed by something better, simply because the ordinary is more likely. Even if the criticism and the praise have no effect at all, that is what we should expect to see. The coaches' natural tendency to expect their actions have some effect will mislead them if they do not take into account the phenomenon of regression to the mean.

I have noticed that students who do very well on the first exam in my course often do much worse on the second exam. It is tempting to think that they get over-confident and slack off. Perhaps, though, I am just observing a consequence of re-gression to the mean.

Consider the Dropout Rate

Most studies, especially long-term studies involving people, have some "drop-outs"—individuals who leave the study and are not figured into the final data. In evaluating a report of the outcome of some procedure, you should always consider whether the dropout rate affects the conclusion to be drawn.

For example, suppose that a course is designed to teach people perfect pitch, the ability to identify by name the pitch of any note played for them. If it is reported that 95% of people who complete the course are able to identify the pitch of any note played for them, you should find out the dropout rate. If most people drop out because the course becomes too frustrating for them, then the course has not had nearly the success that the 95% figure would suggest. It may merely have eliminated all of the people who have difficulty acquiring perfect pitch, leaving only those who need little training.

Similarly, there are several reasons to be suspicious if an ad for an SAT course cites the high scores of people who complete the course. The course may screen out those who don't care enough to continue or who can't follow the instruc-tor. As a result, it may end up with a population of high achievers and may, in fact, add little to their performance. In Chapter 9, we will mention other reasons to be suspicious.

Visibility

Because of the number of airline disasters we hear about, you might get the impres-sion that air travel is not safe. But for a trip of any length for which air travel is rea-sonable, air travel is much safer than any other type. Air fatalities are statistically in-significant, even though they receive national news coverage. If you consider a state anywhere in the United States, it is likely that more people died from auto accidents there last year than died from air crashes in the entire country.

Simpson's Paradox

In a study at a well-known university, it was found that women had a lower accep-tance rate than men for graduate study at the university, but in every department, the acceptance rate for women was as high as or higher than that for men. How can this be? This type of problem, in which the rate for the aggregate is very different from the rates for the sub-groups, is known as *Simpson's Paradox.*

The answer to the paradox here was fairly simple: Women applied in larger numbers to more popular programs—programs that had a much lower acceptance rate. To see how this might happen, consider the simple example of two departments, each of which accepts 10 students. If Department A has 100 applicants and Department B has 20, then we could have the following results; where W stands for women and M for men.

	APPLIED	**W**	**M**	**W ADMITTED**	**M ADMITTED**	**RATE W**	**RATE M**
A	100	70	30	8	2	11%	7%
B	20	4	16	3	7	75%	44%
Total	120	74	46	11	9	15%	20%

Women have a better acceptance rate in each department, but a lower acceptance rate overall. Even though there is no evidence of discriminatory decisions against women, if admission decisions are made at the department level, women get into graduate programs at a much lower overall rate.

This situation has a direct parallel in exploring wage discrimination. On average, women are paid less than men. Is this a result of discriminatory wage decisions within companies? We can't tell this just from the fact that women are paid less. It could be (and in fact is) true that women predominate in many jobs with lower pay. Thus discrimination does not need to take place at the level of individual wage decisions to make women get lower average pay. Of course, one might become very curious about the social forces that produce conditions where jobs in which women predominate are jobs that pay less. That, however, is a very different kind of issue from intentional discrimination in individual pay decisions.

Consider the Right Statistic

In 1983, 4.3 million people over the age of 25 lived with their parents, though in 1970, the number was only 3.4 million. What caused this increase? Many thought that difficulty in getting a good job at a young age was to blame.

Looking at the numbers just given, however, is looking at the wrong numbers. Evidence of job difficulty would require that there be a different *rate* of people over 25 living with their parents. But the rate was not different—it was about 4% in both 1970 and 1983. Because of the baby boom, there were many more people between 25 and 40 in 1983 than in 1970. No social force other than an increase in the population in this age group is needed to explain the increased number of people living with their parents.

Incumbent political candidates often mention the number of new jobs in their jurisdiction (the state or the nation) while they were in office. ("Six million new jobs were created. . . .") The main things that interest voters are, however, the extent to which the number of jobs increases and the quality of those jobs. Evaluating the first of these requires also knowing how many jobs were lost during the same period, and evaluating the second requires much more information about the new jobs and the lost jobs. The raw number of new jobs does not offer the comparative information that we need about the number of jobs. (Even if there is a net increase in the number of jobs, of course, we need to know more before we can conclude that the actions of the politician were causally responsible for the increase.)

Make Sure That the Quality of Statistics Compared Is Uniform

When we compare numbers, we need to make sure that they apply in comparable ways. Most obviously, financial figures need to be corrected for inflation. A house that appreciates 10% in its price in dollars in 15 years has been a very poor investment if it was necessary for it to double in price in order to keep up with inflation. In general, dollar figures from different years must be adjusted for inflation before they can be compared.

A recent student newspaper report at a university was rendered useless because it failed to correct for this inflation factor. The report said that the number of journals in the university's library had gone down over the last 15 years, while the amount spent had gone up. Because the reporters did not correct for inflation, we do not know from the report whether the inflation-adjusted expenditure on journals went down or up. (In other words, inflation alone would make the dollar amount go up. We want to know whether it went up even more than inflation would require.) Thus all we can really tell from the report is that the number of journals went down.

Crime statistics vary considerably in quality, so comparison from place to place or time to time is difficult. Most such statistics are statistics for reported crime or for arrests. Reported-crime statistics can vary in whether prostitution, street vendors without licenses, minor assaults, gambling, public drunkenness, and marijuana possession count as crimes. Arrest statistics will vary further, depending on whether there are police "crackdowns" on such crimes or not. Thus a claim that crime has gone up or down needs to be looked at carefully.

Still another gap between crime and reported crime was alleged in Philadelphia in the 1970s. A reduction in reported crime was for a time cited as a positive outcome of police action. However, the FBI, studying the situation, concluded that reported crime went down because in many neighborhoods people had become mistrustful of the police and so did not report crimes that occurred.

Averages Hide a Lot of Information

Averages hide a lot of information. Simpson's Paradox is one manifestation of this, but there are others. The average yearly rainfall is approximately the same in Kansas City and in Seattle. This fact, though, reveals little about the vast differences between these cities. Kansas City is susceptible to huge storms, great floods, and droughts. In Seattle rain is frequent all year long, but large storms, floods, and droughts are much less common in most years.

CHAPTER SUMMARY

Arguments That Generalize

All observed A are B, so all A are B.

Criticisms

Dispute the premise that all observed A are B.

Make a case that there is another explanation for the fact that all observed A have been B. For example:

Coincidence: the sample is *too small* to rule this out

Alternative explanation of the uniformity in the observed cases (e.g., a *bias* of the sample)

Show the conclusion to be false directly (find an A that is not B).

Arguments With Causal Conclusions

(1)   Observed A and B have been correlated.

(2)   ∴ A and B are generally correlated.

(3)   ∴ A caused B.

There are several steps. For this to succeed, each conclusion must be the best explanation of the truth of the statement that is used as evidence for it.

Criticism

Criticize (1): The observed cases do not exhibit the claimed correlation.

Criticize the claim that (2) is the best explanation of (1).

Accidental correlation (sample too small to rule this out)

Other account for uniformity of observed cases (bias)

Criticize the claim that (3) is the best explanation of (2).

Non-causal account for general uniformity

B causes A

Common cause

Complex causal relationship

Statistical Arguments

Consider the data that serve as a source for any explanatory (usually causal) claim and the rhetorical goal of the claim. See whether the explanatory claim is a part of the best overall explanation for the regularities observed.

Watch out for special statistical problems: claims based on the correlation of broad trends or on unspecified or inappropriate comparisons; causal claims based on observations that simply reflect regression to the mean; faulty inferences that rely on the visibility of phenomena rather than on their true frequency; Simpson's paradox; the effect of population bulges, such as the baby boom, on averages and other statistical comparisons; and comparison of statistics that differ in quality.

EXERCISE 8A

Evaluate the arguments and explanations presented or reported here.

1. Although John has been sitting at the computer for hours today, trying to write a paper, he can't think of anything to write. It must be because he has writer's block.

2. Some psychologists say that we catch colds because we want to. That's why people in the same family or the same office do not always get colds at the same time. A virus is present when you have a cold, but unless there is also a desire to catch the cold, the virus will have no effect. We are not normally aware of the desire that leads to the cold, because the desire is usually subconscious.

3. A curve showing the increase in behavioral disturbances and learning disabilities over the past 25 years parallels the increase in the dollar value of food additives used over that time. This makes it clear that there is a causal link between junk-food diets and antisocial behavior.

4. After a five-week doctor strike in Los Angeles in 1976, a study by the California State Department of Health found that the death rate in Los Angeles County declined significantly during the strike. The department said that fewer people had non-emergency surgery, so there was less risk of dying. These findings were taken to support the view that people might benefit if less elective (non-emergency) surgery were performed in the United States. The authors of the study concluded that greater restraint in the performance of elective surgical operations might improve U.S. life expectancy. In other words, more people would be alive if surgeons performed fewer operations.

5. I am sure that class attendance is an important factor in getting good grades. Whenever I grade exams, I find that the students who attend class often get better grades than those who don't.

6. Spending more money on education will strengthen the economy. We can be sure of this, because the countries that spend the most on education are the ones with the strongest economies.

7. On a bus trip to Albany, David wondered why the bus had not gone through the city of Utica. The bus driver explained that the bus was bypassing Utica on that day.

8. One might suspect that the price of food in inner-city stores causes people in the inner city to pay more for the same food. In a study done in 1967, investigators concluded otherwise. They used the following sample:

   Inner city: 3 supermarkets, 81 neighborhood stores

   Higher-income suburbs: 84 supermarkets, 72 neighborhood stores

   Average food prices:

	SUPER-MARKET	SMALL STORE
INNER CITY	8.54	9.25
SUBURB	8.60	9.38

9. A recent study has shown that, on average, a graduate of an Ivy League college will make more money over the course of his or her career than a graduate of any other college. Also, a graduate of an East Coast college will make more than a graduate of a college in the Midwest, South, or West. It seems clear that if you want to enhance your earning power, you ought to get into an Ivy League school or at least go to college on the East Coast.

10. My son is learning to ride a bicycle. Usually, he goes about thirty feet and then falls down. When he goes significantly farther than that, I make sure to praise him, telling him how well he is doing. Even so, he hardly ever does as well on the next try. When he does much worse than usual, I make sure to tell him that he is not trying hard enough and that I expect more from him. He almost always does better on the next try. Evidently, criticism is much better than praise in motivating him to do a better job.

EXERCISE 8B

The Karl Tool Company recently opened a factory in our area, offering 300 new jobs: 100 office openings and 200 openings working in the factory or in general maintenance. The company had applications in two separate categories, for office positions and for other positions, with one group of personnel officers making decisions for office jobs and a separate group making decisions for the other jobs. Exactly 400 college graduates applied for a job, and 400 people who were not college graduates applied for a job. The company hired 100 college graduates and 200 others.

Does this information show that there was discrimination against college graduates in the hiring process? Why or why not? If not, then what further information do you need to determine whether there was discrimination?

EXERCISE 8C

This exercise focuses on exploring a persistent error.

1. The following account is based on a story by Joelle Tessler in the *Post-Standard,* September 12, 1992.

Vowing to Wait

STATISTICS SHOW THAT BOTH MEN AND WOMEN ARE CHOOSING TO MARRY AT AN OLDER AGE

Fewer people are marrying these days, statistics show. And those who do marry are waiting longer.

Mirroring a nationwide trend, statistics from the New York State Bureau of Biometrics show that the average age at which men and women are getting married in upstate New York has slowly but surely increased over the past dozen years.

In 1979, for example, 2795 men married at age 19, whereas 2952 men married at age 29. In 1989, 1407 men wed at 19, and 4710 at age 29.

Trends among women are similar.

. . .

What all this adds up to is couples vowing to wait before saying their vows. Across the country, the average age for a first marriage for women climbed from 22.3 in 1978 to 24.6 in 1988. For grooms, the average age rose from 24.4 in 1978 to 26.5 in 1988.

a. What explanation is offered for the statistical facts in the article?

b. It is possible to propose a clear alternative explanation for the statistics that are presented. Identify at least one alternative explanation. [*Hint*: Think about people aged 19–25: What else (other than the author's explanation) could produce lower numbers of marriages in that age group in 1989 (than in 1979)? What else could produce a higher average age of marriage in 1988 (than in 1978)?]

c. What information would be needed to show that the explanation in the article is correct?

2. In 1996, the *Los Angeles Times* reported two facts that were offered as reasons to believe that people have been waiting longer to get married.

Fact 1. The median age of first marriages is the highest it has ever been: 26.7 for men and 24.5 for women. (The number of first marriages above the median age is the same as the number of first marriages below that age.)

Fact 2. In 1994, there were more than 44.2 million never-been-married adults in the United States—more than twice as many as in 1970.

Explain why neither of these facts is, by itself, a reason to believe that people born since 1947 are waiting longer to get married than did people born before 1947. In other words, what other explanations might there be for fact 1 and fact 2?

CHAPTER 9

TESTING CAUSAL EXPLANATIONS

Claims about the effectiveness of products, medical treatments, exercise programs, and many other things are a regular feature of our daily life. These are all causal claims, and it is important for our planning that we learn how to evaluate them. More generally, our understanding of the world consists primarily of an understanding of the causal relationships that exist there. Our understanding of that world is improved through the systematic testing of causal claims to eliminate those that are false. After our consideration of causal explanations in Chapters 6–8, we are in a good position to consider some of the factors that go into a test of a causal claim.

Suppose we observe that **(O)** students who have studied from a certain SAT preparation guide and followed its study guidelines have done better than other students on the SAT exam.

> **O**: Students who have studied from a certain SAT preparation guide and followed its study guidelines have done better than other students on the SAT exam.

It is tempting to conclude that the guide helps students to do better on SAT exams.

> **H1**: Studying the particular content and techniques in this guide for the prescribed number of hours will help students to do better on the exam than they otherwise would.

> **H1** explains **O**.

There are many other possibilities, though, and in order be more nearly certain that **H1** is true, we need to consider at least two other hypotheses as possible explanations for the successes already observed. Until we consider these alternatives and rule them out, we cannot have much confidence that **H1** is true. For example, in this situation, we might identify the following alternative explanations of the successes that have been observed.

> **H2**: Studying as prescribed in this guide will help you do better on the exam, but the particular content and techniques prescribed are irrelevant. A

student could buy any SAT study guide and do just as well, as long as he or she put in the study time.

H2 explains **O**.

H3: The students who used the guide were better students than average before they started their study. The guide and the study time made little or no difference.

H3 explains **O**.

When there is more than one possible explanation for something we observe, the observation does not enable us to know which explanation is correct; when theories agree about a prediction, that prediction is useless in deciding which theory is correct. The observation that students who used the SAT preparation guide did well is not a sufficient basis for distinguishing among the three explanations **H1**, **H2**, and **H3**. All of the theories make the prediction that people who used the guide do better on the exam than people who didn't use the guide, and that tells us nothing about which theory to adopt; it eliminates none of these theories. We are trying to decide which is the *best* explanation of the observation (in our IBE inference). Because observation **O** is the initial observation that all of the theories explain, it does not help us to distinguish among them.

If we wish to know what explanation is correct, often we can devise a test of our explanatory hypothesis or theory. The first step in testing it is to identify alternatives: other hypotheses that could explain the observations that have been made so far. We proposed **H2** and **H3** above as alternatives to consider along with **H1**. Such an identification of explanatory alternatives may be incomplete or uncertain, but without it we cannot begin to evaluate an explanation.

After we have identified a set of possible explanations for what has been observed so far, we can try to devise a test to produce some observable outcomes that are explained better by one theory than by its rivals. We try to create or discover situations that have features that are predicted by one theory but not by the rival theory or theories. Thus to create a useful test, we must check predictions the theories do not agree about: predictions that will be relevant to falsifying or showing other inadequacies in one or more of these explanatory hypotheses or theories. The new situations examined in such a test will enable us to select among the possible explanations that are available.

In our example of the SAT preparation guide, we might try to set up a test in which some students take the guide and others just study on their own, with a different study guide. Then a comparison of their results might show that **H2** is false, or it might show that **H1** is false.

Ruling out **H3** as an explanation requires another kind of care. We must make sure that our comparison groups are as much alike as possible before the test starts. We don't want the differences between groups at the end of our test to be merely a reflection of differences that existed before we began to test our hypothesis. We want the causal factor that we introduce in the test to be a determining factor. In our example, we don't want prior academic differences between the students who used the guide and students who didn't to be the main factor in whether students do well on the exam. If only the top students used the guide, then maybe they got good grades because of their general abilities and past study, and maybe the study guide made no difference. For this reason, we must assign people to test groups in a way that is most likely to maintain a high degree of similarity between the group that uses the guide and the group that is assigned to study a different guide. This is the essence of a *controlled* study, and we will discuss that in more detail in this chapter.

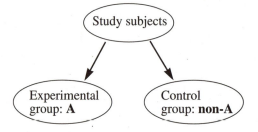

We need to divide the study subjects into an experimental group and a control group by a random method, so that there is no relevant difference between the groups (other than the presence of **A**). Otherwise, that other difference between the **A** group and the non-**A** group might serve as a basis for an alternative explanation of any subsequent differences. In our SAT study example, we must make sure that all types of students are equally represented in the group that gets the study guide and in the group that doesn't.

Comparing Predictions of Theories

The predictions of two theories can differ because they conflict, they can differ because one is more specific than the other (predicting a value of 12.23 rather than "around 12," for example), or they can differ because one makes a prediction about something that the other theory says nothing about (even though they make similar predictions in the cases already observed). Any of these three can be a significant basis for selecting one theory in favor of another, although, as we emphasized in Chapters 7 and 8, the selection of a theory involves considerations (such as integration with other theories that we have) that require that we examine a very broad context when deciding what theory to adopt.

We can test a theory H1 by finding something that H1 predicts that at least some alternative theories do not predict. An unexpected prediction that is successful at least establishes that H1 has some scope. In the most useful kind of test, if the prediction of theory H1 holds, then some of the alternative theories will be falsified (when the predictions of theory H1 actually conflict with those of an alternative theory and when no way is found to accommodate the conflicting theory with the new observations). If the prediction does not hold, then H1 will be falsified (if we find no way to accommodate the data with H1).

To do a test in our SAT example, we would divide a large population of students into two groups, where the characteristics of the two groups were the same before the test. We would then have one group of students use the study guide in the prescribed way while the other group followed a different prescribed pattern of behavior that is the desired comparison. (We may wish to compare the study guide to other study guides, or to no studying at all, or to taking a study class. Each of those would require that we have a separate group of comparable students following that prescribed behavior.) If we find that the study guide group does significantly better than a group that does no studying, for example, then we can conclude that using the study guide and studying is better than not studying at all. We have falsified the hypothesis that using the study guide and studying will make no difference. On the other hand, if we find that the groups show very similar performance, we will have falsified the hypothesis that using the study guide and studying makes a difference.

As we know, however, falsification is not generally as clear-cut as this ideal picture suggests. A result that conflicts with a theory can sometimes be accommodated by modifying the theory slightly or by accepting the result as due to some unexplained interference. We have already mentioned how *ad hoc* theoretical devices such as epicycles can insulate a theory from falsification. Overuse of this is inimical to good practice in ways that we considered in Chapters 7 and 8. Modest elaboration of a theory to accommodate data, however, can be an important means of developing adequate theories. Balanced judgment is needed to decide when to modify an existing theory to fit data and when just to give up a theory and accept that an explanation of an entirely different kind is more successful. (This is discussed in more detail, with examples, in Chapter 7, in the section on falsifying theories and in the discussion of the Copernican revolution.) If the study guide group and the group that doesn't study do equally well, it might be appropriate to hypothesize that the test just didn't go on long enough to show a difference, and hence a longer test should be done. One must be careful, though, about such reluctance to accept the results of tests.

It is also important to note that when we are devising a test, we must make some auxiliary assumptions about the test conditions, and those might be wrong. In simply comparing the weights of two objects, for example, I must assume that no forces other than gravity affect the reading on my scale—neither object emits electrical fields that affect my scale, neither object is being pulled up or down by a magnetic field, and so on. Replication of results under slightly different testing conditions is important in the testing of theories; it minimizes the likelihood of unsuspected interfering factors. Dismissing anomalous results because of interference that is unaccounted for is very dangerous, but it is sometimes completely appropriate if an otherwise powerful theory comes up against a small number of problem cases. A single test of a theory does not usually decisively falsify a theory.

Often people speak of tests *confirming* a theory. But a test confirms a theory in a useful way only if it creates problems for (and in the best case, falsifies) alternative explanatory theories. As long as something else qualifies as a reasonable explanation of the phenomena that theory H explains, theory H has not been established. In checking *unexpected consequences* of a theory H, we are checking for things that conflict with, or at least were not predicted by, other theories that overlap H in the range of phenomena that they explain.

Causes and Correlations

We can say that A causes Z if A is a part of a set of (actual) conditions S* that is causally sufficient for Z, and the set S* without A is not causally sufficient for Z. (This was discussed in Chapters 7 and 8.)

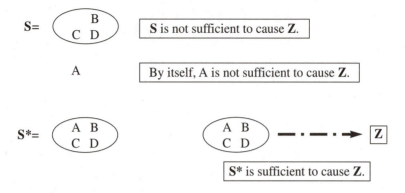

A is a necessary part of a set of conditions (S*) that is sufficient to cause **Z**. It is a necessary part, because without A, the set is not sufficient (that is, **S** is not sufficient) to cause **Z**. Thus we can say that A is a cause of **Z**.

When we do not know all of the other elements of S*, the set that is sufficient to bring about the effect under consideration, statistical correlations can be important in establishing causal relations. A statistical correlation between A and Z is discovered by examining two groups of test subjects (or situations, etc.), those that are A and those that are non-A, and then finding that Z is significantly more prevalent among the A than among the non-A. This will have greater importance in supporting causal conclusions if the two groups, the A and the non-A, do not differ in any other relevant respects, because then there will be no way to find an alternative explanation of the relative prevalence of Z among the A's. When the A and non-A groups do not differ in other ways, and when Z is then produced much more often among the A than among the non-A, the conclusion that A causes Z becomes attractive. When the A and non-A groups differ in other ways, though, then we cannot move so easily from the observation of a correlation to the conclusion that a causal relationship exists. The other differences between the A group and the non-A group may provide a basis for other explanations of the correlation.

For example, if most individuals who are exposed to a virus subsequently get a rash, and if individuals who are not exposed do not get a similar rash, then, if there are no other relevant differences between the groups, there is very good reason to think that the virus causes the rash. But the clause "if there are no other relevant differences between the groups" is very important, and ensuring that is a major goal of a good experiment or study. If the people exposed to the virus all visited a certain forest (and the comparison group didn't), then there may be other possible sources for the rash, such as a plant in the forest, and so there is an alternative explanation that has not been ruled out. Eliminating other relevant differences between the groups is necessary if alternative explanations are to be eliminated.

Let's consider some of the various kinds of tests that can be done concerning causal hypotheses, where we wish to see whether A plays a causal role in the production of Z, and yet we do not know all of the factors relevant to the production of Z. For example, we might wish to determine whether taking a particular freshman writing course actually improves people's writing. In such a case, we do not know all of the factors that go into improving writing, but we still wish to know whether taking a course is actually valuable for a significant number of students.

FULLY CONTROLLED EXPERIMENTS

The ideal experiment to determine whether A causes Z is a **controlled experiment**. Such an experiment is based on the random selection of an **experimental group** and a **control group**, with an **introduced test factor A**. This is sometimes called a "randomized experiment."

0. We begin with an hypothesis, such as "A causes Z in population P." (This test will be useful if other theories do not predict that A causes Z in population P.)

1. We find a representative sample of P's in which neither A nor Z exists.

2. We divide our sample of P's into two groups on the basis of some feature that is not relevant to A or Z.

3. We introduce A throughout one group (the experimental group, EG) but not the other (the control group, CG).

4. We see whether the groups are significantly different in the instance of Z. Is #(Z & A)/#A significantly greater than #(Z & non-A)/#non-A?

5. We make sure that A causing Z is the best explanation of any observed difference.

(In step 4, we use #A to refer to the number of A's, etc. That means that #(Z & A)/#A refers to the number of A's that are Z's divided by the number of A's—that is, the proportion of A's that are Z's. For example, if there are 1000 A's and 357 are Z's, then 357/1000 is the proportion of A's that are Z's. Hence the phrase "#(Z & A)/#A significantly greater than #(Z & non-A)/#non-A" is just another way of saying that the proportion of A's that are Z's is significantly greater than the proportion of non-A's that are Z's. For example, if there are 2000 non-A's, and 433 are Z's, then 357/1000 is significantly greater than 433/2000.)

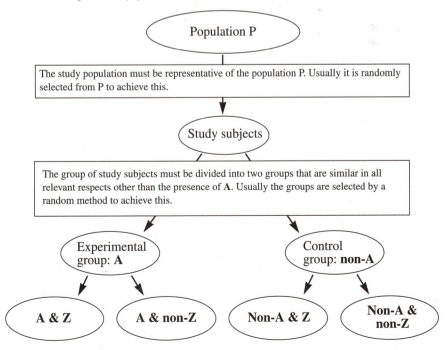

To know that A causes Z, we must at least be sure that the proportion of A's that are Z is significantly greater than the proportion of non-A's that are Z.

In an ideal test of a causal theory or hypothesis, we wish to divide a population into two subgroups, an experimental group in which feature A is introduced and a control group in which it is not. Then, to determine whether A causes Z, wait to see whether Z develops in the experimental group but not in the control group. We need to have the control (non-A) group for comparison, because without it we would not know whether A has anything at all to do with the development of Z within the test population.

The ideal test procedure works beautifully if all of the A individuals develop Z and none of the non-A individuals develop Z. Usually, however, we do not know all of the factors involved in causing a particular effect Z, so some of the individuals in which A is introduced will not develop Z, because other necessary factors are not present in those individuals. In addition, some of the non-A individuals might develop Z for reasons other than A. (The chicken pox virus causes a rash; but not everyone who is exposed gets a rash, because some people are immune, and some people who are not exposed get a rash for some other reason.) Accordingly, we must usually have large enough groups so that we can consider the difference in the prevalence of Z in the two groups to be significant. The control group and the experimental group must also both show *the same range of variation in all of the properties that might be relevant to producing effect Z* except, of course, for the property A being tested. Only then is it clear that the presence of A is the best account for the presence of Z.

We try to achieve an even distribution of all other properties by dividing the population to be observed into groups **randomly**—that is, on the basis of properties that are not at all relevant to the features (A and Z, in our schema) that are involved in the test. For example, whether a person is in an even-numbered position on an alphabetical list is not at all relevant to whether that person will develop a rash if given a certain virus. Thus a random division for such an experiment could be based on the method of going through an alphabetical list and assigning individuals to the experimental and control groups alternately.

If we have made a random assignment of individuals to the groups, and if the groups are large enough, then we can expect those groups to show the same range of variation in the properties other than A that might be relevant to the production of Z. In other words, if these groups were left alone, Z would occur with the same frequency in the two groups. The only explanation for any difference in the frequency with which Z occurs will then be the presence of A in the experimental group.

Let's consider randomness a bit more. In many experiments, it might be all right to divide the population alphabetically, putting the first half in the experimental group and the second half in the control group. Position in an alphabetical list is irrelevant to many kinds of tests. However, suppose we wish to test the hypothesis that a letter to students supporting a full week for an Easter break (with a later end to the academic year as a result) could influence students to favor such a break. The alphabetical distribution could be undesirable if, for example, the ratio of Christian to non-Christian students is different in those two parts of the alphabet. (Perhaps there are more Muslim and Jewish names in the first half of the alphabet than in the last.) We might suspect that Christian students would be more apt to desire the proposed change, so position in the alphabet is related to something that might be relevant to our test. Thus the suggested alphabetical division cannot be used as a basis for assigning people to groups. Relative to this test, we cannot regard that division as random.

Ordinarily, randomness enters twice into the plan of an experiment. To test whether a factor A brings about an effect Z in a certain population P, I usually must first take a sufficiently large *random sample of the population P* (because I usually cannot use the entire population in my experiment). I must then *divide that sample, randomly,* into two groups, the experimental group and the control group. Then I introduce A into the experimental group (and withhold A from the control group), and I observe whether Z occurs significantly more in the experimental group than in the control group.

To do a controlled test of whether a freshman writing course is effective in a certain population of students, I must take a sufficiently large random sample of that population (or use the whole population, if that is feasible). Then I must randomly assign half the students in the sample to the experimental group and the other half to the control group. I must next make sure that the students in the experimental group complete the freshman writing course and that those in the control group do not take the course. Then I must have a clear test of course effectiveness; perhaps I will have all the students write several essays, under the same conditions, and have impartial graders evaluate the quality of the essays. I will next check to see whether the students who took the course did better than those who did not take the course. If they did significantly better, then the only reasonable explanation may be the fact that the students in the experimental group took the writing course. If they did not do better, then we may have falsified the hypothesis that the course is effective in producing better writing in the test conditions.

Problems with Controlled Experiments

Introducing factor A can introduce other differences

In doing a controlled experiment, we must try to make sure that *A is the only difference* between the experimental group and the control group (the only difference that is relevant to the production of Z). It is sometimes difficult to do this, because the process of introducing A may introduce other differences that are relevant. Even in the example of the freshman writing course that we just discussed, there is a problem of this kind. Do all or most of the students in the control group (those not taking freshman writing) take some other course instead? If so, then there will be a relevant difference between the groups, and that difference might play a role in explaining the results that are observed. On the other hand, if they do not take another course instead, then that group differs from the experimental group in that they are taking fewer courses, and that too could play a role in the explanation of the results. Taking the freshman writing course is not the only possible explanation of differences, no matter what happens.

In studies of humans, another factor is important. We know that many people will feel better if they are given a pill to treat an illness, even if the pill has no effective ingredients. This *placebo effect* is especially significant in studies involving pain, mood disorders, and diseases that often go away on their own, but it can appear in many other cases as well. Usually the relief derived from the placebo effect is only temporary, but it can be a significant confounding factor in medical studies. Therefore, if we wish to test the real effectiveness of a new medicine, the experimental group and the control group must both receive pills under similar conditions. The placebo effect should then be equal in the two groups, so that any difference in the groups is due to a real difference in the pills they take. If only the experimental group received pills, then there would always be a possible alternative explanation for the difference between the groups: The difference could be a placebo effect. Just receiving pills might have an effect, even when the pills have no special influence on the biological processes under study. We introduce a placebo pill into the control group to equalize the placebo effect in the two groups.

The power of the placebo effect was shown in a recent study involving 613 men who had enlarged prostrates. An enlarged prostate can cause weak urine flow. The men who received a placebo tablet showed better urine flow (checked with a meter) at the end of the test than at the beginning, even though their prostates had enlarged 8.4%. (The experimental group, in this case, had a 21% reduction in prostate size.) The only apparent explanation of the change is that the men knew that they were part of a study of a drug that might increase urine flow, so their urine flowed better (even though they did not receive the drug and even though their prostates had enlarged).

Just being in an experimental group creates change, and that can alter results in unanticipated ways. Many incidental effects of manipulation can be significant. For example, if we are testing whether a certain kind of monkey will learn when given some kind of explicit training, we must make sure that the control group is managed in the same way as the experimental group. If the training involves two hours of interaction with humans each day, then the monkeys in the control group must also get two hours of interaction with humans each day, but without the specific training program. Otherwise, we will not know whether it was the explicit training program or just general contact with humans that produced any result that occurs in the experimental group.

Experiments with humans need to be double-blind whenever possible

In human cases, to make sure that the introduced factor A is the only difference between the experimental group and the control group, we ordinarily must make the experiment *double-blind*: Neither the subject nor the person recording the results should know whether the subject is in an experimental group or a control group.

The fact that the subjects do not know whether they are in the control group or the experimental group helps to eliminate the placebo effect. Knowing about the experiment can often affect the subject's behavior in other ways as well. For example, patients who know that they are being treated for a condition will generally believe that changes in their condition, even small ones, are due to the treatment; on the other hand, if a patient knows that he is not being treated, then he will probably regard small improvements as insignificant. The result of this could be that small improvements that occur in both populations are recorded only for the experimental population, yielding results that are incorrectly biased in favor of the treatment.

Similarly, the people recording the results of a test must not let their views about the test influence their recording of results. If the person who is recording results knows which group a subject belongs to, the results in the experimental group can be regarded as significant (a very slight reduction in acne, in an acne remedy test, for example) when those same results (a very slight reduction) in the control group are ignored or set aside. The best remedy for this problem is to make sure that the person recording the observations does not know whether the subject is in the experimental group or the control group (though this is not always possible). This idea—that the recording of results should be "blind" if possible—applies in all experimental situations. And as we have said, when we have human subjects, then the subjects, too, must not know which group they are in.

Another experimental problem is also limited by the double-blind method. Patients often "cooperate" with doctors, reporting the results that they believe the doctor wishes to hear. If neither the patient nor the recording physician knows whether the patient is in an experimental group or a control group, then this effect will not be different in the two groups, so any difference between the groups will be due to the suspected causal agent being tested.

Of course, there is also the possibility of ordinary fraud in the collection of data, and true double-blind experimentation helps to limit some kinds of fraud as well.

Often it is impossible to make an experiment double-blind. People will know whether or not they have been forced to wear a patch over one eye, exercise for twenty minutes per day, take a freshman writing course, or the like. But if we do not make the experiment double-blind, the results are less convincing. An alternative possible explanatory factor exists. Subjects may behave differently because they realize that they are in the experimental (or control) group, or the results may be perceived or recorded differently because of the recorder's expectations about the experimental results. In such cases, it is especially important to have a very clear set of guidelines for detecting and observing possible effects.

Ethical barriers

Another barrier to effective studies is that tests with experimental and control groups cannot always be done ethically. Disease agents, helpful drugs, and anything else that is likely to be harmful or helpful must be administered with the subjects' welfare in mind, but that can mean that it is impossible to begin an experiment or that it is impossible to maintain a control group. It can be unethical to introduce factor A if A is or may be harmful. It can be unethical to withhold A if A is found to be beneficial. This problem has seriously impeded AIDS research, for example. If a new treatment is tested with an experimental group and a control group, then as soon as there is a hint of a positive finding, it becomes ethically important to consider discontinuing the control group so that the treatment may be administered to everyone. This makes it difficult to know whether the treatment has lasting or continued beneficial effects.

Some ethical barriers have been significantly breached. For example, the so-called Tuskegee experiment (staring in the 1940s) left some men with syphilis untreated (the control group) while others were treated with penicillin, the commonly recognized treatment. Even if a study of penicillin was needed, withholding this accepted treatment from the control group was an abominable breach of medical ethics.

In the 1950s, placebo surgery was done: An incision was made but no treatment was done for the control group, to test the effectiveness of the arterial surgery performed on the experimental group. Actually making an incision in order to have a genuine placebo treatment (where the patient will not know whether she is in the experimental group or the control group) may make for a better test of the treatment, but it is very difficult to justify inflicting the dangers involved in anesthesia and incision. Nevertheless, in this case, the placebo surgery had positive short-term benefits just as great as the benefit of the real surgery done for the experimental group. Surgery that was of no real benefit was abandoned because of this comparison.

Our ability to do controlled studies is thus ethically limited. Potentially helpful treatments for serious diseases often cannot ethically be withheld (so setting up a good control is difficult), and potentially harmful treatments should not be administered to an experimental group. We cannot do a controlled study of whether long-term tobacco use increases energy levels, because forcing our randomly selected experimental group to smoke (while preventing the randomly selected control group from smoking) would be unethical. We know that long-term smoking leads to debilitating diseases, pain, and premature death in many cases, so the benefits of the experiment cannot be sufficient to justify it.

Economic barriers

Controlled experiments cannot always be done economically. The process of finding, recruiting, and maintaining adequate experimental and control groups can be very costly. Consider the problems in an experiment that requires the long-term observation of the experimental and control groups in order to determine the effects of a certain drug. One must have large enough groups so that a few drop-outs won't matter; one has to find a way to administer the treatment to all in the experimental group (and an appropriate placebo to all in the control group); one must keep thorough, coded records, get changes of address, and bring people in for follow-up observation. All of this is expensive—in some cases, too expensive to justify the research.

If an effect takes a long time to develop, that compounds the problems of cost. It also introduces another, related problem. It may make it unrewarding for any experimenter to undertake the project. Even if the results would come in during the experimenter's lifetime, such investigations might take too long to contribute to the experimenter's professional recognition, and that can be an important barrier to their being done.

Other problems

Not all causally relevant factors can be introduced. For example, introducing Protestant ideology, gender, or kinds of sexual activity is ordinarily impossible, even though we might like to know the effects of these characteristics. Thus, not every hypothesis about causal influence is testable by a fully controlled experiment.

LESS THAN IDEAL: STATISTICAL STUDIES

Conducting a controlled experiment is a very effective way to get information about causal claims. If all goes well in a test of a claim that A causes Z, there will be only one difference between the experimental group and the control group that can explain a difference between the groups in the occurrence of Z. That difference will be the difference in whether A, the hypothesized causal factor, is present, so the experiment will provide a good test of whether A causes Z.

However, because it is often expensive, difficult, or impossible to do a fully controlled experiment, it is useful to try to find alternative ways of making causal judgments. Often we see reports of statistical studies that consider whether individuals with some hypothesized causal factor are more likely to exhibit a hypothesized effect. Our knowledge that cigarette smoking causes lung cancer, for example, is largely based on statistical studies. Even so, there is a general problem to watch out for in statistical studies. Because there is no random assignment of individuals to the comparison groups, there are often other initial differences between the groups that might account for any observed difference in the presence of the hypothesized effect. Statistical studies usually constitute much weaker evidence for a hypothesis than do controlled experiments, because statistical studies do not show as effectively that the hypothesis is the best explanation for the effects observed.

Let's look at this issue in more detail.

0. We begin with an hypothesis, such as "A causes Z in population P."

1. We identify the cases of A in some population and the cases of Z in that population.

2. We see whether a significantly larger proportion of A become Z than in the non-A part of the population. (Is #(Z & A)/#A significantly greater than #(Z & non-A)/#non-A?)

3. We make sure that A causing Z is the best explanation of any observed difference.

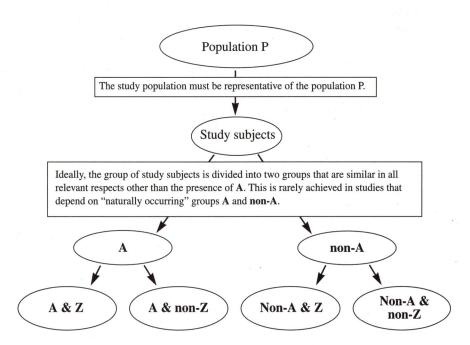

To know that A causes Z, we must at least be sure that the proportion of A's that are Z is significantly greater than the proportion of non-A's that are Z.

We can think of this in two different ways. Looking at possible causal factor A, we can wait to see whether Z occurs with more frequency among the A than among the non-A (that is, whether a significantly greater percentage of the people who were exposed to virus A have symptoms Z). If we look first at the end results, we will identify the cases of Z in the population and look to see whether A occurred more frequently among the Z than it did among the non-Z. These are ultimately equivalent, once all of the information is in.

In some cases, we focus more on the causal agent, waiting to see whether the effect occurs. If a group of people all eat a certain product that is suspected of containing a bacterium that causes an illness, we can wait to see whether the illness develops in them (and not in others who were not so exposed). This is sometimes called a "prospective" study, because we begin with introduction of the causal factor and look into the future (prospectively) for the effect.

In other cases, we focus on the effect first and look for the cause. If a number of people have food poisoning, we may trace back to find the common factor in their diets that led to it. This is sometimes called a "retrospective" (backward-looking) study.

In either case, though, we justify the causal claim (A caused Z) on the grounds that #(Z & A)/#A is significantly greater than #(Z & non-A)/#non-A. We can think of the non-A as being like the control group in a fully controlled experiment, because we must compare the A and non-A populations. However, this kind of study is very different from the controlled studies we discussed earlier, because we have not randomly assigned individuals to these groups. Because of that, we are not able to ensure that the groups are alike in all features except A, the proposed causal factor (and those things that are results of A). There may be other differences between the A and non-A groups, and those differences may serve as possible explanations for any difference in the groups, such as a greater prevalence of property Z (the hypothesized effect).

Problems with Statistical Studies

The principal difficulty here is that the population is "naturally" divided into the A and the non-A, rather than being divided on the basis of random assignment. As a result, there will probably be many differences between the A and non-A populations, and these other differences may provide the basis for other plausible explanations of any observed difference in the frequency with which Z occurs.

Students who take SAT courses do better than average on the SAT exam. However, such students may differ from other students in many ways. On average, they may

be more committed to studying and doing well in schoolwork

be smarter

study more hours for the SAT

have more concern about doing well on the SAT

have more money and go to better schools

etc.

Those other factors, rather than their taking the course, may account for these students' SAT success. A study based on available statistical information will be much weaker than a good controlled study (unless all of the other relevant differences can be identified and filtered out).

If we are looking for a cause of poisoning, we may find that all of the victims drank milk from the same store. But because they all went to the same store, they may have all bought some other product (bread, potato chips, or something else), or there may have been an environmental pollutant in the store or nearby. When we do not have a controlled study, we have no way of automatically eliminating such possibilities.

Other problems also plague statistical studies:

1. Whether we can do a statistical study at all depends on the existence of adequate records. Often the records we have do not correspond to the questions we wish to study.

2. Nothing eliminates placebo effects.

3. Ethical problems arise if Z is either good or bad and this study begins to be successful in linking A to Z. (These are problems that we already discussed in connection with controlled experiments.)

Advantages of statistical studies. On the positive side, statistical studies sometimes enable us to overcome some of the problems of controlled experiments, such as ethical problems, numbers, costs, and long-term continuation, because we rely on existing records or on the observation of phenomena that are not experimentally produced.

Overcoming some problems. Picking a population of non-A's that *match* the A's in all other factors thought to be relevant to Z can produce a better comparison. (This works only if we have a pretty good idea what else is relevant to the production of Z.) We do not need to compare the A group to the entire non-A population. It is better to compare the A's with a similar sub-population of the non-A's. We can even use a matching technique, pairing each A with a non-A that is like it in all other respects that are relevant to Z (if we know what else is relevant).

The need for similar populations is fairly evident. If we were trying to figure out whether watching MTV is good for your health, it would be misleading to compare the health of the group watching MTV to the health of the general population of people who do not watch MTV. We would find a much lower incidence of strokes, arthritis, and bed wetting in the MTV-watching population simply because not all age groups are equally represented in that population. Instead, we would want to compare the MTV group to a group in the general population that is as similar as possible in age and in other factors that might be related to health. Matching individuals in the A and non-A populations gives a much better comparison.

CHAPTER SUMMARY

When we are trying to establish a causal claim, statistical differences between groups can be relevant evidence, because most causal factors interact with a large number of other factors in producing an effect, and because different causal factors may have the same effect. (There is more than one way to get a rash.) A fully controlled experiment is the best way to establish a causal relationship, because in such an experiment the comparison groups—that is, the experimental group and the control group, should differ only in whether the hypothesized causal factor is present. The fact that individuals are randomly assigned to these groups should eliminate all differences that are not a result of this causal factor.

Fully Controlled Experiments

The ideal experiment to determine whether A causes Z is a **controlled experiment**. Such an experiment is based on the random selection of an **experimental group** and a **control group**, with an **introduced test factor A**. This is sometimes called a "randomized experiment."

0. We begin with an hypothesis, such as "A causes Z in population P."

1. We find a representative sample of P's in which neither A nor Z exists.

2. We divide our sample of P's into two groups on the basis of some feature that is not relevant to A or Z.

3. We introduce A throughout one group (the experimental group, EG) but not the other (the control group, CG).

4. We see whether the groups are significantly different in the instance of Z. Is #(Z & A)/#A significantly greater than #(Z & non-A)/#non-A? (Here #A refers to the number of individuals in the experimental group, and #non-A refers to the number of individuals in the control group, etc.)

5. We make sure that A causing Z is the best explanation of any observed difference.

Problems to look out for, even in controlled experiments, include the placebo effect and observer bias.

In a *double-blind* procedure, neither the experimental subject nor the person recording results know which individuals are in the experimental group. This solves some of these problems.

In many situations, it is difficult or impossible to do a fully controlled experiment. We can instead do statistical studies that consider whether individuals with the hypothesized causal factor are more likely to exhibit the hypothesized effect. Because there is no random assignment of individuals to the comparison groups, there are often other initial differences between the groups that can account for any observed difference in the presence of the hypothesized effect. Such studies constitute much weaker evidence for a hypothesis, because they do not show as effectively that the hypothesis is the best explanation for the effects observed.

Less than Ideal: Statistical Studies

0. We begin with an hypothesis, such as "A causes Z in population P."

1. We identify the cases of A in some population and the cases of Z in that population (or in a representative subset of that population).

2. We see whether a significantly larger number of A become Z than in the non-A part of the population. (Is #(Z & A)/#A significantly greater than #(Z & non-A)/#non-A?)

3. We make sure that A causing Z is the best explanation of any observed difference.

Ethical and economic problems sometimes make controlled experiments difficult or impossible. Although statistical studies can occasionally overcome some of the problems in doing controlled studies, one must still strive to avoid placebo effects and observer biases. The greater problem, however, is the fact that other possible explanatory factors have not been eliminated, as they would be in an ideal, fully controlled experiment. The A group will usually differ from the non-A group in many ways (not just in whether A is present), and some of those other differences may provide the basis for alternative explanations of any difference between the groups in the occurrence of Z.

EXERCISE 9A

1. The makers of Simon's Sunburn Soothing Salve (SSSS) claim that SSSS reduces the pain from severe sunburn. SSSS is a cream, and they say that applying SSSS to the sunburn and leaving it for six hours will lead to a significant reduction or elimination of the pain and itching that severe sunburn would ordinarily cause.

   Describe two studies, a fully controlled experiment and a statistical study, designed to determine whether these claims about SSSS are correct. **For each study, answer the following questions**.

   a. Exactly what hypothesis will be tested?

   b. What observations will tend to show that the hypothesis is true? Why? Could there be other explanations for those observations? If so, what?

   c. What observations will tend to show that the hypothesis is false? Why? Could there be other explanations for those observations? If so, what?

   d. What are the principal problems with the experiment you have described?

2. Many people claim that one of the advantages of a college education is that it increases a student's intellectual sophistication (IS) and knowledge of the world (KW). Suppose we had a satisfactory test of these qualities (IS and KW).

   a. What would be the design of a controlled experiment to test the hypothesis that college attendance increases IS and KW?

   b. Could we run an experiment of the type you described in answering question a? What problems would we have?

   c. What would be the design of a prospective experiment to test the same hypothesis?

   d. What problems would there be in using results from the prospective experiment to make a convincing case for the hypothesis?

3. [The following is one paragraph of a long article, "Your Child's Brain," by Sharon Begley, published in *Newsweek,* February 19, 1996. Gordon Shaw is a professor at UC Irvine. Reprinted by permission of Newsweek, Inc.]

"If you're working with little kids," says Gordon Shaw, "you're not going to teach them higher mathematics. . . . But they are interested in and can process music." So Shaw and Frances Rauscher randomly selected 19 preschoolers from a class of 40 students and gave them piano or singing lessons. After eight months, the researchers found, the children "dramatically improved in spatial reasoning," compared with children given no music lessons, as shown in their ability to work mazes, draw geometric figures and copy patterns of two-color blocks. The mechanism behind the "Mozart effect" remains murky, but Shaw suspects that when children exercise cortical neurons by listening to classical music, they are also strengthening circuits used for mathematics. Music, says the UC team, "excites the inherent brain patterns and enhances their use in complex reasoning tasks."

a. What did Shaw and Rauscher observe as a result of their study?

b. What theory is offered to explain these observations?

c. Are there any alternative explanations of the observations that should be considered? If so, what?

d. What information could help to show the correctness of the explanation(s) mentioned in the article?

4. At the close of the following article, based on a story in the *Post-Standard* (from the *Washington Post*), March 9, 1994, an experiment is described. Answer the following questions as well as you can, on the basis of the article. Indicate any lack of clarity in the article that makes it difficult to answer any of the questions.

a. What hypothesis (or hypotheses) is (or are) being tested by Ekman and Davidson?

b. Is their experiment a fully controlled experiment (with randomly selected experimental and control groups)?

c. What do they observe?

d. What conclusion do they draw from what they observe?

e. What alternative explanations for their observations should be considered?

That Certain Smile: Can It Trigger a Brain Response?

A spontaneous smile shows the good feeling of its bearer. Could it be that some smiles do more than just show good feeling—that they actually bring it about?

One particular kind of smile, which has become known as "Duchenne's smile," is thought to be an especially good indicator of inner pleasure. This smile involves the simultaneous use of two muscle groups: the person who smiles flexes the zygomatic muscles while contracting the orbicularis oculi muscles. Recent studies have confirmed that when this particular smile occurs, there is a distinct pattern of activity in the front of the brain, associated with pleasurable feeling.

Psychologists Paul Ekman and Richard Davidson tested whether this expression could be a cause of good feelings, rather than the other way around. They tested whether imitating Duchenne's smile could trigger the same physiological reactions that spontaneous good feelings give rise to.

They found 14 University of Wisconsin undergraduates who could learn to imitate Duchenne's smile voluntarily (a fairly rare skill).

The students' EEG's bore out the researchers' hypothesis. The patterns of brain activity for spontaneous Duchenne smiles and the deliberate Duchenne imitations were clearly similar.

5. Therapeutic touch (TT) is a practice that has been taught to over 43,000 health professionals. It is practiced by many registered nurses and supported by some nurses' organizations. Proponents of TT describe three basic steps, none of which actually requires touching the patient's body. The first step is centering, in which the practitioner focuses on his or her intent to help the patient. The second step is assessment, in which the practitioner's hands, from a distance of 5 to 10 centimeters (2 to 4 inches), sweep over the patient's body from head to feet, attuning to the patient's condition by becoming aware of changes in sensory cues in the hands. The third step is intervention, in which the practitioner's hands repattern the patient's energy field by removing "congestion," replenishing depleted areas, and smoothing out ill-flowing areas. The resultant "energy balance" purportedly stems disease and allows the patient's body to heal itself. (Based on a description in "A Close Look at Therapeutic Touch," Linda Rosa, BSN, RN; Emily Rosa; Larry Sarner; Stephen Barrett, MD, *Journal of the American Medical Association,* Vol. 279, No. 13, pp. 1005–1010. Abstract and full text available at: http://www.ama-assn.org/public/journals/jama/past_iss.htm#1998.)

a1. Describe a fully controlled experiment to test the effectiveness of TT in preventing and healing disease. Be sure to specify how observation would be done. If you wish to focus on a particular ailment, consider its use in treating foot pain.

b1. What observations would suggest that TT works?

c1. What observations would show that TT does not work?

d1. Are there any serious obstacles to carrying out the experiment you have described? Are there potential obstacles to interpreting its results?

a2. Now describe a statistical study that might be done to evaluate the effectiveness of therapeutic touch in preventing and healing disease.

b2. What observations would suggest that TT works?

c2. What observations would show that TT does not work?

d2. Are there any serious obstacles to carrying out the study you have described? Are there potential obstacles to interpreting its results? How does this compare to the controlled experiment in terms of the value of its results?

6. Suppose that a manufacturer of baby foods has begun to market a new line of baby food (ClearUp Baby Foods) containing a natural product that is said to reduce diaper rash when consumed with baby food. We would like to know whether this additive is really effective.

   Describe *two* different studies, one a fully controlled experiment (with random assignment) and the other a statistical study. For each experiment, answer these questions:

   a. What hypothesis will be tested?
   b. What observations will tend to show that the hypothesis is true? Why? Could there be other explanations for those observations? If so, what?
   c. What observations will tend to show that the hypothesis is false? Why? Could there be other explanations for those observations? If so, what?
   d. What are the principal problems with each type of experiment that you have described?

7. [The following account is based on a story published in *Newsweek* on October 24, 1994.] Studies by Linda Stroh find that men from traditional families, in which the wives stay home to care for the household, earn more and get higher raises than men from two-career families. Stroh based her study on 348 male managers at twenty Fortune 500 companies, where she found that for men with working wives, salaries were significantly lower and raises less frequent than for men with wives who did not work. These differences showed up even when age, experience, and time working for the company were equal. Stroh concludes that discrimination is the cause of the salary differences that she discovered; most of the companies are run by men whose wives do not work, and those bosses reward managers who fit the same mold.

   a. What did Linda Stroh observe?
   b. What conclusion(s) is (or are) based on these observations?
   c. What alternative explanations of the observations should be considered?
   d. What information would be needed to show that the explanation(s) mentioned in the article are correct?

8. In a yearlong study at Stanford university, researchers attempted to determine the effects of different types of exercise on people over 65. These researchers tested the members of a sample population for cardiovascular fitness, ability to walk significant distances, ability to lift weights, and levels of comfort and flexibility in their daily lives. Then the sample population (67 women and 36 men) was divided into two groups.

Group A did exercises designed to improve endurance and strength: brisk walking, low-impact aerobics, and strength-building exercises with large latex bands.

Group B did exercises designed to retain and improve flexibility: stretching and other moderate exercise.

Results for group A: exhibited better cardiovascular fitness and were able to walk farther and lift heavier objects than those in group B. Reported a higher degree of physical pain in their daily lives than they experienced before the study.

Results for group B: reported more comfort and flexibility in their daily lives than they experienced before the study.

a. Judging on the basis of this report, there was no true control group in this study. A true control group would be a randomly selected group that was tested at the beginning and the end of the study but that did no significant exercise during the year of the study. What additional information would be available if there had been a true control group?

b. Why do you think there was no control group in this case?

c. On the basis of these results, doctors recommended that people over 65 do all of the exercises that were done by groups A and B. Are there any reasons to be cautious about this recommendation?

9. Some people think that running regularly helps to prevent colds. In particular, they say, after you run regularly (at least three times per week, at least 20 minutes each time) for a few weeks, you will have additional cold resistance that is maintained as long as you continue such regular running.

a1. Describe a fully controlled experiment to test the hypothesis that running helps to prevent colds. Be sure to specify how observation would be done.

b1. What observations would support the hypothesis?

c1. What observations would show that the hypothesis is false?

d1. Are there any serious obstacles to carrying out the experiment you have described? Are there potential obstacles to interpreting its results?

a2. Now describe a statistical study that might be done to evaluate the hypothesis.

b2. What observations would support the hypothesis?

c2. What observations would show that the hypothesis is false?

d2. Are there any serious obstacles to carrying out the study you have described? Are there potential obstacles to interpreting its results? How would this compare to the controlled experiment in terms of the value of its results?

CHAPTER 10

DECISION MAKING

In making decisions about what to do, we are guided by our desires and our beliefs. What would be a desirable outcome of the actions that I can do now? What
do I value? What will be the outcome of my action? What can I achieve?

At this point, we are ready to formulate explicitly some of the procedures and
principles that should go into decisions about what to do. We will consider procedures for determining what you value, and we will look at some ways of deciding
what to do when you are uncertain about the outcome of your action. For most of
the chapter, we will focus on individual decisions, though in the last few pages, we
will consider some of the special issues that come up when the decisions of several
individuals affect each other.

This chapter is also related to issues that we considered in Chapter 2. There
we said that you could justify a *should* conclusion if you could justify SC (the
premise that says that your action will achieve your goal), OMC (the premise that
says that your action is the best way to achieve your goal), and EJM (the premise
that says that achieving your goal in that way is worth it). Two key elements of this
need a further look, though.

One is the question of **uncertainty**: What if you think that it is likely but not
certain that your action will achieve the desired goal? Is there a way to balance ra-
tionally the possibility of failure with the value of a goal? We will look at this question and consider some ideas that have been applied. In other words, what should
you do when SC is not strictly true, because the action *might* not work, though there
is some reasonable probability that your action will achieve the goal?

When we are uncertain about the outcome of our actions and yet still must
choose, we need some ways to take this uncertainty into account. How can we
choose most safely? How do we maximize the value of our actions when we are not
sure what will happen? When should we gamble? We will look at these questions
and try to devise reasonable procedures for answering them. In doing this, we are
filling in the big gap that we mentioned in Chapter 2. There the arguments generally
assumed that you knew what the outcome of your actions would be. Here we will
consider how to decide what you should do even when your information about the
outcome of your actions is imperfect.

Even before we consider the issue of uncertainty, though, we need to consider how we can decide what we **value** and how we can compare the value of various goals. (Because OMC and EJM are about the value of various actions and outcomes, this material can also be seen as helping us to see how we decide whether OMC and EJM are true.)

Knowing what you value is not always easy, but you cannot begin to make decisions about what to do without some beliefs about what you would like to have happen. The procedures we will consider rely on two different kinds of information about your values. Some procedures use *rankings* of possible goals; you may like chocolate cake more than pecan pie, and pecan pie more than apple pie. They are ranked 1, 2, 3. Other procedures will require more: a weighted *rating* or *preference scaling*. For example, you might need to know whether the difference in desirability between chocolate cake and pecan pie is greater than the difference between pecan pie and apple pie. You might rate them 10, 8, and 3 (as distinct from, say, 10, 5, and 3) on a scale of 1 to 10 (with 10 being the best). Just ranking our preferences can be difficult in many situations; preference scaling is almost always difficult. We will examine some ways of working around these difficulties so that we can create rankings and preference scalings that can serve as the basis for reasonable decision making.

The procedures and principles to be considered here are not magic. They are guidelines for making decisions, but we must make some value estimates and guesses about probabilities of outcomes in making decisions. We will have to learn to deal with some pitfalls of such approximation.

For important decisions, I think you will find it useful to have spent some time thinking about the elements of good decision making.

FRAMING THE DECISION PROBLEM

Suppose that you are ordering dessert at a restaurant. If there are three desserts on the menu—chocolate cake, pecan pie, and apple pie—then you will usually see your decision as a relatively simple one: Decide which of those you prefer, and then order it. Even though this is a simple procedure, it is worth our time to think about what goes into framing the problem this way.

You probably have many more options available than just these three. You could order these things for dessert, for example: green peas, pecan pie and green peas, pecan pie and apple pie, pecan pie and apple pie and pot roast, etc. In restricting yourself to the three things in the standard dessert list, you have already passed over two kinds of decisions.

If you restrict yourself to the three items on the dessert list, you have left green peas and pot roast (and all the other things in the other sections of the menu) out of consideration. This may be a perfectly reasonable thing to do; in fact, our dining practices lead us to do this without having to make explicit decisions about it, and most of us use these practices to help us narrow down the options available. We *identify the set of possible actions that are worth considering* at this point by eliminating all the non-sweets from consideration. But it is worth keeping in mind that in important decisions, we may wish to expand or contract the set of possibilities available for consideration. Our list then should be *exhaustive*; it should include all the possibilities that are worth considering so that we can make a fully informed decision about what to do.

If you restrict yourself to choosing one of the three dessert items, you have left some other possibilities out of consideration. You have not considered the possibility of ordering two or three (or more) desserts, sampling more than one type and perhaps even making multiple orders of some. Again, you may feel that this is a beneficial limit on your options, for reasons of finances, health, time, or social respectability. In the broader perspective, however, the three choices of dessert are *not mutually exclusive*; you could order more than one. Ordinarily, when we make a careful choice, we want our list of options to have *mutually exclusive* actions; doing more than one action on the list should not be a possibility worth considering. If you have already decided that having more than one dessert is definitely not worth considering, then you have four choices:

> Order nothing.
>
> Order chocolate cake.
>
> Order pecan pie.
>
> Order apple pie.

If you are willing to consider ordering up to two desserts, then you have a much wider range of options:

> Order nothing.
>
> Order one piece of chocolate cake only.
>
> Order one piece of pecan pie only.
>
> Order one piece of apple pie only.
>
> Order two pieces of chocolate cake.
>
> Order two pieces of pecan pie.
>
> Order two pieces of apple pie.
>
> Order chocolate cake and pecan pie.
>
> Order chocolate cake and apple pie.
>
> Order pecan pie and apple pie.

And if you are willing to order up to three desserts, your range of choices expands enormously (along with your waistline).

In listing the choices in the way I did, I was making sure that they constituted an *exhaustive* set of *mutually exclusive* options. After you chose to limit yourself to the dessert menu, and after you chose a maximum dessert limit, these lists contain all of the options that were under consideration, and no two could be done together within the limits determined. Often we accept limits (like the limit of one item from the dessert list) without considering those limits. This is helpful in keeping our decision making reasonable, but in important cases, we should be careful to slow down to think about possible actions that we may have overlooked.

If you work in a large company that wishes to expand your department, you might have the task of finding an excellent person to add to your staff. If you find two excellent people, don't spend time trying to decide between them until you check to see whether hiring A and hiring B are really mutually exclusive options. Perhaps you can hire both of them. People sometimes take it for granted that two actions are exclusive when they really are not. (Neglecting the possibility of hiring both may be a case of false dilemma, in other words.)

If you have to move to San Francisco to accept a great job that you were just offered, don't assume you have to choose between staying with your boyfriend John and moving to the new job until you make sure that these are really mutually exclusive choices. Maybe John will move to San Francisco with you.

FRAMING THE PROBLEM

To frame the problem is to identify the set of possible actions. It should be an exhaustive set of mutually exclusive possibilities.

Mutually exclusive actions: They cannot be done together. Your options should be mutually exclusive—otherwise, you wouldn't have to choose among them; you could do more than one. (People really do make mistakes because of this, by choosing between X and Y without adequately considering whether they can do both.)

Exhaustive set: At least one action in the set will be done. The set does not omit any possible actions.

It is not always possible to organize our decisions into an exhaustive set of mutually exclusive alternatives that is manageable. For example, if you are choosing courses, and you have no requirements to fulfill, and you are going to take up to five courses, then you have 5^n possible combinations (where n is the number of courses offered). This is not a surveyable set of options. To choose courses, you need to eliminate many possibilities before you can begin to organize your set of options into an exhaustive set of mutually exclusive alternatives.

Even worse, consider the problem of balancing revenues and costs in a large institution, such as a university that needs revenues from student tuition and that must make financial cutbacks. You have many options to consider.

Fire employees? How many, and which ones?

Decrease salaries? How much? Which ones?

Increase tuition? How much?

Decrease financial aid? How much?

Increase housing costs? How much?

And *any combination of these.*

There will ordinarily be no way to organize these choices into a tidy set of options—an exhaustive set of mutually exclusive options.

In this chapter, we consider only those kinds of decisions that can be organized into an exhaustive set of mutually exclusive options.

DECISIONS WITH KNOWN OUTCOMES

If you are limiting yourself to a single dessert, then you have four choices in our example. Suppose you prefer chocolate cake to pecan pie and to apple pie and to no dessert. Then you are ready to order. You know what your set of choices is, you know what you prefer, and you know what the outcome of your action will be (if the waiter is still paying attention and they haven't run out of chocolate cake while you were deciding). Go for it!

Not all choices are so easy. Even when you know the outcomes of the possible actions under consideration, in complex cases you may have difficulty determining what you prefer. For example, you know that if you pull the lever for Sanchez at the election place, then you will have voted for Sanchez. You may have trouble deciding what your preference is, though; you may have trouble deciding whether you prefer to vote for Sanchez or for Wong. Perhaps Sanchez holds the same opinion as you about abortion but has different opinions about health policy, whereas Wong agrees with you on health policy but disagrees on abortion policy. In the case of decision outcomes with multiple attributes, there are several methods for deciding.

Satisficing

If you are selecting from among a large number of options and it is not important to make the very best choice, you can follow a procedure called *satisficing*. This term refers to the procedure of picking the first action you consider that has an acceptable outcome. This is a good procedure to use in ordering at a Chinese restaurant or in choosing among multiple brands of tuna fish at the supermarket. You have a very wide range of options available, and probably many of them will fulfill your needs well. If you follow the satisficing procedure, you can choose without considering all of the available options, so your decision is more efficient. As long as you are sure that the first dish you pick at the Chinese restaurant will provide a satisfying meal at an acceptable price, you can chat with your friends instead of spending more time looking over the menu. As long as you are sure that the differences in price, quality, and portion size are not great, this method for choosing tuna is fine. Your outcome will be acceptable, it will differ little from the best possible outcome, and you will have saved some time.

Elimination by Aspects

Satisficing is not usually appropriate in the case of voting. There are usually not very many candidates, so you can consider all of them, and even the best of your options may not fulfill all of your important criteria. Studies suggest that many people use the method of *elimination by aspects* when deciding how to vote. When you follow this method in selecting a candidate, you first *rank the issues* (the important *aspects* of evaluation) in order of importance, $A_1, \ldots, A_n$; then you eliminate all candidates who are unacceptable with respect to the most important issue,

A₁; then you eliminate all candidates who are unacceptable with respect to the next most important issue, A₂; and so on until you have only one candidate left. If Sanchez and Wong are the only candidates, and if health policy is the most important issue to you, then you will pick Wong (who agrees with you on health policy) over Sanchez (who doesn't), if you follow this method.

However, elimination by aspects will not always produce the choice that optimizes your total set of preferences. For example, if Wong agrees with you on health policy but disagrees radically with you on almost everything else, then Sanchez may be a much better choice for you, all things considered. If you use elimination by aspects as your method of choice, you will have eliminated Sanchez from consideration without taking all of the relevant, available information into consideration, and you will not have made the best choice.

Multi-attribute Utility Theory

A method called *multi-attribute utility theory* (MAUT) can lead to a better outcome. This procedure brings together considerable information about the possible outcomes of your actions and produces a preference scaling. More information is needed to get the procedure started, and so it is more difficult to apply, but it can produce helpful guidelines for making complex, important decisions. When we have many evaluative factors to consider in making a choice, it is helpful to have a good method for bringing all of these factors into the decision-making process.

Applied to our voting problem, MAUT would work in the following way. You would begin by identifying the important attributes you are looking for in the possible outcomes of your action. You might want a candidate whose positions on important issues are in good agreement with yours and who shows the ability to carry out policies effectively. Next you will need to develop a *preference scaling* for the various important attributes. For example, you might evaluate features of the candidates on the following scale, assigning numbers from 1 to 10 (with 10 being the most important).

ATTRIBUTE

---

10   ability to execute policies

Agreement with you on:

8   abortion policy

7   health care

4   waste disposal

2   tourism development

2   affirmative action policy

To the left I have indicated the value assigned to each of the important evaluative factors. These are numerical values on a scale of 1 to 10; they are not just an ordering. In the MAUT procedure, it may make a difference whether health care receives a 7 or a 5, even though that would not change the ordering of the attributes considered. This kind of rating, in which more than order counts, is called a *ranking with weighted differences* or a *preference scaling*.

Your next step is to assign a value for each attribute in the case of each of the possible outcomes. In this case, you would assign a value for each attribute as it applies to each of the candidates, because the outcome of your decision will be the selection of a candidate to receive your vote. You want a rating of each candidate with respect to each attribute. We can use a scale of 1 to 10 again (or choose some other uniformly applied scale).

ATTRIBUTE	SANCHEZ	WONG
10 ability to execute policies	8	6
Agreement with you on:		
8 abortion policy	10	2
7 health care	3	9
4 waste disposal	2	10
2 tourism development	3	9
2 affirmative action policy	3	8

Now you can assign a preference number to each candidate. For each candidate, multiply the weight for each attribute by the value assigned to the candidate for that attribute, and then add all the values together. For Sanchez, we would have the following calculation:

$$(10 \times 8) + (8 \times 10) + (7 \times 3) + (4 \times 2) + (2 \times 3) + (2 \times 3) = 201$$

If we let $A_1, \ldots, A_n$ be the attributes, and if we let $O_i(A_n)$ stand for the values assigned to outcome i for attribute n, then the general formula applied to the action of voting for Sanchez (O_1) is

$$[A_1 \times O_1(A_1)] + [A_2 \times O_1(A_2)] + [A_3 \times O_1(A_3)] + [A_4 \times O_1(A_4)] +$$
$$[A_5 \times O_1(A_5)] + [A_6 \times O_1(A_6)] = O_1 \text{ preference rating}$$

The general formula for any action with outcome O_i involving attributes $A_1, \ldots, A_n$ is

$$[A_1 \times O_i(A_1)] + \cdots + [A_n \times O_i(A_n)] = O_i \text{ preference rating}$$

When we apply it to voting for Wong, we get the following calculation:

$$(10 \times 6) + (8 \times 2) + (7 \times 9) + (4 \times 10) + (2 \times 9) + (2 \times 8) = 213$$

Wong (213) comes out with a higher preference rating than Sanchez (201), so it appears that your preferences would be served better by a vote for Wong.

You might not feel very confident about this result. After all, it relies on some fairly arbitrary numerical assignments, and you might not be sure that you got those right. And you are probably wise to be suspicious in this case. Sanchez and Wong get different ratings, but the difference is not huge. Small changes in just a few of the numbers would affect the outcome. Because of the many approximations involved, a difference like this (less than 15%) in the final preference rating is probably not a very strong indicator of preference.

Still, even when you get this kind of result, showing little difference, you have gone through a useful process. You have closely considered the relevant attributes of your possible action outcomes, and you have decided what is important to you. If you get an inconclusive result, you can expand the range of attributes considered and see whether doing so makes a difference. There is little more that you can do in making a decision, and this procedure will help you to consider what is relevant and will enable you to bring all your thoughts to bear in generating a single result. If a large difference shows up, you can expect it to be a good indication of how you can make a choice that optimizes what you value. If the difference is small, then if you really have considered everything that is relevant, it will not matter very much what you choose.

Let's look at another example to see how we might apply this procedure. Suppose you have just finished your degree and you have three job offers:

A job as a computer programmer, at $42,000 per year, in Rochester, New York

A job as a program checker, at $35,000 per year, in Boston

A job managing the software library of a large firm, at $30,000 per year, in San Francisco

Suppose further that you feel you have all of the information you need about these jobs. It still might not be immediately clear what to do. Perhaps the Rochester job is the most interesting job, and it certainly has the best pay, but we will imagine that you would prefer the other locations. Let's try MAUT. Suppose that these three factors are the main things worth considering (no other factor could make a significant difference). Then you will need to weight the three attributes and assign a rating to each job for each attribute. Suppose your preferences worked out as follows:

ATTRIBUTE			
RATING	JOB A	JOB B	JOB C
WHERE	Rochester	Boston	San Francisco
2	5	8	10
WHAT	programmer	checker	librarian
5	10	8	7
HOW MUCH	$42,000	35,000	30,000
3	10	9	8

For each job, we can now determine a rating.

A $(2 \times 5) + (5 \times 10) + (3 \times 10) = 90$

B $(2 \times 8) + (5 \times 8) + (3 \times 9) = 83$

C $(2 \times 10) + (5 \times 7) + (3 \times 8) = 79$

Job A is slightly ahead of the other two, and they are about even. Thus A appears to be the best choice if you have assigned values correctly. MAUT suggests that A may be better, but the difference is not great enough to regard this as a reliable stopping point in your deliberations.

One way to carry your deliberations further would be to think of other attributes of the jobs that might be significant: Job security, opportunities for advancement, opportunities for further education, fringe benefits, and vacation time could be additional factors to consider. Then you could apply MAUT to this fuller set of attributes.

Another possibility is that you might look at the result of applying MAUT in the first place and see immediately that it is wrong. You are sure that you want to go to San Francisco, no matter what this calculation tells you. Then you have discovered something about yourself. Evidently, the place where you live is more important to you than you first thought it was. That attribute deserves a greater weight, or perhaps the values assigned to the three cities should show a greater difference.

ATTRIBUTE			
RATING	JOB A	JOB B	JOB C
WHERE	Rochester	Boston	San Francisco
5	4	7	10
WHAT	programmer	checker	librarian
3	10	8	7
How Much	$42, 000	35, 000	30, 000
2	10	9	8

For each job, we can now determine a new rating.

A $(5 \times 4) + (3 \times 10) + (2 \times 10) = 70$

B $(5 \times 7) + (3 \times 8) + (2 \times 9) = 77$

C $(5 \times 10) + (3 \times 7) + (2 \times 8) = 97$

If you have it right now, then you can head for San Francisco. You have thought the issue through and come to see how much it means to you to go to San Francisco. MAUT has helped you to focus on the relevant features of the problem and bring them together.

In the case of a real decision of this kind, you are likely to have many other factors to consider, such as job security, opportunities for advancement, opportunities to find other positions, and so on. In addition, you might wish to make finer categories. Our category "where," for example, might include many factors, such as proximity to family, climate, and a city's ambiance. That means more calculation, but as the factors proliferate, MAUT becomes more useful. It allows you to consider the attributes one at a time and then bring together the results of those deliberations in a sensible way.

There are two other important "rules" of good decision making. The first is *Eliminate unsatisfactory options.* If you have a range of acceptable choices, then at any stage of your deliberations, you can eliminate any option that is clearly unacceptable with respect to some attribute. For example, living in Rochester may be quite unacceptable to you. If so, then you can eliminate job A immediately, because you have some acceptable options. Or if earning $30,000 per year in San Francisco is clearly too little for you, then you can eliminate job C at an early stage. Making these eliminations as early as possible will help to simplify your deliberations.

The other important rule is *Eliminate dominated options.* In our example, if your preferences for places were slightly different, and you preferred Boston to San Francisco, then you could eliminate the San Francisco job from consideration. The Boston job would rank higher with respect to every attribute being considered (location, job responsibilities, salary). In fact, if the cities of Boston and San Francisco were tied in your preference ranking, that would be enough to justify eliminating the San Francisco job, because the Boston job would rank higher with respect to some attributes (quality of job and salary) and would not be lower with respect to any attribute. The San Francisco job is dominated. You can eliminate it from consideration in this kind of a situation. (Note that this rule can be applied on the basis of rankings, before a preference scale is created. Thus it may enable you to simplify your decision at an early stage.) Following this rule will not ordinarily determine what to choose; you may still have more than one option, even after you eliminate the dominated options. But following this rule can simplify your decision problem.

You should notice that MAUT produces more than just a ranking of the options. It produces a preference scaling, with numbers that indicate the ordering of preferences *and* the relative "distance" between adjacent items on the list. If job A receives 97, B receives 77, and C receives 70, then we know that the difference between A and B is large and that the difference between B and C is not large. (Of course, you need a preference scaling of attributes to get MAUT started.)

Some of the methods we will consider for deciding what to do under conditions of uncertainty will require preference scaling, not just a ranking, and MAUT can be useful because it determines an appropriate input (a scaling or rating of preferences) for these methods.

SUMMARY: DECISIONS WITH KNOWN OUTCOMES

To select an action *when the outcomes are known,* we need only *rank-order* the outcomes (with costs) of the actions. We do not need preference scaling (rankings with weighted differences). In other words, we need a preferential ordering, but not the strength of the preferences.

But sometimes we have difficulty rank-ordering outcomes, because they have multiple attributes, and outcome X may rank high on attribute A and low on B while Y ranks high on attribute B and low on A. Then careful comparison requires some procedure for selecting outcomes. Here are some ideas.

(continued on next page)

Eliminate unsatisfactory actions: If one attribute of the outcome of an action A is unsatisfactory, then action A *is an unsatisfactory action.* If there are some actions with outcomes that are satisfactory with respect to all attributes, then action A can be eliminated from consideration. (This can simplify your decision problem.)

Eliminate dominated actions: If the outcome of action A ranks higher than the outcome of action B with respect to some attributes worth considering, and if A ranks at least as high as B with respect to every attribute, then action A *dominates* action B. Action B can be eliminated from consideration. (This simplifies the decision problem.)

Satisficing: Pick the first action you consider that has an acceptable outcome— that is, the first that exceeds an established acceptability level with respect to every important attribute. (This saves time.)

Elimination by aspects: Put the *attributes* of each action in order of importance, $A_1, \ldots, A_n$. Eliminate any actions that are unacceptable with respect to attribute A_1; then do this for A_2; and so on until only one is left or until all are acceptable in every way. (In the latter case, choose arbitrarily or apply MAUT.)

MAUT: Weight the relevant attributes and devise comparable scales (such as 1 to 10) for each attribute. Then apply MAUT by adding the weighted values (attribute weight times scalar value) for the identified attributes of the outcome. This determines a *ranking* of the outcomes, and it also determines a *preference scaling* (a rating). Only the *ranking* is really needed for decisions with certainty of outcome, but a *preference scaling* is useful in other decision situations.

EXERCISE 10A

1. Rachel is a student who lives in an apartment off campus. She wants to buy a bicycle so that she will be able to get to campus more easily during the school year and so that she will be able to get to her summer job. Getting a bicycle that is light in weight is very important, because it will be much easier to ride and much easier to move in and out of the storage area in her apartment building where she will be parking it. She must also be careful of cost, though. She could spend up to $600 for a bicycle, but if she spends more than $300, she will have to cut down on her purchases of other things she enjoys (such as compact discs, movies, and dinners out). She would also like a bike that is easy to maintain, because she doesn't know much about bicycles. After eliminating the very expensive bikes and the inappropriately specialized bikes, she has narrowed her choice to two at the bicycle store. She also knows of one used bike that she could buy.

   The **Italia**: This bicycle is very lightweight, and it would fit Rachel's riding needs perfectly. On the down side, however, it costs $560, and it requires some maintenance operations that Rachel feels she would not do well.

The **Ralston**: This bicycle is significantly heavier and bulkier than the Italia. Because of this, it would be much harder to ride and a little more awkward to move into and out of her building, though she could manage it. The Ralston costs $290, and it is very easy to maintain.

The used **Schwein**: This bike is very heavy, so riding would be hard, and it would be very awkward to move into and out of her building. In addition, because it is used, it will require significant maintenance effort. It costs $70.

a. Indicate how Rachel might try to come to a solution by using the method of *elimination by aspects*. Assume that, among bikes priced under $600, her most important criterion is weight, a very heavy bike being unacceptable with respect to this attribute. Her next most important criterion is price; any difference over $100 would eliminate the bike with a higher price. Ease of maintenance is third in importance.

b. Indicate how multi-attribute utility theory would be used to try to make a selection. Assign the numbers that you need to make calculations in accordance with this selection method. Does this process yield a clear choice?

2. Ralph is trying to decide which of three cars to buy. He wants a car with good fuel economy in the city, but it is more important to him that it look nice so that he can impress his friends. It is also important that it be comfortable. Of principal importance, however, is that the car run well. He has found three cars that are all about the same price.

The **Albatross**: This car has good power and runs very well, but it gets only 15 miles to the gallon in the city. It looks OK, and it is pretty comfortable.

The **Buzzard**: The Buzzard looks much nicer than the Albatross, and it also gets 15 mpg in the city. It has good power and runs very well, and it is pretty comfortable.

The **Chicken**: The Chicken gets 22 mpg in city driving, has good power, and runs all right, though it is not as smooth and consistent as the other two cars. It is definitely not as nice-looking as the Albatross and the Buzzard, but it is significantly more comfortable inside.

Show how multi-attribute utility theory (MAUT) could be used to help Ralph decide. Show your calculations, and indicate what he should decide and why. Fill in any reasonable details of the story that you need in order to apply MAUT. (Any reasonable specification will be acceptable.)

3. Doug is trying to choose among three colleges at which he has been accepted, and he is having trouble deciding which he prefers. Doug doesn't know what he wants to major in, and all of the colleges he is considering seem to have adequate programs for any major that he is interested in now. He would like a college that is not too challenging academically but that will keep him interested. He wants a relaxed student atmosphere and good opportunities for study abroad, and he really wants to study Japanese. In addition, he would like to be able to work at the radio station while he is on campus.

Herbert College: Not too challenging. Has interesting topical seminars for freshmen. Very friendly students. Special problems in using his financial assistance if he takes a semester abroad, so he probably couldn't take a semester abroad. Offers just one year of Japanese. Friendly assistance and good opportunities for working at the radio station.

Beaufort College: A little bit more challenging than he would prefer. Students not as friendly as at the other colleges. Good program in Japanese, well integrated with an appealing semester abroad. Friendly assistance and good opportunities for working at the radio station.

St. Sigmund U.: Not too challenging. Special projects associated with freshman courses provide for interesting study opportunities. Students not as friendly as at Herbert College. Good program in Japanese, well integrated with an appealing semester abroad. Friendly assistance and good opportunities for working at the radio station.

Indicate how multi-attribute utility theory (MAUT) could be used to help Doug make this decision. Fill in the details so that you can show how to get a MAUT evaluation of his various options. (Creating a suitable chart will be helpful. It is not necessary to discuss your specification of Doug's preferences in great detail, as long as they are reasonable.)

4. Sarah is trying to decide how to vote in a senatorial primary campaign. There are four candidates, and she would like to vote for the candidate who best represents her views. Sarah holds the following views, her views on abortion being the most important to her, welfare next, affirmative action next, and foreign policy next. Sarah does not have strong opinions on other issues.

Abortion: Sarah favors the availability of abortion, with no restrictions. She also favors government payment for abortion for women who are not able to pay for those abortions themselves.

Welfare: Sarah believes that healthy people should not be able to continue to get welfare payments for prolonged periods.

Affirmative action: Sarah believes that affirmative action programs should be continued, with regard to both educational opportunities and employment opportunities.

Foreign policy: Sarah believes that the United States should never send troops into troubled areas, such as Somalia, Bosnia, and Rwanda. If they are to go at all, she would want them to be a part of a UN mission.

There are four candidates, who hold the following views:

Alvarez: Believes it is important for the government to take action where it can help people. He favors the continued availability of abortion, with government payment for abortion for women who are not able to pay for those abortions themselves. He also favors a welfare system that continues to provide financial assistance as long as a person needs it. He favors continuing affirmative action programs. He thinks that the United States should "live up to its responsibilities as the only superpower" and should send U.S. troops into world trouble spots even when the United Nations does not support the mission.

Baranoff: Favors the availability of abortion for those who can pay, but does not favor government payments for abortions. Believes we should drastically limit the length of time during which healthy people can get welfare payments, except in the case of single parents of young children. Would eliminate all affirmative action programs. Believes that the United States should never send troops into troubled areas, such as Somalia, Bosnia, and Rwanda.

Chen: Opposes the availability of abortion. Believes that we should not limit the length of time during which healthy people can get welfare payments. Would eliminate all affirmative action programs. Favors U.S. participation in UN missions to trouble spots, but opposes independent U.S. action.

Davidson: Favors the availability of abortion for those who can pay, but does not favor government payments for abortions. Agrees that we should drastically limit the length of time during which healthy people can get welfare payments. Would eliminate all business affirmative action programs, but would encourage educational institutions to continue affirmative action programs. Thinks the United States should send U.S. troops into world trouble spots even when the United Nations does not support the mission.

a. How might Sarah use elimination by aspects to make her decision? Are there any problems with applying that method in this case?

b. Can any candidate be eliminated from consideration because that option is dominated?

c. Show how multi-attribute utility theory (MAUT) could be used to help Sarah decide. Show your calculations. Fill in any reasonable details of the story that you need in order to apply MAUT. (Any reasonable specification will be acceptable.)

d. Indicate what she should decide and why.

5. Carl would like to buy a nice sound system, with an AM/FM receiver. He wants to be able to play both CDs and cassettes, and he wants the best possible sound, but he is not a sound "perfectionist" and would settle for less than the best if there were other advantages. He would like to be able to have good sound in several different rooms in his house. Once in a while, he likes to listen to music when he is doing something outdoors. Being able to play multiple CDs would be a nice feature. He could spend up to $1000, but finding something that costs less would be a definite advantage.

He is considering three options:

The **Voce**: This little radio and (single) CD player gets great sound for such a small unit, though not the best possible sound. You can also hook it up to a walkman (for cassettes), and you get pretty good sound. Hooking up is a little inconvenient, but the walkman can of course be used separately, with headphones, for full portability. The central radio unit is small enough to move around easily from room to room in the house, though the cables get awkward when the walkman is connected. Cost: the Voce radio with CD player costs $480; the walkman and connecting cables come to $70.

The **Boomer:** A single large boombox player would include a radio, single CD player, and cassette player for $320. Although heavy, it is portable from room to room (and even outside if he wants to put eight batteries in). It would have the advantage of having no connecting wires to carry around for the cassette, but the sound is not nearly as good as that of the Voce.

Components: He can buy separate components: an amplifier, multi-disc player, good cassette player, and speakers. This gives him the best sound, a little bit better than the Voce. This system is not portable at all. With the used and new equipment he has found, he could put the system together for $950.

a. Explain how Carl could make a decision using elimination by aspects. (Add any additional information that you would need to apply this method.) Is there any problem with this method?

b. Is any option dominated? Explain.

c. Explain how he would make a decision using multi-attribute utility (MAUT) theory. Show your calculations. (Fill in any reasonable details of the story that you need in order to apply MAUT. Any reasonable specification will be acceptable.)

d. What should he do? If you need any other information to decide what he should do, then say how the decision depends on that information.

6. Michael is trying to decide which set of dining room furniture to buy. He is at a secondhand shop that has three sets (each with a table and six chairs) that he is considering, and they are somewhat different. (He is sure that this is the best place in town to buy his furniture; he won't get as good a deal anywhere else.)

The **fifties look**: This is a set of metal furniture with aqua-colored seats, seat-backs, and table top made of some kind of an artificial substance, probably Formica. Michael doesn't like the look very much, and he would like to have something that is more impressive, but the seats are comfortable enough, and the set is very durable, so he wouldn't have to worry about scratching it up. It costs only $100.

The **pseudo-wood finish**: This set is made of a substance that looks like wood (unless you look very closely), and it is pretty durable (though not as durable as the fifties look). This set looks nice, though it is not as nice-looking as the real wood. The chairs are not as comfortable as in the other two sets. It would not scratch easily, and it costs much less than the wood set. It sells for $200.

The **wood set**: This looks beautiful, and it would certainly make a nice impression when he invites friends over for a special dinner. In addition, the chairs are very comfortable. But this set scratches very easily, and Michael would be worried about that. It costs $500, a bargain for a set in perfect condition like this one.

Michael is not rich, and the differences in price among these purchases is significant to him, but he could afford any one of them. How the set looks is very important to him. He has problems with anxiety, and a table that scratches easily would be a serious problem for him. (The option of covering it up all the time is not attractive, either, because then there would be no point in having a nice-looking table.) Michael likes a comfortable chair at the dining table, but that is less important than the overall appearance of the set.

a. Is any option dominated? Explain why or why not.

b. How could Michael use MAUT (multi-attribute utility theory) in making a decision? Provide the details of a MAUT calculation, based on the information we have. (Fill in details of the story if you need to do so.)

7. Juan has the responsibility for making a recommendation to the mayor concerning a city contract with ambulance companies. Juan will consider the ambulance companies that want the contract and make a recommendation based on which will be best for the people of the city. He must consider the condition of the companies' equipment, the training of their staffs, and their past performance. Cost is also an important factor in the minds of many taxpayers, but it is certainly not the only thing to consider. Three companies are under consideration.

Agreeable Ambulance: Judging in terms of response time and "alive on arrival" statistics, this company is slightly better than the others, but the difference is not great. Agreeable has excellent equipment, and its staff is adequately trained. It will charge $1.5 million per year for the services that the city requires.

Bet-Your-Life Ambulance: This company's response time and "alive on arrival" statistics are very close to those of Agreeable Ambulance and slightly better than those of County-wide. Its equipment is excellent, and its staff is especially well trained, with considerable experience and expertise guaranteed in the team for every call. It will charge $1.3 million per year.

County-wide Ambulance: This company has a good response time and "alive on arrival" record, but not quite as good as the other two. Its equipment is good, and its staff is adequately trained. It will charge $1.35 million per year.

a. Is any option dominated? Explain why or why not.

b. How could Juan use MAUT (multi-attribute utility theory) in making this decision? Provide the details of a MAUT calculation, based on the information we have. (Fill in details of the story if you need to do so.)

c. Is there anything else that Juan should consider that would help him with his decision?

DECISIONS WITH UNCERTAINTY ABOUT THE OUTCOME

So far, we have been considering cases in which you know all of the important features of the outcome of your action. We have assumed that you know what will happen when you order dessert, how your vote will be recorded when you pull the lever marked "Wong," and what the relevant features of your job choices will be. In many important choices, though, we do not know for sure what our action will lead to. When you plant crops, you don't know how the weather will be. When you buy a used car, you don't know how reliable it will be. When you take a new job, there are usually many unknowns—for example, how you will like the location, your chances of promotion, what you will learn, and how you will get along with co-workers.

In conditions of uncertainty about the outcome of actions, each choice has *a set of possible outcomes,* each outcome having some probability (given that action). We must find some way of balancing the *probabilities* of the possible outcomes and the *values* (or *utilities*) of the possible outcomes, selecting the action that produces the best balance of likelihood and value of outcome. There are different ways to do this, depending mainly on

1. How well we are able to determine relative value (with a ranking only, or with a preference scaling)
2. What risks we are willing to take
3. How confidently we can estimate the probabilities of the possible outcomes

Sometimes we can make a decision when we have only a *ranking* (not a preference scaling) of possible outcomes to work with and when we have *no definite probability assignments* for the various possibilities. Methods like these have great value, because applying them means there will be less guesswork going into the deliberations.

Eliminate Unsatisfactory Choices

If an action might lead to a completely unacceptable outcome, eliminate that action from consideration. Sometimes this is sufficient to narrow the set of options to just one possibility. Even if the elimination of unacceptable actions leaves more than one option available, the process can help to narrow the field and simplify subsequent deliberations. (If the process leaves *no* options, then you should probably choose in a way that maximizes the *probability* of a satisfactory outcome. This will require probability assignments, and we will discuss methods for making such assignments in the next section.) Application of this procedure requires only the determination of a definite *level of minimal acceptability* for the possible outcomes of your actions, so that you can eliminate all actions with outcomes that fall below that minimal level.

In the job example already considered, you may decide that possibilities for job advancement and mobility are important factors for you to consider. Even if you do not know the exact probabilities of various possibilities for each job, you might feel that there is a significant chance that in the Boston job, you will meet few people in connection with your work and that, for this reason, you will have little opportunity for advancement within the company and little opportunity to find out about other job possibilities. If this is unacceptable to you, then you can eliminate that position from consideration. Even though it is not certain to be a problem, it might be; and eliminating the Boston job from consideration can serve to narrow your set of options if an unacceptable outcome might really occur. If you can eliminate all but one job on the grounds of unacceptability, then you will have made your choice ("by default," as they say). Thus, if you have information that the Boston job might make you too isolated in a way that you cannot avoid, and if the San Francisco job would not enable you to maintain an adequate standard of living, for example, then you can head for Rochester. Your choice is made.

Of course, it is possible that every option you consider will have some unacceptable possible outcomes. If so, the method of eliminating unacceptable options will leave you with no possible action to select. You will have to use some of the methods we will discuss later to decide what to do in such a situation. If you are lucky, there may be more than one option that has only acceptable possible outcomes. Again, you must have some other basis for your choice, but if you eliminate some options, you will simplify your decision.

Eliminate Dominated Actions, if There Are Any

If the outcomes of one possible action, A_1, are at least as highly ranked as the outcomes of another possible action, A_2, in every possible situation, and if A_1 ranks higher in at least one situation, then you should select the action with more highly ranked outcomes (A_1). We say that A_1 *dominates* A_2. (We talked before about *attribute domination;* here we are talking about *possible-outcome domination*. These concepts are structurally similar.)

Suppose that your main goal is to make money, and you are considering three possible careers: being a high school English teacher, being a real estate agent, and being a bank manager. (Assume that these are mutually exclusive.) Suppose that you believe the following:

> An English teacher makes $30,000 per year, with modest raises as time goes on.
>
> A real estate agent: makes $35,000 to $200,000 per year, depending on the state of the real estate market.
>
> A bank manager: makes $32,000 per year, with very significant raises each year and many opportunities to move into positions with better pay.

If money is your only goal (an unrealistic assumption, of course), then you can eliminate the teaching job. Both of the other jobs dominate it; no matter what happens, you will earn at least as much from one of the other jobs. Neither of the other jobs can be eliminated by this method, however, because a significant advancement in the banking business will quickly get you above $35,000 per year, so banking might be more lucrative than the real estate business in some situations. To decide between them, you will need to consider the probability of significant advancement in banking and the probability of a poor real estate market. Sometimes the elimination of dominated actions can lead to a choice; sometimes it merely simplifies the deliberations. Here we say that the option of being a school teacher is *dominated* (by each of the other choices), because the maximum value for that choice is lower than the minimum possible in the other cases. But neither of the other jobs is dominated, so this method would not enable you to choose between them.

There is another way in which one action can be dominated by another. If their value responds to the same outside factors, then we might be able to tell that there is one that will be better than the other no matter what happens. For example, suppose you are a farmer planning to plant crops. If there are two crops that you are considering, and if they respond similarly to weather conditions, then you might have the following situation, where the dollar amounts represent your net profit from that crop.

	POOR WEATHER	NORMAL WEATHER	EXCELLENT WEATHER
Crop A profit	$10K	$30K	$50K
Crop B profit	$5K	$30K	$40K

Clearly you should plant crop A. In every kind of situation it does at least as well as B, and in some situations it does better. Even though crop B has a maximum possible value that is much higher than A's minimum possible value, we know that a comparison of those values is irrelevant. Because the crops respond similarly to weather conditions (and because your choice of a crop does not affect the weather), we need not consider the possibility that the weather is good for B but poor for A. (Nothing comparable could be said about the job selection we just considered, unless, for example, there is some link between real estate markets and the probability of advancing in the banking business.)

ELIMINATE DOMINATED (WORSE) ACTIONS

Case 1. If the minimum possible value for some action A_1 is at least as high as the maximum possible ranking for A_2, and if some possible value of A_1 is higher than the maximum value for A_2, then A_1 *dominates* A_2. Eliminate A_2 from consideration.

Case 2. If the value of the outcomes of A_1 and A_2 can be represented as responding to the same external states of the world, you can refine this. Then, if A_1 has a higher ranking than A_2 in at least one possible state of the world, and if A_1 always has a ranking at least as high as A_2's, no matter what happens, then A_1 *dominates* A_2. Eliminate A_2.

If the elimination of dominated actions leaves just one option, then that option is a *best action*. Choose it. Even if there is no best action, eliminating dominated actions can simplify the choices to be made.

Maximin and Maximax

There are two other ways of choosing on the basis of preference rankings, even when the probabilities of various outcomes are not known. These are the *maximin* and *maximax* choices.

Using the maximin method of choosing is playing it safe. You *maximize* the *minimum* possible value of the outcome of your action by selecting the action that has the highest minimum. For example, if Ed is trying to decide whether to become an English teacher, a stock broker, or a musician, then Ed might be considering these possibilities:

If I become an English teacher, I will make at least $30,000 per year, with job security and summers off.

If I become a musician, there are many possibilities and I can't tell what will happen. I could become a star and earn millions each year. Or I could have just a modest success, earning big for a few years and then living off my past earnings, along with giving lessons or whatever. Or I could have no success at all and end up barely earning a living giving music lessons or even working in restaurant kitchens or something.

If I become a stock broker, I could have earnings anywhere from $20,000 per year to $300,000 per year, depending on the market and my luck (and on whether I can get people to order through me rather than using the Internet to place their own orders).

If Ed is cautious ("risk averse"), he will take the maximin choice and become a school teacher. You can figure out the maximin answer without knowing about the probability rating of these various possibilities, so it can be a good method for choosing when there is no best action and probability values are uncertain.

The maximax (risk taker's) solution is also available under the same conditions: The outcome possibilities are envisioned and ordered, but the probability values are not known. The maximax solution is to pick the option that provides the highest possible payoff (no matter what its likelihood is). Pick the choice with the *max*imum possible *max*imum. Ed could choose to become a musician, for example, if he sees that as having the highest possible payoff.

Both the maximin and maximax solutions have serious drawbacks in many situations, however. If the worst possible outcome (for example, $20,000 as a stock broker) has a very low probability, and if, as a stock broker, you are very likely to earn more than $180,000 per year, then if money is your principal goal by far, and if you are willing to take some risk, you should prefer being a stock broker to being a school teacher. The maximin answer is too cautious, leading you to forgo likely benefits. Similarly, if stardom is very unlikely, then the gamble of the maximax solution is too great.

Most of the time it is desirable to try to find a better balance of risk and value than either the maximin or the maximax method provides. The *expected utility* method can provide such a balance, but we need more information before we can employy it.

MAXIMIN: Choose the action with the highest possible minimum utility. This choice is *risk averse*. Information about probabilities of outcomes is not needed. (For ties, use maximax, reapply maximin to utilities other than the minimum, make an arbitrary choice, or add information about weighted differences or probabilities.)

MAXIMAX: Choose the action with the highest possible maximum utility. This is the choice of those who are *risk takers*. Probabilities of outcomes are not needed. (For ties, use maximin, reapply maximax to utilities other than the maximum, make an arbitrary choice, or add information about weighted differences or probabilities.)

The Expected Utility Method

To use the expected utility method, you need two kinds of numerical information. You need to know the *probability* of each of the outcomes of each action under consideration, and you need to know the *value* (the *utility*) of each possible outcome of every action on a uniform preference scaling (not just a ranking, but a preference scaling). If you have this information, the expected utility method will provide a way to bring this information together into a decision that will provide an optimal balance of likelihood and value. If you followed this procedure over a long run of decisions, and if your luck was not very unusual, then you would achieve a higher total value for your choices than you would by employing any other decision method.

We need to look at the two elements required for the expected utility calculation.

Probabilities

When we are not certain what will happen, we can often still assign probability values to the various possibilities. In some cases we can be quite certain about the probabilities, even when we are very uncertain about the outcome. When I flip a coin that I know is fair, I know that the probability of heads is .5, and I do not know how it will come up. Rolling dice, I can know the probabilities of various totals, but I do not have any idea what my total will be.

We will follow the usual practice of assigning probability values between 0 and 1 to events. When we have an exhaustive set of mutually exclusive alternative events, their probability should add up to 1. Because the set is exhaustive, at least one of the events is sure to happen, so their probabilities add up 1, which represents certainty of occurrence. (Each side of the coin has a probability of .5, and it is certain that one side or the other will come up. Each face of a die has a probability of 1/6, and it is certain that one will be up.)

Of course, our probability assignments for most events are much more speculative than our probability assignments for a coin toss or a roll of dice. We bring together all of the information we have about what might happen, and we divide the total (1) among the various possibilities. In trying to decide what car to buy, I might want to know whether fuel prices will go up dramatically so that I can determine how important fuel economy is. Although I don't know for sure what the prices will be, I might be pretty sure that the political situation would not permit a dramatic rise in consumer prices for gasoline in the next six years, and I may believe that the political situation is not likely to change drastically in that time. In that case, I can assign a low probability, perhaps .1, to the possibility of a dramatic rise in fuel costs. Even though this is a very rough estimate, it may provide an adequate basis for applying the expected utility method.

Preference scales (utilities)

"On a scale of 1 to 10, how would you rate that dessert?" When we ask questions like this, we are asking for a utility rating, a rating on a preference scale. This kind of rating is the other major input to an expected utility calculation. For this calculation we will need real preference scales, not just rankings. This means that if we rate three possible outcomes, O_1, O_2, and O_3, by the numbers 10, 8, and 3, that represents something different from rating them 10, 5, and 3, even though their order is the same in both cases. The differences in value matter, not just the order.

In making utility assignments, we could use any numerical range as the basis for the scale. In rating three items, 100, 50, 30 would represent the same utility assignments as 10, 5, 3, because the differences relative to the overall scale are the same.

The word *utility* should suggest the important idea here. The numbers assigned should represent any value or usefulness of the outcome that you think is worth considering in your deliberations about what to do.

Sometimes we will deliberate about financial outcomes. Should I buy the $40 battery or the $30 battery? In such cases, we can usually let the saved dollars represent the utility value (if there are no other important differences). However, if the numbers are very high or very low, this method will not be useful. A lottery in which I earn $20 million (after taxes) is better than one in which I earn $10 million (after taxes). But it is not twice as good. $10 million would make an enormous difference in my life; $20 million would make a bigger difference, but not twice as much. Utility is not a smooth function of dollar value. As the amounts increase, the value of each added dollar is less.

Similarly, finding two pennies does not have twice the utility of finding one. Neither of these acquisitions would make any difference in my life. When values are very small, utility can be insignificant, so monetary units do not indicate real value relationships.

Expected utility

Expected utility rule: For each option, multiply the utility of each possible outcome by the probability of that outcome, and add the product values together. Compare the resulting *expected utilities* assigned to the various options, and choose the option with the highest expected utility.

The expected utility rule provides the highest utility in the long run if your luck is not much better than average, and it avoids low utility in the long run if your luck is not much worse than average. (In the long run, your luck is not likely to be much better or much worse than average.) Thus, if actual utilities and probabilities can be assigned with reasonable accuracy, this is a good method to use.

Expected utility method

ACTIONS	POSSIBLE OUTCOMES	PROBABILITIES	UTILITIES
A_1	$A_1O_1, A_1O_2, \ldots, A_1O_m$	$p(A_1O_1), p(A_1O_2)$, etc.	$u(A_1O_1), u(A_1O_2)$, etc.
A_2	$A_2O_1, A_2O_2, \ldots, A_2O_s$	$p(A_2O_1), p(A_2O_2)$, etc.	$u(A_2O_1), u(A_2O_2)$, etc.
:			
A_n	$A_nO_1, A_nO_2, \ldots, A_nO_r$	$p(A_nO_1), p(A_nO_2)$, etc.	$u(A_nO_1), u(A_nO_2)$, etc.

Expected utility of A_1 (with m possible outcomes):

$$[p(A_1O_1) \times u(A_1O_1)] + [p(A_1O_2) \times u(A_1O_2)] + \cdots + [p(A_1O_m) \times u(A_1O_m)]$$

General: expected utility of A_k, with j possible outcomes:

$$[p(A_kO_1) \times u(A_kO_1)] + [p(A_kO_2) \times u(A_kO_2)] + \cdots + [p(A_kO_j) \times u(A_kO_j)]$$

Let's consider how to apply all of this in some sample cases.

Example 1. Suppose that a farmer is deciding which of three crops to plant, and some are more weather-sensitive than others. The farmer's goal is to plant the crop that brings the largest net profit, and she has estimates of what those profits will be in each of several different kinds of weather situations. The following chart might represent this decision situation, where the utility values are measured in thousands of dollars of profit. We will also imagine that the farmer could invest her money in planting crop B in a hothouse, instead of planting A, B, or C in the field. (We assume also that the farmer can plant only one type of crop. This is a simplification; for a large operation, a strategy that involved planting several different crops should ordinarily be considered as well.)

	POSSIBLE STATES OF THE WEATHER		
	PERFECT (**PROB: .2**)	**FAIR** (**PROB: .5**)	**BAD** (**PROB: .3**)
Plant crop A	15	6	−2
Plant crop B	10	8	4
Plant crop C	8	7	6
B in hothouse	6	6	6

Before doing the expected utility (EU) calculation, we can sometimes simplify by using the methods mentioned in earlier sections. Principally, you should apply those two familiar simplifiers: *eliminate unsatisfactory options* (options with the possibility of an unsatisfactory outcome) and *eliminate dominated options.*

> *Eliminate unsatisfactory options:* If the farmer is entirely unwilling to take the risk of a loss, for example, she can eliminate the option to plant crop A, which has a .3 probability of a loss. If profits under $5000 are completely unacceptable, then she can eliminate both A and B. But if she is willing to take a risk, even as big a risk as A entails, then this method will not limit her choices.
>
> In considering this example, we will imagine that she is willing to accept the risk of a $2000 loss, so that she will not eliminate any option on the grounds that it is unsatisfactory.
>
> *Eliminate dominated options:* She can, however, eliminate the hothouse from consideration, because that is a dominated option. Planting crop C is always at least as good, and is sometimes better, so we can simplify our options, considering only A, B (planted in the field), and C.

Now we can apply EU. (*Note:* Obviously, A is the maximax choice and C is the maximin choice, but we have enough information to make a more balanced choice, using EU.) Each option will have a calculated EU value.

$$EU(A) = (.2 \times 15) + (.5 \times 6) + (.3 \times -2) = 5.4$$

$$EU(B) = (.2 \times 10) + (.5 \times 8) + (.3 \times 4) = 7.2$$

$$EU(C) = (.2 \times 8) + (.5 \times 7) + (.3 \times 6) = 6.9$$

Clearly, B and C are better crops to plant than A. The choice between B and C, on the other hand, is close. The farmer may wish to see whether the limitation to those two possibilities gives her a basis for thinking about the weather possibilities in more specific detail, to get a better assessment of the relevant probabilities. She may wish to bring in other information to help her decide, as well.

Example 2. Arnie works for an insurance company with substantial assets (many billions). He must decide whether to insure fully a shipment that is worth $15,000, when there is a .1 chance that the shipment will be destroyed. The fee he sets will hold for all such shipments, and the cost of doing business (employee time, postage, etc.) in such cases averages $100. Should he insure the shipment for a fee of $1700?

$$\text{EU(insure)} = [(\text{fee} - \text{costs}) \times .9] + [(\text{fee} - \text{costs} - \$15,000) \times .1] =$$

$$= (1600 \times .9) + (-13,400 \times .1)$$

$$= 1440 - 1340$$

$$= \$100$$

Thus Arnie's company will, on the average, make $100 per shipment after costs (if its luck is neither unusually bad nor unusually good). If that is an acceptable profit, then Arnie can offer to insure the shipment at that price, if he has included every relevant factor.

SUMMARY: DECISIONS WITH UNCERTAIN OUTCOMES

In conditions of uncertainty about the outcome of actions, each choice has *a set of possible outcomes,* each outcome having some probability. We must find a way of balancing the *values* of the possible outcomes and the *probabilities* of the possible outcomes, selecting the action that produces the best balance. There are different ways to do this, depending mainly on

1. How well we are able to determine relative utility (ranking only or ranking with weighted differences)
2. What risks we are willing to take
3. How well we know the probabilities of the possible outcomes

Sometimes we can make a decision when we have only a *rank ordering* to work with and when we have *no definite probability assignments.*

Eliminate unsatisfactory choices: If an action might lead to a completely unacceptable outcome, eliminate that action from consideration. Sometimes doing this is sufficient to reduce the actions to just one possibility. Even if it leaves more than one, it can help to narrow the field. (If it leaves none, then you should probably choose in a way that maximizes the probability of a satisfactory outcome. This will require probability assignments.) Application of this procedure requires the determination of a definite *level of minimal acceptability* for the outcome.

(continued on next page)

Eliminate dominated choices:

Case 1: If the minimum possible value for some action A_1 is at least as high as the maximum possible ranking for A_2, and if some possible value of A_1 is higher than the maximum value for A_2, then A_1 *dominates* A_2. Eliminate A_2 from consideration.

Case 2: If the value of the outcomes of A_1 and A_2 can be represented as responding to the same external states of the world, you can refine this. Then, if A_1 has a higher ranking than A_2 in at least one possible state of the world, and if A_1 always has a ranking at least as high as A_2's, no matter what happens, then A_1 *dominates* A_2. Eliminate A_2.

If the elimination of dominated actions leaves just one option, then that option is a *best action.* Choose it. Even if there is no best action, eliminating dominated actions can simplify the choices to be made.

Maximin: Choose the action with the highest possible minimum utility. This choice is *risk averse.* Probabilities of outcomes are not needed. (For ties, use maximax, reapply maximin to utilities other than the minimum, make an arbitrary choice, or add information about weighted differences or probabilities.)

Maximax: Choose the action with the highest possible maximum utility. This is the choice of those who are *risk takers.* Probabilities of outcomes are not needed. (For ties, use maximin, reapply maximax to utilities other than the maximum, make an arbitrary choice, or add information about weighted differences or probabilities.)

Adding information about numerical probabilities and preference scalings makes it possible to balance probabilities and utilities in other ways.

If it is not possible to eliminate the possibility of an unsatisfactory outcome, we can at least *minimize the probability of an unsatisfactory outcome* (when a definite satisfaction level has been determined).

Instead of the maximax and maximin methods, we can apply the *expected utility* method for balancing utilities and probabilities of outcomes.

Expected utility rule: For each option, multiply the utility of each outcome by the probability of that outcome, and add the product values together. Compare the resulting expected utilities assigned to the various options, and choose the option with the highest expected utility.

The expected utility rule provides the highest utility in the long run if your luck is not much better than average, and it avoids low utility in the long run if your luck is not much worse than average. (In the long run, your luck is not likely to be much better or much worse than average.) Thus, if actual utilities can be securely assigned, this is a good method to use.

Expected Utility Method

ACTIONS	OUTCOMES	PROBABILITIES	UTILITIES
A_1	$A_1O_1, A_1O_2, \ldots, A_1O_m$	$p(A_1O_1), p(A_1O_2)$, etc.	$u(A_1O_1), u(A_1O_2)$, etc.
A_2	$A_2O_1, A_2O_2, \ldots, A_2O_s$	$p(A_2O_1), p(A_2O_2)$, etc.	$u(A_2O_1), u(A_2O_2)$, etc.
$\vdots$			
A_n	$A_nO_1, A_nO_2, \ldots, A_nO_r$	$p(A_nO_1), p(A_nO_2)$, etc.	$u(A_nO_1), u(A_nO_2)$, etc.

Expected utility of A_1:

$$[p(A_1O_1) \times u(A_1O_1)] + [p(A_1O_2) \times u(A_1O_2)] + \cdots + [p(A_1O_m) \times u(A_1O_m)]$$

Expected utility of A_k, with j possible outcomes:

$$[p(A_kO_1) \times u(A_kO_1)] + [p(A_kO_2) \times u(A_kO_2)] + \cdots + [p(A_kO_j) \times u(A_kO_j)]$$

We have considered a number of ideas for making decisions. Another way to look at these is to organize them into a flowchart. Facing a decision in which we would like to postpone assigning probability numbers and utility numbers to outcomes for as long as possible, we might create a flowchart like the one that follows. (We can move to the expected utility method much more quickly and simplify this procedure if we have a problem in which we can assign probabilities and utilities with confidence at an early stage.)

EXERCISE 10B

1. Frank has inherited $200,000, and he has to decide whether to invest in a mixed group of stocks or a mixed group of bonds or both. He will leave the money in these investments for 20 years, until he retires, so his main concern is what he will have at that time. If the value of these investments does not increase by at least 50%, it will be disastrous for his retirement plans. Naturally, any greater increase will be a real benefit.

   He expects that money left in stocks will probably triple (increase 200%) in that time, but there is a significant chance (maybe 20%) that it will only double (increase 100%), and there is a small chance (maybe 5%) that it won't increase at all.

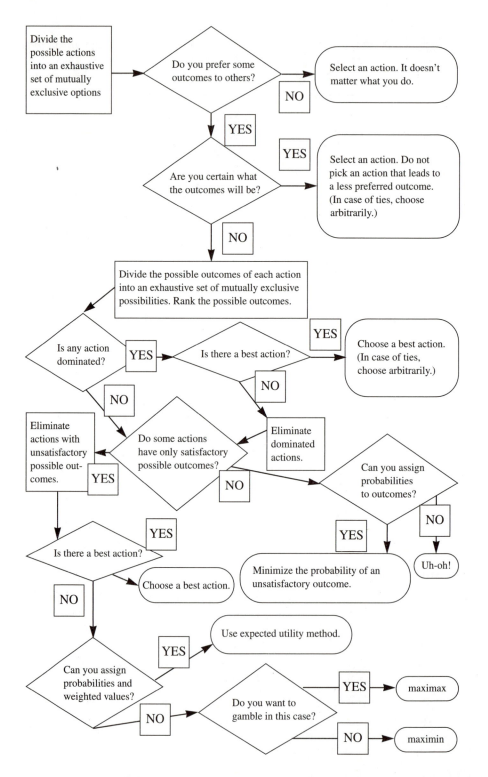

Money left in bonds will double (increase 100%) in that amount of time. There is no significant chance that it will do worse, and it might do a little better (increase 120%).

Compare three possible investment strategies:

Strategy A. Invest all the money in stocks.

Strategy B. Invest it all in bonds.

Strategy C. Invest half ($100,000) in each.

In answering the following questions, you may assume that the payoffs in the bond market are independent of the payoffs in the stock market. That is unrealistic, but it will simplify our problem.

a. What is the maximax choice? Explain why that is a poor choice for Frank.

b. What is the maximin choice?

c. What is the expected utility calculation?

d. What should Frank do? Why?

2. Arnie is trying to decide what to do this summer. The money he makes this summer will be his spending money for the next school year, and he has three jobs to consider.

   Arnie could have a job bussing tables in the dining room at a resort hotel. He has heard that the tips are good: He would make at least $1500 for the summer and would have a chance of making up to twice that much. He will get room and board at the hotel, and he won't have very much free time to spend his money, so he will bring home nearly all of the money he earns. But it will be very hard work, long hours, and not much fun.

   He could also work as an assistant ranger for the park service, working in a national park out west. If the weather is generally good, this will be a very enjoyable job for Arnie, working outdoors and helping people see the sights. However, if there is a long stretch of hot, dry weather, then he will be miserable and will be spending much more of his time working on fire prevention. If the weather is unusually cool and rainy, that would be better than hot, dry weather, but it would be uncomfortable and not much fun— only a little better than working at the hotel dining room. After expenses, Arnie figures that he would come home with about $1000. The National Weather Service says that there is a .2 (20%) chance of a long stretch of very hot, dry weather and a .1 (10%) chance of unusually cool and rainy weather in that part of the country.

   Arnie could also stay with his parents and work at the local bank. After his personal expenses, he would probably have about $1000 at the end of the summer. The whole summer would be very boring.

   a. Show how Arnie can use a calculation of expected value as a basis for deciding what to do. (If necessary, fill in details of the story in a plausible way so that you can assign the needed values.)

b. Does the expected value calculation give a clear indication of what to do? How or why not? Are there are other factors that Arnie should consider in making his decision?

3. Alice is a college student who would like to grow some crops this summer. She thinks it would be fun to plant some flowers or some interesting varieties of vegetables (white eggplant, bok choy, and arugula) this year, and she would have a chance of making good money at the market if the weather were just right. But it is risky. Growing the old standard vegetables (tomatoes and cucumbers) would be fun enough, and less risky, with a reliable (though small) payoff at the market. Alice could instead work as a clerk at the local pharmacy and make a predetermined amount of money ($1800 for the summer), but this wouldn't be very much fun. Considering interest, fun, money, and time, Alice ranks her preferences this way:

Grow interesting vegetables with very good weather	12
Grow flowers with very good weather	11
Grow interesting vegetables with normal weather	10
Grow flowers with normal weather	9
Grow old standards with very good weather	8
Grow old standards with normal weather	8
Work at the pharmacy	5
Grow old standards with poor weather	5
Grow interesting vegetables with poor weather	2
Grow flowers with poor weather	1

a. Do these preferences provide a clear basis for action? Why or why not? (To answer this and the questions that follow, you should make a chart showing what Alice's four choices are and how each depends on the weather.)

b. What is the maximax (risk taker's) choice?

c. What is the maximin (safe) choice?

d. Are there any actions that Alice can eliminate from consideration?

e. Can you figure out the *expected utility* solution? If not, why not? If so, what is it? (Show any calculations.)

Suppose that Alice figures out some comparative utilities (on a scale of 1 to 20), considering the outcomes in the best and worst weather (.2 probability each) and in the likely normal run of weather (.6 probability). (These utility assignments consider interest, fun, money, and time.)

Grow interesting vegetables with very good weather	20
Grow flowers with very good weather	17

Grow interesting vegetables with normal weather	14
Grow flowers with normal weather	12
Grow old standards with very good weather	10
Grow old standards with normal weather	10
Work at the pharmacy	8
Grow old standards with poor weather	8
Grow interesting vegetables with poor weather	4
Grow flowers with poor weather	3

a2. Do these preferences provide a clear basis for action? Why or why not?

b2. What is the maximax choice?

c2. What is the maximin choice?

d2. Can you figure out the *expected utility* solution? If not, why not? If so, what is it? (Show any calculations.)

Suppose now that Alice takes a closer look at her financial situation and determines two things that may change her preferences: She absolutely must make at least $1200 this summer, and if the weather is very bad, she will not make that from gardening (no matter what she plants).

a3. Does this provide a clear basis for Alice to act? Why or why not?

b3. Are there other options that Alice should consider? If so, what are one or two examples?

4. Alex runs a flower shop. He is trying to decide whether to expand by renting the floorspace of the shop next door. This wouldn't require any extra work on his part (other than a little planning). His net income (income after all expenses) is now $100,000 per year. If he makes the move, his expenses will increase by $20,000. He figures that if he makes the move, there is a 20% chance that his gross income will increase by $70,000 per year, a 50% chance that it will increase by about $40,000 per year, a 20% chance that it will increase about $25,000 per year, and a 10% chance that there will be no increase. His income will remain stable if he makes no change. (Keep in mind that net income = gross income − expenses.)

   a. What is the maximax choice?

   b. What is the maximin choice?

   c. Show the expected utility.

   d. What should Alex do? Is there any other information he should consider when deciding what to do? If so, what?

5. Danielle owns a dry cleaning business in a neighborhood in which real estate values have been slowly declining. She makes a modest living from her business ($35,000 per year), and she also has the advantage of living in an apartment over the business. She has been offered a fair price for the business, including the building, but if she sold, she would need to find another apartment.

If she sells, she will probably have to pay about $800 per month in rent for a comparable place to live. (Or she could buy a house, but the net cost would be similar.)

She can go back to her old job as an accountant in a large firm, where she would make about $50,000 per year. After her work for a few years in the dry cleaning business, the idea of being her own boss has lost some of its appeal, though she still likes being self-employed a little better than her old job.

She has heard rumors that a huge condominium project will be built nearby. That would increase her dry cleaning business so that she would net about $45,000 per year (and, of course, she would still have her apartment over the business). It would also stabilize real estate prices. She thinks that the chance of the condominium housing being built is about 50%.

a. What is the maximax choice?

b. What is the maximin choice?

c. Show an expected utility calculation. (Fill in details if you have to.)

d. What should Danielle do? Is there any other information she should consider when deciding what to do? If so, what is it?

6. Stella is planning to buy a motel, and she is considering three that are on the market.

Adams Avenue Motel: This place (motel A) will produce a net income of about $100,000 per year. It has considerable unused capacity, though, and there is a rumor that the new highway's entrance will be built nearby. If that happens, then the net income will be doubled (starting in three years, after the highway is built). Stella estimates the probability of the new highway exit being near the motel at about 50%.

Berkeley Boulevard Motel: This place (motel B) is doing well, with net earnings of $140,000 per year. It is in good condition, and it has an excellent location, near a thriving amusement park. Its earnings can be expected to be stable.

Coventry Court Motel: This place (motel C) will net only $80,000 per year at first, because it needs extensive renovation. However, everyone expects the new sports complex to be built nearby (90% probability), and after renovation, this motel can earn $200,000 per year if the sports complex is nearby. If it is renovated and there is no sports complex nearby, it can do better than it is doing now, earning about $150,000 per year. It will take three years to renovate, and then the renovations will be complete at the same time the sports complex is completed. It will produce $80,000 during those three years.

Stella decides to consider the earnings over the next ten years, because it is hard to predict what forces might be at work after that. (The price of motel A is $1 million, and the price of motel B is also $1 million. Motel C is priced at $500,000, but it will cost $500,000 to renovate. The result is that this initial-investment factor is the same for each.)

a. What is the maximax choice?

b. What is the maximin choice?

c. Show an expected utility calculation. (Fill in details if you have to.)

d. What should Stella do? Is there any other information she should consider when deciding what to do? If so, what is it?

DECISION MAKING: SOME SPECIAL ISSUES

In what follows, we will note some cognitive impediments to effective decision making, and we will consider several special issues that come up in decision problems.

Creativity and Social Conformity

When we confront an unfamiliar situation in which to make a decision, we often look to the experience of others as a guide. This ability to learn from others, either by imitation or by explicit teaching, is an important human feature that influences almost everything we do. Our lives are strongly dependent on the accumulated wisdom of our predecessors, in a way no other species can match.

Our dependence on social interaction extends beyond its role in learning, of course. Almost every decision we make involves the consideration of how our action will affect other people, and our ties to other people also influence us in deeper ways that evade our conscious deliberations.

The pressures of social interaction sometimes have a negative effect on our cognitive lives. We tend to think in the way our associates do, or at least we tend to want to think in the way our associates do, and that can prevent us from creatively reexamining our situation, it can prevent us from coming up with novel ideas, and it can prevent us from seriously considering novel ideas that do arise (whether from ourselves or from others). Experiments by Solomon Asch (1955) are a simple illustration of the power of social influence. He showed a line segment to a group of eight people and asked each of them to judge which of three lines on a card was closest in length to the given line. The experimental subjects did not know that the other seven people were accomplices of the experimenter, who were all agreeing on an obviously incorrect answer. In all but 20% of the cases, the experimental subject went along with the choice of the rest of the group, rather than making the obviously correct selection.

Generally, the pressure to conform works in much subtler ways, and laziness is a powerful ally, because it is much simpler to agree with the accepted idea than it is to think hard and come up with new ideas that need to be explained, argued for, or tested. For many of our actions, this tendency to conform is valuable simply because accepted limitations on our ideas and options yield satisfactory results without the bother of serious reconsideration of the accepted ways of doing things. (We mentioned before that satisficing is often an acceptable method for making your choice from a large restaurant menu.) For important decisions, however, you should make sure that you have conceived the range of alternatives as broadly as possible and that you are considering all relevant information when making a decision. The decision methods already discussed were introduced to help you to think about the full range of possibilities available to you when you make a decision.

In several other ways, we have emphasized the need for cognitive openness in this book. The most important fallacy we noticed (in Chapter 4) was the fallacy of false dilemma, which simply consists in overlooking relevant alternatives; we learned the importance of thinking creatively in developing counter-examples to show that a general claim is false or that an argument structure is not a validating structure; we learned that the central ability needed in the evaluation of explanations was the ability to develop alternative explanations creatively; and we saw that it is very useful to extend the techniques for creatively evaluating explanations, applying this creative search for alternatives to all cases in which we wish to evaluate the extent to which the available evidence supports a conclusion.

Money and Value

As you probably noticed, the decision procedures we developed in this chapter can apply more smoothly when what we value is easily measured. Often dollars can be used as a measure of utility, producing an immediate preference scaling. If you are considering three jobs in the same city that pay $40,000, $34,000, and $33,000, respectively, you have an easy way to rank these jobs as far as the attribute "initial salary" is concerned, and you even have a very good idea of the relative separation of these salaries in a preference scaling. In a business, dollar values in typical decision situations can be a very good measure of utility.

Nevertheless, $5 does not always have the same value. Most obviously, a seven-year-old child and a rich stockbroker do not get equal value from it. For the child, it may represent an extraordinary opportunity, but having it or not will make little difference to the stockbroker (at least in the good years). We use the more general concept of utility in indicating that the $5 has considerable utility for the young child and almost none for the stockbroker.

In general, utility is smoothly related to dollar value only in a narrow range of values. Although $400 is about twice as valuable to me as $200, 2 cents is not twice as important to me as 1 cent (neither is very important at all), and $200 million is not twice as valuable as $100 million (because the value added by *another* $100 million, though great, would not be as great as that added by the first $100 million).

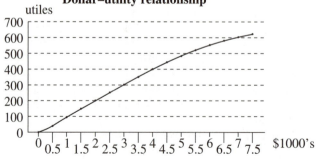

Dollar–utility relationship

This graph shows in one case how dollars are not a uniform indicator of utility. (The word *utiles* is used here to stand for units of utility.) Small numbers of dollars lack significant utility, and in the case of large numbers of dollars (over $5000, in this case), the additional dollars do not contribute as much as the dollars up to $5000 do. In most situations, the dollar–utility curve will have a shape something like this, though the point at which the utility of additional dollars begins to decrease may be very different.

The idea that dollar amounts are not a uniform measure of utility shows up clearly in some unusual cases. For example, when my son was about six years old, he had only one use for money: to buy Star Wars figures. These cost $2.19 each. As a result, the curve showing how utility varies with price would have a step shape, leaping up one notch at every multiple of $2.19.

There are still other cases where it is clear that dollars cannot be a simple measure of utility. Suppose that you are offered the choice of taking one of the following two wagers. In each, a fair coin is tossed.

Wager A: If the coin is heads, you pay $1. If it is tails, you get $3.

Wager B: If the coin is heads, you pay $100. If it is tails, you get $105.

If you are like most of us, you will pick A, even though the expected utility method tells us that B has more than twice the expected utility. (The expected utility of choice A is $(-1 \times .5) + (3 \times .5) = 1$, a pretty good deal. The expected utility of choice B is $(-100 \times .5) + (105 \times .5) = 2.5$, an even better deal.) The problem here is that the risk is not worth the added value in a single play of this game. A frequent gambler might find B more attractive, because she or he can see it as a part of a long run of choices; and B is a favorable game when looked at in this light. If you can play B a thousand times, you are almost certain to win something, and the average winning (among players who do this a thousand times each) will be $2500. This may be part of the reason why frequent gamblers can be comfortable with risks that the rest of us would take care to avoid.

Game Theory

Economists, philosophers, and political scientists have found it useful to explore "game theory," the study of decision-making tasks that involve more than one decision maker, with each "player" trying to maximize his own benefit. Two related examples, the prisoners' dilemma and the tragedy of the commons, will be of special interest to us, because they illustrate some very important features of decision making in situations where there is a potential for cooperation. (Decision theory has its origin in the work of John von Neumann and Oscar Morganstern, whose book *The Theory of Games and Economic Behavior* (1947) is seminal.) It is useful to consider how we interact with others, and a consideration of this also leads us to look at some issues related to the balancing of short-term and long-term interests.

Prisoners' dilemma

A well-known problem in game theory, the prisoners' dilemma, illustrates some important features of decision making in a social setting and can help us to see the importance of considering all of the consequences of an action when making a decision. In the basic version of the prisoners' dilemma problem, two people have been apprehended as suspects in an armed robbery. The district attorney separates them for questioning and says the same thing to each of them:

> I am sure that you committed the crime, but we don't have quite enough evidence to convict you or your partner of armed robbery, so I am going to offer you a deal.

> If you will confess and implicate your partner, I will withdraw all charges against you. If your partner does not confess, then he will take the whole rap, and he will be in for 10 years of hard time.

> If both of you confess, then you will both have to serve some time. (I can't let you both off.) Because of your cooperation, I will agree to a plea bargain, and you will be out in six years or less.

> If neither of you confesses, then I will still be able to get you on charges of carrying unregistered weapons and possessing stolen goods. You will serve two years.

The prisoners are kept in isolation from each other, and both contemplate the deal. Each is making a choice with an uncertain outcome, because they do not know for sure what the other will choose, and their own outcome depends in part on what the other chooses. Their choices can be represented on the following grid. (We will call the criminals Alicia and Barbie.) Alicia's years in jail are in the lower left corner of each box, and Barbie's are in the upper right.

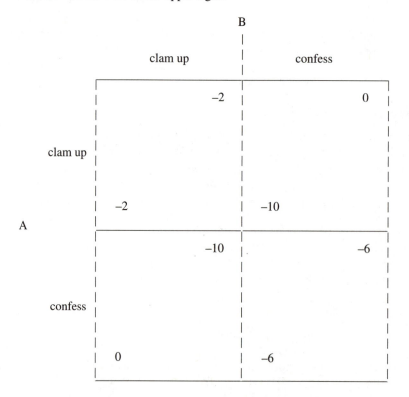

Once you look at the grid, two things should be obvious. The best thing for the pair of them is not to confess: Each will then serve only two years. If we look at the individual choices, however, clearly the best choice is to confess: Alicia will always serve less time if she confesses, no matter what Barbie does (and, similarly, Barbie will always serve less time if she confesses, no matter what Alicia does). In other words, clamming up is a dominated action for each of them: Confessing always yields a better result. We have already learned to eliminate dominated actions when making choices. Thus it seems that each should confess. But then they get six years each, when they could have served just two years each.

Is there anything that could be added to the situation that would make it possible for the prisoners to secure an outcome that they would regard more favorably? Really, there are at least two different ways to enlarge the problem (by considering a larger context for their choices) so that it becomes possible for a different choice to be reasonable. Before you go on to the next paragraph, stop to think about the other factors that could influence their choices.

First, and most obviously, there might be other consequences of their choices, so that the number of years in prison does not reflect the real payoff. If Alicia and Barbie both work for the same gang, then the gang might enforce a discipline on people who confess, and that could outweigh the advantages of confessing. (You can imagine the gory details for yourself.) Or, if Alicia is Barbie's mother, then Alicia might feel that time in jail for Barbie is as bad as or worse than time for herself, thus producing a very different total payoff for her actions. In either case, forces external to the prosecuting attorney's deal would change the payoffs *in this single situation* so that a different result becomes possible, even when selecting the action that maximizes what is valued most.

Even if no external forces change the tangible payoff of this particular choice situation, the choice situation is altered if it is a part of an ongoing relationship. If Alicia and Barbie can expect to be involved in many more "deals" together, then sustaining their cooperative relationship could be more important than securing the best payoff for this one action. If there are repeated rounds of "play" in a game like the prisoners' dilemma situation, then one might secure better results through cooperation than through defection. In repeated rounds of a game like this, however, it is not immediately obvious what to do, because the payoff on any single round is always higher if a player defects in that round. This means that the player must judge the balance between the actual payoff on a particular round of play and the expected value in sustaining a cooperative relationship.

In thinking about the prisoners' dilemma, it might be useful to conceive of it as a game with positive payoffs that could be played for many rounds, with the payoffs (in dollars) indicated on the following grid. On any one round, you will earn more by defecting, but a long run of cooperation will yield much more than a long run of defection. The structure of this game shows more clearly the benefits of cooperation and the payoffs of defection. We can call this the cooperative dilemma game.

The following grid represents the choices in the cooperative dilemma game (a version of the prisoners' dilemma).

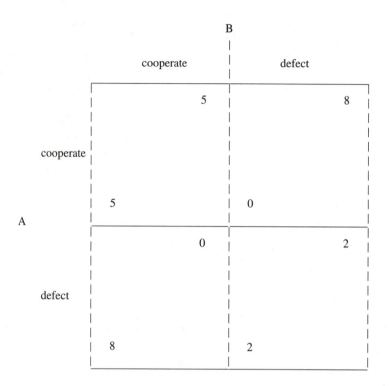

We will discuss this game further after we look at a multiperson variation of this kind of game. Right now, try to think of other situations that are like the prisoners' dilemma (or the cooperative dilemma).

The tragedy of the commons

The tragedy of the commons is a multiperson form of the prisoners' dilemma. Its name comes from the situation of the New England common—a grassy area where everyone in town grazed their cattle. Suppose that the following situation prevails:

> Everyone has ten cows, and everyone nets $100 per month by selling milk. By adding 1 cow, you would raise your net profit, to $110 (let us imagine). If everyone else adds a cow, though, then the grass will be depleted, and the cows will produce less. If you have 10 cows (when everyone else has 11), you will make $80, and if you have added a cow (when everyone else also has 11), then you will make $88.

If we look at this problem in isolation, it is clear what to do: Add a cow. You will always do better with 11 cows than with 10.

	NO ONE ELSE ADDS A COW	INTERMEDIATE CASES	EVERYONE ELSE ADDS A COW
A adds a cow	$110		$88
A doesn't add a cow	$100		$80

Viewing the problem in isolation is unrealistic in this kind of situation, however. In the town, these people will share many interactions, and maintaining a general atmosphere of trust will often be more valuable than the added payoff from one more cow. This one decision is embedded in a network of ongoing relationships that involves many such decisions. Thus factoring in all consequences of a decision may greatly alter the long-term payoffs.

Further exploration of these "games"

Once we understand the prisoners' dilemma situation, we can see how it is a useful model for other kinds of situations. Think of the cold-war problem of nuclear escalation, for example. Clearly the abolition of such threats to the planet would best serve the general good. However, as in any prisoners' dilemma situation, each side got the most immediate benefit from the course of action that is not most beneficial in the long run. For decision makers on each side, developing and maintaining nuclear arms always seemed more beneficial, no matter what the other side did. There is no greater sovereign power to change the payoffs through enforcement of regulations; and there are no personal ties sufficient to prevent continued escalation. The only solution would seem to be in breaking the problem down into many smaller agreements, increasing the number of cooperative interactions until an ongoing cooperative relationship makes continued reduction more beneficial than escalation. Unfortunately, as more countries become players in this weighty "game," it becomes harder to secure the total cooperation that is necessary for complete success.

In thinking about the nature of social relations, philosophers have used the prisoners' dilemma situation and the tragedy of the commons as models. These models were not explicitly formulated until the middle of the twentieth century. Even so, Thomas Hobbes (1588–1679), for example, seems to have viewed the "state of nature" as a large number of independent, two-person prisoners' dilemma situations ("the war of every man against every man" in which life is "nasty, brutish, and short"). On this basis, he argued that we need a strong "sovereign" power that alters the payoffs, so that we get more from cooperation than from defection. (This sovereign power would function like the gang we discussed in connection with our first prisoners' dilemma involving Alicia and Barbie.) The sovereign power's laws and enforcement encourage cooperation, enabling us to get out of the prisoners' dilemma and into a situation in which cooperation is the mode of behavior with the best payoffs.

In arguing that we need a strong sovereign, Hobbes was neglecting the other factors that can alter the prisoners' dilemma situation. Sustaining cooperative relationships can be a long-term goal that significantly changes the value of cooperation and defection.

We mentioned that a concern for others, like that of a mother for her daughter, might also alter the payoffs. If there is an even broader general concern for others, this could, of course, change the choices in the prisoners' dilemma situation. If I am as concerned about the welfare of the other prisoner as about my own, and if I can expect that of him, then we will cooperate with each other. Hobbes, though, argued that we are all rational egoists, looking out just for ourselves, and he did not consider the possibility of altruistic action to be an important aspect of social interaction. (Hobbes leaves room for a small exception to rational egoism where family matters are involved, because he speaks of a man looking out for the good of his wife and children. But he does not seem to think that this exception could extend beyond the family to become a significant social force.)

More important, however, Hobbes ignored the significance of repeated rounds of play, especially when there is information about people's record of play. To see the significance of this, suppose we were to play many repeated rounds of the two-person cooperative dilemma game, with these two features: You would know the past record of all players, and you could choose your playing partner for each round. In a long run of play, it would clearly be to your advantage to establish a good record of cooperation if you wanted to be in on subsequent rounds and you wanted to play with cooperative partners. In a small town, a business that cheats its customers will not last long, because there will usually be a good network of information about its business record. The situation is favorable to cooperation because of the repeated, public nature of interactions.

This model of social interaction as a network of very public two-person interactions also has its limits when we try to apply it. Such complete information about previous transactions is not available for most of our business and social decisions, and we do not always have a wide selection of alternative "partners" for our transactions. Nevertheless, in considering this model, we are able to see immediately that there are situations in which it is evidently beneficial to choose cooperation. Even if the narrow modeling of a single decision process makes it look like a prisoners' dilemma situation in which cooperation does not pay, the consideration of cooperative possibilities in future interactions might lead one to choose to establish a record of honest, cooperative actions.

Even practices like gift giving make egoistic sense in the context of a network of ongoing relationships, because gift giving increases the number of interactions that show, in an evident way, a long-term interest in maintaining a beneficial relationship, without concern for a maximal payoff from each action. (This is not to say that this is the only reason for giving gifts.)

Repeated play in the tragedy-of-the-commons situation illustrates some additional features of social interaction. As in the repeated prisoners' dilemma, cooperation can be much better than defection if it helps to maintain an ongoing cooperative relationship. In a multiplayer situation like the tragedy of the commons, it can also be worthwhile to continue cooperation even when there is limited defection. Even if no direct action can prevent some townspeople from introducing new cows, it may still be in the interest of the majority to maintain the standard of not adding their own cows to those already grazing the commons. This tolerance of limited defection can be worthwhile as long as it continues to play a role in encouraging a sufficient number of people to cooperate. (What constitutes a sufficient number depends on details of the situation.)

As we have seen, though, it is not an easy matter to find the balance between cooperation and defection. If there is a stable, cooperative group of adequate size, then defection will pay off well, as long as it does not undermine the cooperative base it depends on for success. This makes maintaining the stable, cooperative group very difficult, because whenever cooperation exists, everyone has a motive to defect—to take advantage of the base of value that the cooperative core provides.

CHAPTER SUMMARY

If you have an *exhaustive set of mutually exclusive* actions to consider, then you have determined what your options are. You are in a position to begin deciding what to do.

When you know the outcome of each action, you want to pick the outcome that you value most. When it is not obvious what outcome you value most, use one or more of these methods as a guide to selection:

Satisficing

Eliminating dominated options

Eliminating unsatisfactory options

Elimination by aspect

MAUT—This is the best selection method if you can

1. Identify the important attributes of the outcomes of the actions

2. Rate the attributes

3. Rate each outcome with respect to each of the important attributes

When you don't know the outcome of an action, there are several methods of selection that you can use. Instead of a single outcome to consider for each action, you have a set of possible outcomes. You want to select an action that provides an optimal, or at least acceptable, balance between value of occurrence and probability of occurrence. The extent to which you can do this will depend partly on the quality of information you have about the possible outcomes of your actions. Do you know what the possible outcomes of your action are? Can you rank the possible outcomes of the actions that are open to you? (That is, can you say which you prefer?) Can you put them on a preference scale (give them a rating rather than just a ranking)? Do you know the probability of each of the outcomes of a particular action?

Here are some of the methods that can help in your decision process.

Eliminating unsatisfactory actions (actions that have a possibility of an unsatisfactory outcome) if satisfactory actions are available. *Requires that you set a satisfaction level; does not require rankings or probabilities. Will not usually produce a decision all by itself, and if the probability of an unsatisfactory outcome is low, this method may be too cautious.*

Eliminating dominated actions. *Requires a ranking of the possible outcomes of the actions available. Does not require information about preference scaling (rating) or probabilities. This can often simplify problems; it will not ordinarily lead to a unique choice of action.*

Maximax or maximin. *These methods require a ranking (or at least a partial ranking) but do not require a preference scaling (rating) or information about probabilities.*

Expected utility method. *This method provides the best balance of value and probability, but it requires the most information. You need preference scalings (ratings, not just rankings), and you need to be able to assign probabilities to the possible outcomes of each action that is available to you.*

In the last part of this chapter, we took up some special issues concerning impediments to good decision making, concerning money and value, and concerning decisions whose outcome depends on the decisions of other people.

EXERCISE 10C

1. You have invited a good friend out to dinner. You have $30, so you can't go anywhere very expensive. But Mary, a high-rolling acquaintance of yours, has offered a bet. You will flip a (fair) coin, with these outcomes:

   If it is heads, Mary will give you $40. (Thus you will have $70.)

   If it is tails, you will give Mary your $30. Mary will give you a peanut butter sandwich. (You will have to call your friend and cancel dinner.)

   Consider whether you should take the bet.

   a. What is the maximax (risk taker's) decision?

   b. What is the maximin (safe) decision?

   c. If dollars were a good measure of value, what would the expected value solution be?

   You were hoping to have more than $30, so you could go to a better restaurant. Still, you want to go out with the friend rather than eating peanut butter by yourself.

   d. Will you take the bet? Why or why not?

2. Suppose you are in Las Vegas and you have $60 (and a ticket home) left. You are trying to decide whether to play the following game, which costs $50 to enter.

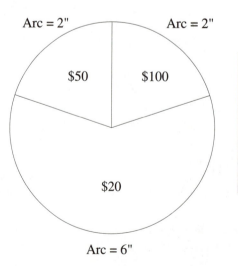

Arc = 2"   Arc = 2"

$50 $100

$20

Arc = 6"

Spin the pointer on the wheel and win the prize in the region in which it comes to rest. (Spin again if it stops on a line.) It is equally likely to come to rest pointing in any direction.

a. What is the maximin (safe) solution?

b. What is the maximax (gambler's) solution?

c. What is the expected value solution, assuming that dollars are here a good measure of value?

d. Should you play if it costs $60 to bet? If it costs $40?

Suppose there was a restaurant where you would like to take a friend who is with you. But you feel that you should have at least $90 before going in so that you can order your appetizers, wine, and dinners "in proper style." (It won't be worth going if you go with less.)

e. How might this affect the maximin and maximax solutions?

f. How might this affect the expected value solution?

3. You are considering two games at the casino, trying to decide whether you should play one of them. Each game cost $50 to enter.

Game 1:   You are to draw a card from an ordinary deck of 52 cards (no jokers).

If the card is a club, you get $120.

If the card is a spade, you get $80.

Otherwise, you get nothing.

(*Note:* An ordinary deck with 52 cards is divided into four suits: clubs, spades, hearts, and diamonds. There are 13 cards in each suit.)

Game 2:   You will throw an ordinary six-sided die.

If it comes up 6, you get $180.

If it comes up 5, you get $90.

Otherwise, you get nothing.

a. Tell us what these various decision methods recommend that you do, assuming that dollars are a good measure of value in these games. (Show your work for any calculations that you do.)

(1) Maximax
(2) Maximin
(3) Expected value (expected utility)

b. What should you do if it costs $40 to enter each game?

c. What should you do if it costs $60 to enter?

Consider the following variation on game 1.

Game 1*:   It costs $500 to enter.

You are to draw a card from an ordinary deck of 52 cards (no jokers).

If the card is a club, you get $1200.

If the card is a spade, you get $800.

Otherwise you get nothing.

d. How does the expected value calculation here compare to the expected value calculation for the original version of game 1?

e. If you had $500 to gamble, would you rather play game 1 ten times or Game 1* once? Why?

4. Cape Halibut Bay supports a fishing industry based solely on small boats that are able to navigate the shallow waters near the harbor. There are 40 independently owned boats that fish in the bay. There is a new technology that can increase a boat's catch by 40%, and only a 5% increase in a boat's catch would be needed to pay for the installation and maintenance of the new equipment. Unfortunately, if more than half of the boats adopt the new technology, the stock of fish will be depleted so quickly that every boat will experience about a 1/3 (one-third) reduction in its catch. That means that the boats with the new technology will be catching a little less than they would have if no one had introduced the new technology. (The boats with no new technology, of course, will be getting even less.)

a. What should the individual boat owner do to maximize productivity?

b. What could the boat owners do together to avoid losses?

c. Be sure to indicate why cooperation is difficult in situations like this.

d. What do you think is likely to happen? Why?

5. It is Sunday night, and John must decide whether to study hard for his Monday morning class, watch TV and skim his notes, or go to a concert (with no studying at all). He has no idea whether there will be a quiz the next day, and if there is, whether it will be easy or difficult. John knows that he would like it best if there were no quiz and he went to the concert. These are his rankings of the possible outcomes:

Concert and no quiz	9 (best)
Skim notes and no quiz	8
Study hard and no quiz	7
Study hard and easy quiz	6
Skim notes and easy quiz	5
Study hard and hard quiz	4
Concert and easy quiz	3
Skim notes and hard quiz	2
Concert and hard quiz	1 (worst)

a. Do these preferences provide a clear basis for action? Why or why not?

b. What is the maximax (gambler's) choice?

c. What is the maximin (safe) choice?

d. Can you figure out the *expected utility* solution? If not, why not? If so, what is it? (Show any calculations.)

6. Suppose John finds out that there will be a quiz for sure. (The teacher had announced it when John was asleep. A friend told John about it.)

a2. Do these preferences provide a clear basis for action? Why or why not?

b2. What is the maximax (gambler's) choice?

c2. What is the maximin (safe) choice?

d2. Can you figure out the *expected utility* solution? If not, why not? If so, what is it? (Show any calculations.)

7. But now John learns that his teacher may have postponed the quiz. (John can't find anyone who went to the last class, so he can't check for sure.) John thinks that the probability of a quiz is about 50%, and he thinks that it is very likely to be difficult. John places these utilities on his preferences.

Concert and no quiz	100 (best)
Skim notes and no quiz	70
Study hard and no quiz	60
Study hard and easy quiz	55
Skim notes and easy quiz	50
Study hard and hard quiz	45
Concert and easy quiz	35
Skim notes and hard quiz	20
Concert and hard quiz	5 (worst)

a3. Do these preferences provide a clear basis for action? Why or why not?

b3. What is the maximax (gambler's) choice?

c3. What is the maximin (safe) choice?

d3. Can you figure out the *expected utility* solution? If not, why not? If so, what is it? (Show any calculations.)

e. Is there any reason why John should hesitate to act on the result of the expected value calculation in this case?

8. Suppose that John has no real interest in the material for this course, but he would like to get as high a grade as possible on the quiz. If John's teacher grades "on a curve," guaranteeing that there will be approximately 10% A's, 30% B's, 30% C's, 20% D's, and 10% F's, does this affect what John should do? Explain why or why not. If John knows some other people in the class, what should he advise them to do? If this is different from what he should do himself, explain why. (Consider all of John's options.)

SOME SPECIAL CASES OF VALIDITY

This appendix is a note on the concept of validity. In Chapter 1, we identified the key idea of validity as one that we could explain in several ways:

d1: The premises support the conclusion.

d2: If all of the premises were true, then the conclusion would also be true.

d3: It is impossible for the premises to be true with the conclusion false.

For the most part, these definitions of validity amount to the same thing. Concerning a few special cases, though, they differ, and here we call your attention to this.

In several special types of arguments, d3 clearly applies: It is impossible to have the premises true with the conclusion false, and yet it is very questionable whether d1 applies.

The Conclusion Is a Premise

First consider "arguments" of the following form:

A   Alice will give Bill a present.

∴ A   ∴ Alice will give Bill a present.

It is not at all clear whether we should say that the premise supports the conclusion, because we have not been clear enough about what we mean by *support*. One couldn't use such an argument to make a convincing case for the conclusion, because a person would have to believe the conclusion already in order to believe the premise (they are the same thing). The argument is circular (see Chapter 4). Nevertheless, we will still want to call it a *valid* argument, because it clearly meets the conditions of d2 and d3. Why do we favor those over d1? Because they are clearer, and because employing those definitions gives us a notion of validity that is more useful in analyzing arguments in general. This is not something that can be shown by a simple argument; one must see the overall coherence of the systems of logic associated with one definition rather than another.

The Conclusion Is a Logical Truth

The definition d3 also yields odd consequences in two other cases. Consider arguments of the following sort:

A	Alice will give Bill a present.
∴ B or not-B	∴ Charlie is angry or Charlie is not angry.

Here the premise is irrelevant to the conclusion. In fact, the conclusion is a logical truth—something that stands on its own—because it is true in every possible situation. Since the conclusion of this argument is a logical truth, there is no way for the premise of this argument to be true with the conclusion false, simply because there is no way for the conclusion to be false. Thus if we adopt d3, we must say that this is a valid argument, because it meets the conditions of d3. (It is impossible for the premises to be true with the conclusion false.) It seems very odd to say that the premise supports the conclusion in this case, because it is completely irrelevant to the conclusion.

No information is needed to support this conclusion, though, because the conclusion contains no information about how the world is (or at least none that requires more than logic alone to establish it). The conclusion stands on its own, and the premise is gratuitous. In general, when the conclusion of an argument is a logical truth, something that stands on its own as a truth, the argument is valid. Any premise that we have is superfluous information not needed to establish the conclusion. Logic should provide a basis for establishing the conclusion even if there are no premises. In other words, the argument would be valid even if there were no premises. Adding information is superfluous, but it does not affect the question of whether the argument is valid.

The Premises Are an Inconsistent Set of Statements

The other case in which d3 yields an unexpected consequence is now predictable. We just said that an argument with a logical truth as its conclusion is valid: It is impossible for the conclusion to be false, so it is impossible for the premises to be true with the conclusion false, no matter what the premises are. Similarly, if it is impossible for all the premises to be true (that is, the premises are an inconsistent set of statements), then it is impossible for the premises to be true with the conclusion false. Hence any argument with inconsistent premises is valid!

A	Alice will give Bill a present.
not-A	Alice will not give Bill a present.
∴ B	∴ Charlie is tall.

No doubt it will seem even stranger at first to call this valid. Definition d3, though, certainly has the consequence that such arguments are valid. (It is impossible for the premises to be true with the conclusion false.) Such a finding has led some logicians to seek new systems of logic to try to avoid this consequence, but the general consensus is that the standard systems of logic, based on the d3 definition of validity, work the best. Arguments like these are terrible arguments for logical reasons: There is no way for them to be sound, because there is no way for all premises to be true. This just shows that invalidity is not the only logical problem an argument can have.

These issues are of some interest in considering the general applicability of our definitions of validity and of some importance for any discussion of formal logic. For further discussion, see Paul Tidman and Howard Kahane, *Logic and Philosophy,* 8th ed. (Belmont, CA: Wadsworth, 1999), p. 60; or *Modern Formal Logic,* Thomas J. McKay, (New York: Macmillan, 1989), pp. 59–61.

INDEX